KINGS
over
ACES

The Insider's Guide to Angel and VC Investing in The Next Billion Dollar Startups and IPOs

ROSS BLANKENSHIP
Founder, AngelKings.com

Copyright © 2015
Authored By Ross D. Blankenship
All rights reserved
ISBN: 1512008184
ISBN 13: 978-1512008180

THANK YOU

I want to thank my family for always being there. Through the ups and downs, the stress and the tireless work, we will achieve victory together. My love for you is endless. Although the planets will come and go one day, we will always be bonded by our passion and energy to make the best of life.

To my better half (DWB), and the most amazing daughters in the world.

Thank you to my team, especially Melissa Bojos. We have a bright future ahead and, with patience, we'll be able to show the world the amazing opportunities we've discovered together.

Thank you to my father, Dr. D. Michael Blankenship. Through your words we speak, by your mind we think, and with your soul we feel. There will never be a wake so strong.

Thank you to Bradford B. Rossi and Michael J. Blankenship, for giving great advice and counsel.

I always remember how much faith the first investors put into my first deal. Thank you to these amazing people: Dr. D. Winslow Blankenship, Doe Browning, Jinny ("Jinx") Browning, Doug Hendrickson, Gina Browning, Reza and Ali John Ghassabeh, Eric Andalman, The Edgar Family, John VanMeter and Karen Edwards.

To my buddies at Signature DC who made for quite entertaining company while writing a good portion of the book: Pops, Granville, Mikey, Dr. Stiglitz and the crew. And to my new coffee mentor, Hudai Yavalar.

And to you, the reader… though we make no guarantees for any returns, we can confidently say that the wave of the future is startup investing, angel advising and venture capital; using this approach, you're much more likely to make serious returns on your investments than by paying some broker to do it for you. The next check you write must be backed by data and driven by knowledge and the confidence that you're making a difference in the American economy.

Let's go find the next big, billion dollar startup, together!

***To learn about Angel Kings, and one of our startup and venture capital funds, visit <u>AngelKings.com</u> today.**

CONTENTS

Preface		1
Pt. One:	**Angel Kings' Billion Dollar Startup Formula**	**17**
1	Introducing the Angel Kings	18
2	The X Factor: How to Invest in the Right People	33
3	The New in Nothing New: How to Find the Next Billion Dollar Products	48
4	How to Know a Company will Execute	65
5	How to Know When the Timing is Right	84
6	Financial Case Study of Startups	101
Pt. Two:	**The Official Angel Kings Rankings**	**116**
7	The Next Billion Dollar Startups	117
Pt Three:	**The Best Articles on Angel and VC Investing**	**185**
8	Articles for the Investor	186
Final Thoughts		366
*BONUS:	**How to Get Started in Venture Capital**	**368**
Index		370

PREFACE

"It ain't got nothing to do with God, Mr. Cash. It has to do with believing in yourself."

In 2012, one of the premier media companies in the world, AOL TechCrunch, invited me to San Francisco, California to speak at a major event called "Disrupt." Only a select group of companies had been invited to pitch, and my startup was one of them. I had just spent two years building StudyHall.com, an "online university meets social network" that helped millions of students connect online; our website allowed universities around the world better access to collaborate and share academic research. I knew it was a big deal that one of the largest tech events in America had invited me to speak, but wasn't sure just how big it would be for my future.

At the event, I was scheduled to speak after Mark Zuckerberg. He was an icon of the industry; the Founder of Facebook, global titan and billionaire many times over. Mark would discuss the rise of social media and the impact Facebook had in changing the world. Of course, as he concluded his Facebook update, the audience cleared out; about 10,000 people winnowed down to only 5,000. At the time, I remember thinking, why couldn't they all just leave? Even though I was nervous and anxious, I was ready to make an entrance.

I remember standing on stage in front of this massive audience; with sweat on my brow, my heart visibly palpitating, and my mind reciting thirty times the same pitch I had practiced in front of the mirror; I had never pitched any idea, when there were more than five people in the room.

But it was a huge success! As my loud voice echoed in that conference auditorium, the previously departed audience came back into the room to listen. I knew that people wanted to see a passionate person; that ideas come and go, but that leaders can lead from anywhere. So I would make it happen.

Mark Pincus, Ross Blankenship and Rohit Gupta, Zynga Party, 2012.

The pitch went great. All five minutes of it. Even though I don't remember the questions many of the judges asked, I do remember that insanely emotional experience – and remember looking out onto the audience thinking, *I had made it*. Hundreds of people approached me after the pitch. Many eager angel investors wanted to write checks even though they hadn't seen anything more than a Power Point presentation. It was absolute hysteria, but my startup had finally launched!

* * *

So how did I go from startup on stage pitching my startup to thousands, to writing a book on becoming a venture capitalist that judged these similar startup events? And where did I get my passion for startup investing? Its roots go back to my student days at Cornell University, where I enrolled after moving from Texas – my home state - to the far Northeast. At Cornell, I developed three immeasurable traits that have guided my entire career path: listening, observing and always surrounding myself with people whose skills complement or exceed my own.

And using these learned traits, I would become skilled at two things: rowing and making money. My academic advisors might cringe at the thought that students at Cornell, an Ivy League University would do anything other than study, but the truth is that I always managed to do just enough schoolwork to get by. Though it might seem like these two activities – rowing and making money– were unrelated, both required the most immense amount of listening and observing that I would be remiss to not explain their connection.

LISTEN

My best friend from Cornell taught me how to **listen** – a bright-eyed, affable Canadian guy named Tobin Ireland. Tobin was just above 6'2" and about 175 lbs; I stood at 6'6" and had a sizeable weight advantage at 220 lbs. However, Tobin was always a better rower; he grew up in St. Catharines, Ontario, where Olympic rowers made their homes, and most rivers and lakes had a boathouse on the shoreline. We grew up in different parts of the world. Whereas I grew up in Texas where boats were used for bass fishing, in Canada, rowing is the national pastime. We had both been recruited to join Cornell's crew team in 2001. Immediately, Tobin was selected to be the "stroke," or leader, in the eight seat of the boat. I was selected as his seven-seat where I sat right behind him.

Ross Blankenship (bow), Tobin Ireland (stroke), Cornell University Rowing Team, 2002 Eastern Sprints Championship.

OBSERVE

From this position, I **observed** every move and rowed in perfect unison. With one wrong move, our boat could stray off course. Rowing is a sport of tiny margins and fractions of a second can lead to victory or defeat. So, I always listened to his seat and watched his back as his cadence increased or decreased; our oars splashed the calm Cayuga Inlet. We rowed thousands of miles and never missed a beat during our years together. We won many races together against top crews like Stanford, Boston University, the University of Pennsylvania, and the University of Michigan.

Tobin and I both faced challenges during our first year at Cornell, but his were greater than mine. He had tragically lost his mother just a few months after he started Cornell. I was so inspired that Tobin was able to maintain his composure – to keep calm and row on, so to speak, that I wanted to learn how he overcame such adversity. We shared thousands of meals together, won a hell of a lot of races together, and even debated Canadian politics in the packed dining halls. By listening and learning from my Canadian friend, I began to expand my mind from those Texas roots. Where I was loud and boisterous, his calm demeanor guided me through some tough experiences for the remaining years at Cornell, and beyond.

We also shared the experience of not having a mother. Although, Tobin's loss was much later in life, my loss also created serious adversity. But this, too, is something I've been able to overcome.

We both would look to our fathers as navigators and compasses to be the best in life.

From left to right: Dr. D. Michael Blankenship, Tiamo Blankenship, Ross Blankenship and Michael Blankenship, 2010 Wedding of D. Winslow Blankenship & Ross Blankenship.

We challenged each other – not just on the water with our crew – but also on land, where we constantly debated politics, life, and women too.

Our differences complemented each other well. He loyally stayed home every night to telephone his girlfriend (now amazing wife), while I stayed out late, partied and picked up the game of poker in our college town. I eventually found a wonderful woman worth staying home for too!

SURROUND

I'm glad I surrounded myself with people like Tobin, my best friend Rohit Gupta (formerly of High Line Venture Partners), and Nick Kavanagh (Google Inc). They've made a huge difference in my life's path to venture capital and startup investing.

Tobin Ireland and Ross Blankenship, while in St. Catharines Ontario (Canada), 2004.

To this day, I've written down everything I've learned from each of my friends on this journey into venture capital.

And these days when an entrepreneur is either pitching me for an investment or want my advice on a startup, I evaluate what kind of listening, observing and surrounding they do too. These are critical, learned traits that everyone must do to win in the business world.

FROM CORNELL TO LAW SCHOOL

During my senior year at Cornell, I decided to apply to law school. Even though I had no interest in becoming a lawyer, it seemed like the right decision at the time. Receiving a full scholarship to attend Washington University School of Law in St. Louis, I dove headfirst, thinking that law was the answer.

However, from Day One, sitting in the infamous first-year Contracts law, I knew that the legal world wouldn't suit me. I just couldn't imagine how these attorneys could sit through and read volumes of text for clients, only to tell them that there's a gray area – and there's no way to guarantee how some judge would decide a case. It was mundane. Too ordinary and not enough action or impact for me to care, and I didn't want to write someone's deal contract; I wanted to be *the* dealmaker.

So I found other ways to distract me from the law school lecture hall until I could figure out how I would become *that* dealmaker.

Every Wednesday during the school year, I invited a group of students — the "law school truants" — to play poker at my apartment. I learned that these events became great for making money, but not so great for making it to Contracts Law lecture the next day. I also learned fast that poker wasn't about the cards you were dealt. Poker was about the people against whom you played, and I only wanted to invite the best players with whom I could surround myself.

In these fierce late night, law school poker battles, I concentrated on building my observation skills. I was also unlike any other poker player; I kept a spreadsheet of my winnings, took notes about player's moves, and made detailed observations of everyone's facial expressions and body language. While others drank Maker's Mark bourbon, I sipped on a bottle of water so as to not get distracted. I was analytical, mathematically decisive and won the great majority of the hands—cards dealt—that I played. I observed every tick, twitch and habit of each player with shorthand notes in my 8x11 notepad. It worked like a charm.

THE POKER HAND THAT BUILT ANGEL KINGS

However, one hand, in particular, defined my future career as a venture capitalist. With nine people at the green felt table, and my stack growing steadily around 2 a.m., I was dealt pocket Kings—the second-best starting hand in poker, exceeded only by twin Aces. I used my keen observation skills: the player on my right was excited by his cards. His face was glowing, and his heart was palpably beating through his shirt. As I always did, I re-raised him to see whether my "hand" was good or not. He quickly called, and then glanced more at his cards; in poker, this was almost always a sign of strength. Finally, we were together as everyone else folded his or her cards.

When the dealer laid out the three-card flop, two Kings, and an Ace appeared. Now, there was exactly a 0.25% chance or 407 to 1 odds of hitting four Kings. The probability of this happening made me the luckiest man in that room. I knew that even if the player to my right had pocket Aces I was going to win a lot of money. Immediately, this player went "all-in"—he didn't even look around, or observe whether there was a chance I had a better hand. He risked his entire chip stack and all his winnings that night.

That one hand — pocket Kings versus pocket Aces — changed my perspective. It was the defining moment. I pledged to take my $729 in winnings that evening and turn it into millions. I also learned that you need skill before your luck matters.

When we left that early morning, I stored that $729 in my dresser drawer, underneath the Michigan crew rowing shirt Tobin and I won together.

I learned so much from playing poker. One of the most astute lessons: even when you're dealt pocket Aces, your luck can change in an instant. Often, like losing poker players, startup founders with big venture capital investments lose because they overestimate their dealt hand. As in poker, that money can disappear quickly. Most startups fail because they burn through cash, are mismanaged, or don't observe the world around them.

I've also learned that attending an Ivy League school doesn't entitle you to anything. You've got to fight for every victory; entitlement leads to complacency, which leads to failure in the business world.

With startups, ideas don't win; execution plans do. There are plenty of people with good ideas. Some take it a step further and become founders so they can share their ideas. As an investor, you need to see if the founders seeking your investment have execution plans to transform their ideas into successful products.

> **Startups**: Beware of being dealt pocket Aces; sometimes it can work against you long-term. Having venture capitalists invest money in your startup without having a market-proven product or service may be doing your company a disservice. Remember that execution always trumps ideas. Don't think raising massive amounts of VC money, pre-launch, will lead you to success. Customers, clients and traction should always precede your fundraising.

I don't remember much about law school, other than that Poker game. The cases often blended together, and the people seemed too complacent with their paths of becoming future lawyers. I realized that unless I pursue something different in life, I would be just an ordinary guy watching the world pass before my eyes.

The Hard Rock Hotel Poker Invitational with Doyle Brunson, Ross Blankenshp and Scott Ian, 2008.

That's when the entrepreneurial bug bit me like a Texas yellow jacket. I remember being restless because I wanted to get started on my master plan—starting a business and doing some good. Both came to fruition. While my law school classmates wrote countless pages, notes and outlines on court cases, I drafted a plan to use my poker winnings to start my first company. After all, how many full-time lawyers can get to the top of the Fortune 500 list? I needed to dream bigger, but knew being a full-time poker player wouldn't be either big enough or sustainable. So, I decided to take the only other area of expertise I've been working on my whole life where people I respected have also affected me: my education. I wanted to use my academic skills and teach others similar to how Tobin had taught me in college, and how my father taught me growing up.

The plan was simple, and like poker, it involved math and analytics: tutor and teach others how to become better test takers. There was a niche industry called "test preparation," which, I heard from fellow law school classmates, required virtually zero startup capital to advertise, and with which you could use free books from the library to teach. Within weeks of posting on the bulletin boards and local coffee shops, prospective customers and leads were calling me every other hour.

> "Cornell 'Ivy' Grad, tutoring for SAT and other exams – not boring like the rest/ $150/hour or special packages for early reservations."

Along with some tear-offs at the bottom of the page, I spent $15 on advertisements. Within two weeks, I had ten clients and was making thousands of dollars—making more money than my fellow law students would make, and meeting amazing families across the Midwest. Every one of the kids with whom I worked increased their scores. Word got around that I was a "miracle worker" who could listen and observe critical patterns on exams. The parents loved me and I absolutely loved teaching.

Eventually, I built an established education company that evolved from tutoring in person, then to online (B2C), then to actual testing and teaching for large enterprises (B2B). I learned so much about hiring and building new products that I wrote a book about it (*Hire Like a Boss*) and a book on cyber security startups (*Cyber Nation*). However, I had my share of failures thinking that hiring more people equals greater productivity (hint: it doesn't). From the years 2000 until 2014, I built several companies, graduated three times, and would get married and have children.

And then...

TO GO ON TELEVISION OR NOT?

After all those years of hustling and trying to find my way, in May of 2014, I got the call that changed my life...

...from a nationally syndicated television show on a major network. In fact, it was my favorite show on television—one that my wife and I had recorded and repeatedly watched every week since it first aired. The phone call came from a Santa Monica, California phone number, and a producer from this television show exclaimed, "we saw your performance at TechCrunch, we love what you're creating, and want you to come on our television show and pitch the sharks!" I thought this was a prank call from an old Cornell buddy. However, when I asked them to verify their credentials, they did. And after a video chat and three emails, I knew these producers were the real deal. Wow. I couldn't believe they had seen my pitch from a couple years back. It dawned on me that alongside the interested investors among the crowded audience sat interested television producers. I wondered if the phone call would be the final culmination and justification for not practicing law and pursuing my startup journey?

I believed it would. So in preparation, I spent five months practicing and refining my pitch. I learned everything about these investors – what they wanted to hear, which industries they tended to invest in, and how other founders piqued their interest. I was so certain I was going to impress them that I even debated whether to say I was from Texarkana or Washington D.C., not knowing which sounded cooler.

So, I practiced my *listening* skills…

I practiced my *observation* skills….

Watched hundreds of hours of re-runs…

Read every book these television investors had written…

And then I got another **call** that changed my life (eventually for the better). After I had spent months practicing and doing my homework to head out to L.A. from Washington D.C., the producers told me,

"Ross, we're sorry, but we have to push you back till next year."

Hundreds of thousands of dollars and months later, the dreaded nightmare had happened. Many friends knew about the show and how excited I had been, and I felt like I had let them down too.

In hindsight, this disappointment was the best thing that ever happened to me. The day these producers in L.A. called me to say it wasn't going to happen was the day I realized I didn't need them. I recalled something Tobin told me after I had a bad breakup with a girlfriend: "Ross, do you remember that movie *Walk the Line?* Yes, I replied… "Well, Ross, the only person you need to believe in, is yourself."

Tobin was right, again. My company had started with a good idea, so why not pay it forward? Why not take what I've learned and what I know through my own business and investments and help others? Why not? I loved learning from others and then teaching, and wanted to do it on a bigger stage.

Ross Blankenship at the Angel Kings office, Washington D.C. (2015).

And by the way, you don't need to launch your own startup, learn poker (though it would help!) or go to law school; You only need yourself and the ability to listen and observe what we've mastered at Angel Kings and my venture capital group. You need to be able to listen to startups and not get swept away by their ideas if there is no execution plans behind them. You need to accept that your gut may often be wrong, something I know all too well. By doing so, you will ask better questions and make fewer mistakes. Learning from mistakes is great, but sometimes you've got to stop learning and start doing. To become a successful startup investor like me, you only need to listen, believe in yourself and take calculated risks that put you in control of your life's destiny.

PART ONE

Angel Kings' Billion-Dollar Startup Formula

1

INTRODUCING THE ANGEL KINGS

Since the passage of the Jumpstart Our Business Startups Act ("JOBS Act") in 2012, there has never been a better time to invest in startups and get started with venture capital. The doors are opening wider for investors to be a part of the new startup boom, and the conversations between investors and startups have never been so loud and public. The risk and potential reward have always been great. But those investors who keep their eyes open and listen can turn the risk and reward in their favor.

Startup and angel investing is the *new* frontier for you to make maximum investment returns on your money. In fact, the closed-door process of venture capital has changed over the recent years that you are now allowed to invest in a startup during the seed level and get access before it becomes an IPO. You also have the fortunate opportunity of positively impacting society.

Here are examples of two successful angel investors for you to consider. In August 2004, Peter Thiel wrote a $500,000 check for an angel investment in Facebook, giving him a 10.2% stake in the company. By the end of the company's lockout period in August 2012, Thiel had pocketed $1 billion in cash, or thousands of times return on his initial investment.

Ronald Wayne co-founded Apple with Steve Jobs and Steve Wozniak. He received a 10% stake in Apple, which he sold for $800 two weeks later in April 1976. His 10% stake would have been worth more than $70 billion today.

Investing in Angel Kings puts you, the investor, in the best position to write a check, invest in the next Facebook and earn returns like Thiel.

We'll show you how to find top startups like Thiel did, and how not to sell your stake too early, like Wayne did. With our advice, you won't need to start your own company or become a founder, to know how to make smart investments: we've already been there.

* * *

Investors aren't born overnight. They don't come out of the womb with the ability to identify successful startups. They might want you to think they do, but they don't. Some may have the good fortune to have an ample cash flow to invest. But the knowledge that would allow them to pick the right companies in which to invest isn't something learned by intuition. Intuition is expensive. What you need is both strategy and focus to win so you can become one of the incredibly successful angel investors mentioned in this book.

Most people — you may be one of them — are intimidated by the idea that investing is exclusive to "those people" like Peter Thiel or other Silicon Valley tycoons. "Those people" work in tall buildings made of glass. "Those people" wear three colors when it comes to clothing: blue, black and gray. "Those people" look sharp with their shiny, polished shoes, and they walk around with a portfolio in one hand and a cup of coffee in the other. "Those people" talk only to people who look similar to them. They use words like "return of investment," "financials" and "valuation" as easily as you might use the words "ice cream," "coffee" and "sleep." They always know when to invest and when to walk away. They also seem to know about the up-and-coming startup companies that are going to explode in the market. But they never share that knowledge.

At Angel Kings, we know when to invest in a company, not because we have prophetic powers, but because we do our due diligence to find out everything about that company–from the founder to the financials. We look for companies that provide better solutions for everyday problems, not iterations of other companies' successes. It's easier to follow the pack of VC's who invest at the next biggest startup, but it's wiser to take a closer look at startups that are providing simpler and better solutions for problems of everyday people. Our main goal is to reduce your risk—for which there's plenty in the current startup-investing environment—and help you make calculated, wiser decisions about where to place your money.

We wrote KINGS over ACES because you too can be a king or queen. Your story is no different. Who cares if you went to an Ivy League school or know how to play poker? No one does. What matters is that you become skilled at listening to potential investments and observing patterns in successful startups. By doing so, you can make tons of money too and create a life that is unencumbered by a 9-to-5 routine (sorry law school, not interested). Moreover, you'll be able to affect the lives of entrepreneurs who are making major differences for others – think Mark Zuckerberg and Steve Jobs. They at one time had small startups built out of a dorm room and garage, respectively.

KINGS over ACES discusses startups, emerging companies, and the next IPOs… all companies you can get involved with now and make an investment. It discusses companies like Airbnb, Pinterest, Dropbox, GoPro, Uber, and Facebook, and helps you discover the common thread that made these companies successful.

If you had an opportunity to invest in the next Facebook, how would you? We've got the answer.

We want companies who will maintain their success against their competition because they know how to adjust their product or service to fit the needs of the market; they know how to spend their money responsibly; and they know that even when they reach profitability, there still won't be enough time in the day to get everything done. We look at four core ingredients before investing in a startup/company:

1. **People**
2. **Product**
3. **Execution**
4. **Timing**
    + Financials

These four ingredients are critical in mixing together a successful company. And in venture capital, we defined "success" as billion-dollar exits for investors. Thus, each ingredient must pass our smell and taste test, or we won't invest. And neither should you.

* * *

PEOPLE

Behind every great company is a founder who discovered a better solution to an everyday problem, and who is so dedicated, even obsessed, with delivering her better solution to everyone that she has no choice but to commit everything to the success of her company. Behind every great company is a founder who knows the value of every dollar that comes in and every dollar that goes out of her company. We want a founder who knows how to balance being pragmatic and passionate. She won't underestimate the value of her company, but she also pays attention whether there is an actual need for her product or service. We don't want a founder who is so in love with her company that she fails to pay attention to what the market actually needs. Founders need to be focused, but they need to be flexible with their products, as well. At Angel Kings, we also know that founders who are hyper-focused on profit and the marketability of their products only hire people of the same mindset. Therefore, a driven founder, who is supported by an equally motivated and driven team, has a better chance in leading her company on a positive trajectory. As an investor, look for founders who are obsessed with winning, but not blinded by illusion.

You should also look to see whether the founding team has a **hacker, hustler, and social media maven** to lift the company to the next level. I wrote a previous book called *Hire Like a Boss*, which explains the critical fact that every founding team needs these people — or elements — to become billion dollar companies.

1. A perfect **hacker** is an engineer who not only understands how to build a product, but can also teach others how to do the same in the most efficient way. At his or her core, a hacker is someone who not only builds

software or hardware, but can also manage a product team as the company grows to scale.

2. A perfect **hustler** sells you a product and becomes your friend at the same time. It's someone who you didn't even realize was asking you for money — when in fact they were the entire time. Business development is about asking for money, getting paid customers, and then using these customers to refer others. Startup hustling is a three-part process, and you need a hustler on a founding team.

3. A perfect **social media maven** can drive organic traffic to a startup. When a startup company first launches, more money should be spent on search engine optimization ("SEO)" and driving buzz and conversation around a product. A social media maven should be working non-stop to drive campaign traffic; if you see a startup paying for traffic, that's a red flag. Most often, early stage companies already have someone who's a social media maven, but you should find out whether they are leveraging social media and SEO to drive free customer acquisition in this new technological era.

You **need all three elements** to build and scale a company. However, this doesn't mean you need three people doing each role. In fact, early stage startups often have one or two people at most. But each element must be present at the time of your investment; your venture capital investment should not be used to pay for outsourcing or hiring someone else to fill these roles.

PRODUCT

Companies that have withstood the test of time are quite simple in concept. As we mentioned before, the best companies are the ones that provide solutions for everyday problems. Some companies may even address the same everyday problem, but take different approaches to appeal to consumers. Take Apple and Microsoft. They address the same problem of providing people with a platform that connects them to the Internet, while providing an electronic interface for people to do their daily administrative or creative tasks. They address the problem of communication and convenience.

But if we look back at the development of these two giants, which existed before there was Facebook or Google, we can see that Microsoft and Apple products have evolved to fit the needs of their market—both in style and functionality. At Angel Kings, we invest in companies that have the potential to evolve with the constantly changing market. We first recognize the problem that the company is trying to solve with its product. Then, we put ourselves five, 10, even 20 years down the road, and ask ourselves if this company can develop its product to fit the needs of people later on. It requires more foresight and creativity to ask those types of questions, but they are important in assessing the longevity prospects of a company. To illustrate, a company that sells protective cases for cellphones may become obsolete 10 years from now if cellphones are replaced by wearable technology, such as Google Glass.

EXECUTION

Execution is closely tied with the people of the company. Simply put, we want to invest in the founder who has the vision for the company, and who has an organized, realistic execution plan to launch and market the company. A founder who does not have an execution plan on how to make her company profitable by a certain time is a founder who will not be financially responsible with her investor's money.

To quote Robert Herjavec from ABC's Shark Tank:

"A goal without a timeline is just a dream."

Let's face it. Startups are expensive. As investors, we don't have time to invest in dreams. We need founders who know exactly what they will do with the money we provide. Will they use the money to meet the demand of their purchase orders? Will it be used toward a better marketing campaign via Google Adwords? Will it be used to lower the cost of the technology they're using?

If the founder in whom you're investing does not have the answer to execution questions, that's a big red flag. Execution plans are a necessity for a founder to show that she has the commitment, the preparedness and the follow-through to make sure her company succeeds.

TIMING

Timing is all about waiting for the right time to hit the market with the company's product. There must be urgency for a better solution among consumers. This urgency emerges from previous products' failures to address the needs of consumers. Make sure that the company in which you'll invest has a proof of concept and has gone through several iterations to meet the market's needs. Sometimes, this may mean that the company will wait for competitors to launch products first, then wait and see how the market will react.

* * *

We will discuss these four core values in further detail in the following chapters of this book. But what we want to impress upon you is that there is no exclusivity when it comes to investing, especially angel investing. You will need to be honest with yourself about whether you have the

money to become an accredited investor. Do you have the cash flow to invest and the stomach to weather the ups and downs that are guaranteed to come? You don't have to join any clubs, or perform any rituals that would signify you are a part of the "Angel Investors Club."
With this book, we will go over how our four core values, or our formula, will help you invest in the right startup companies. We will provide you with financial case studies of startup companies so you can, as the saying goes, follow the money and learn what questions to ask when assessing startups. We will also provide you with articles that discuss the important names in angel investing, the sectors that are drawing a lot of investor interest, as well as the importance of knowing what to look for in a startup.

At Angel Kings, we've now invested in more than 25 companies, most of which have been in education, biotech, and our favorite industry… cyber security. In fact, we became an expert in cyber security in order to gain an advantage over hackers abroad.

Having gone through the trials and tribulations of launching startups has put us in a perfect, winning position to invest. We know the questions to ask other startups. We know the characteristics to look for in a successful startup. We know the formula that identifies a successful startup. In fact, our first two investments in startups became major returns because we applied the exact investment thesis and the proprietary formula that we've been using to distinguish startup winners and losers from this book.

 Now armed with the knowledge we have acquired as an angel investor and venture capitalist, we can help other people have the same success. We can find the 100*xers* of startups, the next IPO companies, and provide the necessary knowledge to investors looking for the next Uber or the next Facebook. The Angel Kings' philosophy and mission is to teach, while making other people rich. We will guide you on the path of startup success, share our wisdom and give you the same opportunities to win. After all, there are many more startups brewing and ready to be worth billions.

POKER 101:

As you get started seeking and investing in the next billion dollar startups, remember this piece of advice that I learned from my prior days becoming an expert poker player: playing fewer hands is better. You should invest in fewer companies, take less risk, but believe even more in the hands you do decide to play your cards. Often times, I waited patiently for hours at the poker table before hitting a great hand. And you should also patiently wait and apply every element of our startup formula before investing!

THE BILLION-DOLLAR STARTUP FORMULA

Like the S&P, Moody's credit rating systems, or Morningstar research for ranking public companies, we built our own proprietary, private market investing formula and ranking of the next billion dollar startups. Until now, we have never released our proprietary formula; we're sharing this for the first time because you deserve to know how venture capitalists think, and moreover, how you too can make money investing in the right startups. We score every startup we meet on a scale from 0 to 100 using the following investment formula.

Before you make any investment in startups, ask yourself, the startup founders, and others, the following questions:

I. PEOPLE (See Chapter 2)

The fundamental questions:

1. Are the founders all-in?
2. Does the founding team have a hacker, hustler, and social media guru?
3. Does the founding team have a potential "icon," i.e. the next Steve Jobs or Bill Gates?
4. Would you trust the founders with a blank check? (Based on a thorough background & credit check)
5. What experience have the founder(s) had with money?
6. Do the founders listen to your ideas?
7. How many of the founding people are still on board?

II. **PRODUCT** (See Chapter 3)

The fundamental questions:

1. How much do you enjoy using the product?
2. What is the likelihood the product will be around 20 years from now?
3. How favorably do customers speak about the product?
4. How big is the actual market for this product?
5. Can you convince your biggest skeptic to buy the product?
6. Do customers keep coming back to buy the product?

III. **EXECUTION** (See Chapter 4)

The fundamental questions:

1. Does the product create a need or "must-have-it" in businesses or consumers?
2. Does the product spark memorable marketing conversations?
3. Does the product empower a community of evangelists?
4. Has the company become the thought leader, or the follower?

IV. **TIMING** (See Chapter 5)

The fundamental questions:

1. Is this a revolutionary, first-in-class product or the most amazing upgrade to an old system?
2. If it hasn't been done before, why hasn't it?
3. Does the startup have an exit strategy: either staying private and being acquired, or having an Initial Public Offering (IPO)?

V. FINANCIALS (See Chapter 6)

The fundamental questions:

1. How soon will the startup make money?
2. What's the startup's valuation?
3. What equity stake will you obtain and is it enough to stay interested?
4. Will your investment help allow for at least 18 months of sustainability?
5. If there's an exit, what's your potential upside?

We always ask tough objective and subjective interview questions; and we always calculate a "1 to 100" startup score. To learn specific scoring ranges for each question, visit AngelKings.com.

* * *

There's also another part of the decision making process above that's not mentioned: it's called your gut feeling or better known as "intuition." Whether you're a card player, investor, doctor, lawyer, or any other profession, you often rely on your intuition in cases where things don't add up quite right or you don't have enough information to make an informed decision. In fact, when you're investing in startups, you won't have the same publicly released information as you would investing in a company listed on the NASDAQ or NYSE; thus, you have to be more logical and patient in your investment strategy. You need to use your intuition *less* often in startup investing before writing a check. After all, for every startup success story you've heard where someone invested in a "billion dollar" idea because of a purported gut feeling, there are thousands more who lost their money because their gut was dead wrong.

> **POKER 101:**
>
> We look for someone who not only is dealt pocket aces – a phenomenal product, viral growth, massive scale – but someone who knows how to execute. This goes back to my story about playing Kings and beating pocket Aces. Beware of the founders who have always had pocket Aces in life, but never executed.

* * *

(1) PASSIONATE, BUT WITH A PURPOSE

It is vital for every founder to be passionate, since passion is what fuels a startup to success. Think of a startup as a car, and every founder as the driver. That driver's passion is what fuels that car. It's the gasoline that keeps the car running through every bump on the road; every storm it has to weather; every passenger it has to carry. We've been pitched countless times, and 99% of the time, the founder will say how passionate or dedicated he or she is about an endeavor. However, if passion fuels a startup to success, it is purpose that will guarantee that a startup remains headed in the right direction. Every founder that has had tremendous success has had both passion and purpose embedded in their companies.

Take a look at Elon Musk. Having founded some of the most successful companies in modern times – PayPal, Tesla, and SpaceX –Musk perfectly fits each of the Angel Kings' personality traits.

Musk starts each new company with a fundamental question: *will my idea completely revolutionize an age-old industry for the betterment of the people?* Most startups see a personal pain point and decide to fix it for themselves. However, Musk sees fundamental stagnation in an industry, and delves head first into solving a problem that will change commerce. Musk begins to answer his own question by building a product he would use personally, which is important, but he then tests immediately whether others would use it too by asking if they would pay for it… and invariably they do – in droves.

PayPal, Tesla and now SpaceX have changed the financial and transportation industries to the point that traditionally embedded players, like banks and NASA, are forced to rewrite how they can compete within the market they used to dominate. Musk will remain an icon of the VC and angel investors industries because he persists in challenging the classic players with innovative ideas. His passion is complemented by a real desire to purposefully drive change and to produce new solutions to existing problems.

Passion is important as the basic trait, but a better marker of a future icon or success is whether there is a genuine purpose behind an idea.

Passion, purpose and money aren't mutually exclusive, either. What we're saying is that you are more likely to make money investing in someone if he or she has passion and purpose combined.

> **Interview tips: Here are some questions to help you assess a founder's passion *and* purpose:**
>
> 1. Why do you believe your company is the next big thing?
> 2. What's the potential impact of your company on people/businesses around the world?

3. Where have you had an impact already in your life on those around you?
4. How would your friends describe you?
5. When did you fail in life? How did you rebound?

* * *

(2) THE ALL-IN MENTALITY

All passionate and purposeful founders or inventors must be asked whether or not it's their full-time venture or just an idea they're pondering perfunctorily. Why? If it's not their full-time, all-in moment, don't bother writing a check. Not one of the top 10 billionaires in the world ever took on an idea, product or service part-time.

For Musk, his all-in mentality has driven him to a level of obsessive compulsiveness that one could blame for a divorce and much strife within his own life. Musk was all-in to PayPal - and to every venture he pursued. Musk worked day and night, and in fact, slept in the office and shared a tiny apartment to save on expenses. Musk would do everything he could to make sure that his company succeeded.

Reminder: your role as an angel investor is to find the best founders who can bring you a massive return on your angel investment. No, we don't want, wish or hope for any of our founders to suffer personal strife or deal with major pains, but look to none other than Steve Jobs to know it can happen to the best.

When we say all-in, just like in poker we want you to treat any investment – $25,000 up to $10,000,000, which we've seen at Angel Kings – as possibly your only startup investment. A founder expecting you to write a check should be just as committed, if not more so, to building her product as you are in giving precious dollars to help her fulfill her vision. She has to understand that receiving your check does not mean the work gets easier. If anything, she has to become so hyper-focused in making her vision succeed that her level of commitment to both your investment and her vision becomes a bit daunting.

The all-in mentality is a two-sided coin for both investors like yourself and founders.

On the one hand, you need to be willing to go all-in and have enough of a meaningful investment for it to hurt if the startup doesn't succeed. As Mark Cuban says, you need to have enough "skin in the game" to care about whether the startup succeeds or fails.

On the other hand, the founder should be willing to play her cards right, not be distracted by different commitments, and remain fully committed to making your investment profitable. If a founder is hedging her bets by thinking that "if this doesn't work out, we can always do something else," then it's not going to work. There's a limited amount of time during which your startup investment should take off, and the founder can't squander that time bouncing around ideas and splitting her time between different companies. The all-in mentality requires focus, decisiveness and cooperation between the founder and the investor.

As an investor, you have to be discerning about the founders of your startup investments. Although a founder may have a great idea and is brimming with passion, she must be able to shoulder the level of risk that your investment carries. Just as in poker, the founder must play every hand as if it were her last hand to play. For every hand dealt – whether pocket Aces or deuce-seven – a founder must be all-in as though her life is on the line. Even when tired, exhausted and ready to give up because

This is why the Angel Kings' investment formula is important for startup investors and venture capitalists; it makes important decisions more reliant on facts than intuition. Use as much of the formula as you can, ask the questions in the following chapters, but if there's a missing piece that doesn't add up to our 90 score… you've got to be willing to say "no." In the startup world, it's about saying "no" more than saying "yes" that will lead you to higher returns on investment.

As in law, your burden of proof for investing in startups is beyond a reasonable doubt. And thus, our formula too is geared towards investing in companies that score a 90+ or more before we would ever say yes to invest.

*You can find our startup calculator on our website: AngelKings.com.

FACTS:

- Each of these four categories combine to make a 0 to 100 score.
- We invest when a startup reaches a total of 90+ points or more.
- Most startups (98.5%) that have pitched Angel Kings have scored 90 points or less.

Here's a fact: the typical venture capital firm (VC firm) assumes it can beat you investing in startups and amass greater returns than you. VC firms often return up to 25% per year annualized, often beating the average S&P investor by 10% to 20% or more per year.

Now, here's a myth: the old boy networks of VC firms and private equity ("PE") funds are running the show and preventing you from getting in on startups. With platforms like AngelKings.com and crowdfunding sites growing under the JOBS Act, you now have the ability to make smart, calculated investments in the next billion dollar startups.

The old boy networks are gone. **Enter Angel Kings.**

2

THE X FACTOR: HOW TO INVEST IN THE RIGHT PEOPLE

"Trust but verify."

– Ronald Reagan

When Angel Kings invests in startups, we look to the founders first. Our team looks for that future icon: the next Steve Jobs, Bill Gates, or Elon Musk. Those names are pretty big shoes to fill. We want someone who will swing for a homerun every chance he or she gets; someone who creates a new industry or platform to solve a problem; someone with an all-in mentality from day one until the day we meet him or her. And just to be clear: We meet the founders behind every potential investment them before we write a check. And you should, too.

The "People" factor accounts for a large percentage of our investment formula. We're disclosing this not because we want some sycophantic founder to pitch us and tell us how "passionate" and "dedicated" he or she is; in fact, to the contrary.

The investment formula is about selecting the right people, and informing and educating them so that they don't bother pitching us unless they fit our proprietary **"PASS"** Formula.

Here are Angel Kings' **four must have personality factors** before we make an investment in an idea from a founder or founders. We call this the "Angel Kings' Personality Profile" model:

1. <u>**P**assionate, but with a purpose.</u>
2. <u>**A**ll-in to their endeavor.</u>
3. <u>**S**hows no fear of failure.</u>
4. <u>**S**urrounded by equals or those greater.</u>

These four personality traits are hard to define objectively. After all, how do you define passion? What does it mean to be "all-in?" How can you tell if someone has no fear of failure? How do you know if a founder has people on her team just as good as she is? And does this matter?

We'll outline some key questions to ask so that you can spot these founders' traits and make smarter investments in startups. We will take these subjective questions and concepts and put them inside our proprietary formula to make you a better angel investor.

she feels like nothing is going right, the best founder always gets up quickly before the self-pity worms its way in. There is a level of tenacity, shrewdness and optimism that a founder must possess in order to make sure her vision succeeds.

For the investors…

As an investor, your big moment could come at any time. Again and again, you'll be pitched on ideas, products and services that will be the next "big thing." You have to know when and how much you should bet to get a fruitful return, one in which you're not just in the money but you're the grand winner … Yes, it's possible.

For the founders…

View every hand you're dealt as if it's your last. Look at an investment as your ticket. You will never be dealt pocket Aces every hand. You're likely to be dealt just as many terrible cards as the next guy. In fact, you should be happy to even be sitting at the table instead of working a boring job!

If you're distracted or not fully committed to each hand, you will fail.

Here are some interview tips for investors questioning founders to determine whether a founder is all-in or if their startup is a part-time venture:

1. What keeps you busy outside of working with this company?
2. How many other projects/ventures are you working on?
3. When someone asks you for your job title, what do you say?
4. When someone asks you where you work, how do you respond?

5. Do you do better with more things or fewer on your plate?

Each of these questions pertains to what keeps a founder occupied day and night; as an investor, you need to know if your money is going to a startup with focus and a leader who is all-in at every moment.

You should always ask the same question in many different ways to know if someone is telling the truth. And as Ronald Reagan once brilliantly said, "Trust, but verify." Verify that a founder is just as motivated as you are before giving him or her a dime.

* * *

(3) SHOWS NO FEAR OF FAILURE

The most common trait that we see in startup founders is no fear of failure. Entrepreneurs in every startup must be able to hear the word "No" over and over again. The harsh reality is that it's hard to hear "no" for most founders, particularly when these often Ivy-educated, top-of-their-class individuals have soared beyond their peers all of their lives.

But a "No" is ubiquitous in the startup world, and founders must maintain composure and be able to move on to the next customer, VC firm or investor, or else they'll wither away like a flower in the desert. They inevitably discover that hearing the word "no" and facing multiple rejections and objections to their companies are all part of the startup process. The best founders are the ones who learn how to embrace these rejections and turn them into stepping-stones to success.

Can you imagine what it must have been like for Elon Musk at SpaceX to think he had a shot of competing against NASA by launching satellites and rockets into space?

Musk has encountered resistance repeatedly when launching new products – whether it was from large defense companies that feared his companies would take their government subsidies, or from utility companies that were wary of embracing Musk's green energy in SolarCity.

Another unquestionable example of a founder without fear is Mark Zuckerberg. Facebook has been arguably the most impactful company on society in the past 10 years. If it weren't for Zuckerberg's antics at Phillips Exeter Academy and then Harvard University, where he was warned repeatedly about his programming and online activities, Facebook would have never happened.

Rejection and failure go hand and hand with running a startup. The difference between founders like Musk and Zuckerberg and founders who aren't as successful is the ability to recognize that rejection isn't an obstacle or roadblock. Rejection is fuel to keep going, to keep building great things, and to launch what they know will transform industries and make people call them "icons."

BUT LET'S BETTER DEFINE FAILURE...

On selling:

Having no fear of failure doesn't mean a startup founder should continue to build a product that people don't want.

If a founder is blindly stubborn, and she continues to sell her vision to a market that finds no need for it, then as an investor, you should be concerned. There's nothing worse than a founder spending money to build something no one is either going to use repeatedly for free (Facebook) or going to buy out of necessity (Tesla).

Having no fear of failure doesn't mean a startup founder should continue to pitch investors when they continually refuse to write a check. Having no fear of failure can simply mean a founder who takes charge of her own path.

Musk and Zuckerberg were intent on having their ventures change the conversation within industries that have existing dominant players. They didn't care that those players would be upset. Based on their example, having no fear means a founder believes that a fundamental paradigm shift is needed in an industry to make the world a better place, and she's going to take charge to make it happen.

Interview tips: How can you tell if a founder is fearless?

1. When was the last time you were rejected? How did you respond?
2. Has anyone ever told you something was not possible? How did you respond?
3. If you were given a chance to speak to a huge audience for five minutes (example: the United Nations, the State of the Union, or on Wall Street) what would you say? And why?
4. What's your biggest fear in life?

* * *

(4) SURROUNDED BY EQUALS OR THOSE GREATER

Not one startup founder has created a successful company without being surrounded by amazing talent.

When we invest in startups through Angel Kings, we don't just get to know the startup founder, but we also get to know the team. We also don't care whether someone went to an Ivy League or state school, or if the team is stacked with previous successes. Ultimately, we want a founder who has managed to recruit people of equal talent and skill to support her vision and share the same success-driven purpose.

The default question we ask before investing: Is there more than one person on the team who could step up and take over the CEO role if the CEO died, was replaced, gave up or just didn't have it in her anymore? There must be at least one, and preferably two or more, people within a company who could step up to the plate and replace a founder.

Even though an iconic personality ideally should build the startup, someone should be able to take over at a moment's notice. Don't invest in a one-person business, which is often the problem that investors encounter with lifestyle and one-person service companies.

Interview tips: Who else is making it happen on your team?

1. Who's the best person on your team?
2. How do you respond when this person disagrees with you?
3. Can you delegate tasks to him/her and feel confident that he or she will get the job done?

4. When you leave the company for a week, how often do you check in with the office/team?
5. How certain are you that if you were unable to stick with your company the company would still succeed long-term?

* * *

Within the Angel Kings' Investment Formula, we use the following as metrics before deciding to invest in **people:**

- Integrity
- Organic net wealth vs. Age
- Family background
- Education
- Experience
- Credit and Background check

Investors need to interview founders in order to trust but verify the credentials and people with whom they plan on investing. Your intuition is often the best marker for future success.

For example, someone who claimed to have generated more than $10,000,000 in revenue at a previous cyber security startup once pitched to us at Angel Kings. With such profound success in business development, we knew we might have a hit on our hands. However, after speaking with the previous CTO and CEO, we learned that the startup had dissolved after three years and that the company had hit no more than $750,000 in total revenue during that time frame. Be careful with integrity... Trust, but verify.

Investors need to determine how old a founder is and whether or not she has previously earned a living or made money independent of her family's wealth. If a founder has made money by her mid-30s – read: had a liquidity event, IPO'd or sold a previous company – this should catch your eye. However, if a founder is saddled with debt or still struggling financially in her late 20s while using her parents' money to pay her bills, stay away.

Most 20, 30 and 40-year-olds should have learned how to manage their money. But another indicator of success in startup founders is their exposure to affluent people, which may be because many founders come from wealthy families themselves. We believe that it is best to invest in founders who are comfortable having a conversation that deals with large amounts of money, but also do not support themselves using their families' wealth. These startup founders tend to have wealthy parents who taught their kids how to invest but also how to live frugally. As an investor, having a founder who has been taught financial responsibility at a young age yields greater returns. This doesn't mean Angel Kings doesn't invest in some kid who's only 19 years old and is building the next big thing... rather, we tend to ask enough about a founder's background and nurturing to get a sense of how he or she handles money. After all, when we write a $1,000,000 check, this money should be neither overwhelming nor too little for a founder to understand how to manage it.

In fact, look no further than Zuckerberg and Gates. One's father was a wealthy dentist and the other's father ran a bank. Both kids went to private schools and then matriculated at Harvard University.

Why does exposure to money matter? Why are angel investments more successful when the founders come from a family with some means?

The basic reason is two-fold: On the one hand, you get someone who won't spend freely without frugality (a big problem currently in startup investing), and on the other hand, the investors will get someone who's not going to sell out on their first buy-out offer from a larger company.

Larry Page and Sergey Brin of Google exemplify the type of founder we're talking about. They were offered $1,000,000 to sell Google to Yahoo. To most people, $1,000,000 is a lot of money. However, both Page and Brin had been among wealthy students at Stanford, and they both come from families who understand worth, value and how to spend money frugally but with calculated risk. As founders, their backgrounds gave them a far-sighted perspective on what Google would be worth down the road.

POKER 101:

The best poker players each year at the World Series of Poker are those who understand how to take calculated risks under fixed time constraints. Yes, there's a certain amount of luck involved, but on average during the tournament of life you'll be given an equal amount of opportunity to execute and win. The icons of the industry were no different than you and would have been phenomenal poker players. Could you be just as great? Yes.

***Note on Founder Background Checks:**

We realize it's difficult to do credit and background checks on all founders and founding teams. In fact, just asking the question of a founder ("can I see your credit report?") might be awkward. However, just like a bank giving a loan to someone, you've got to ask these questions. If you don't know whether the founders are credible, you shouldn't invest.

To my knowledge, we're one of the only venture capital groups in the world who request a background check during our due diligence process… but it's saved us from making many mistakes! If you're considering investing in a startup and don't know how to conduct a background check on founders, learn how at AngelKings.com.

3

THE NEW IN NOTHING NEW: HOW TO FIND THE NEXT BILLION-DOLLAR PRODUCT

"What has been will be again. What has been will be done again. There is nothing new under the sun."

– Ecclesiastes 1:9

After concerning ourselves with the people behind a startup, we look at the product. Everyone–from investors to literary agents–talks about looking for the next big idea, the new kid on the block who's poised to shake things up. The truth is that there isn't anything new. None of the startups covered in this book solves a problem that hasn't been solved before, and no product idea is universally unique.

At its core, Uber is a taxi service. Taxi services carry people from one place to another, providing a valuable transport service in exchange for money. In 1897, Gottlieb Daimler built a meter-equipped taxi–the first "modern" taxi–over 100 years before Travis Kalanick and Garrett Camp founded Uber. Before Daimler, for-hire carriages and stagecoaches transported people across America and Europe in the 17th and 18th centuries. Even earlier in human history, travelers bartered with wagon owners or merchants for rides.

A history of the taxi could span an entire book; the bottom line is that Uber doesn't offer a new service. As long as humanity has needed to get somewhere, people created solutions–products–that met the transport need.

Instead of looking for the next new thing, we look for people with the next better solution. We invest in products that offer more efficient, economical, sustainable, or convenient solutions. We want products that also have the potential to be a future monopoly. With Uber, the solutions are more efficient than traditional cab services. In many areas, they are more convenient and offer a more luxurious approach to transportation services than a basic yellow cab.

In Peter Thiel's brilliant book, *Zero to One*, he characterizes the best startups as those that start small in a niche, and then monopolize as they scale. He is right. Every day we get pitched on the next "Uber for X." Clones have ruined opportunities for innovation. Products shouldn't be about creating a clone; they should be about creating a new category of innovation.

When evaluating a product-considering whether it's a game changer-we ask:

1. Does the product solve a problem better, or in a significantly different way, than other products or services?
2. Would we pay for the product or service?
3. Does the product create a strong want or is it needed?
4. Does the product benefit from a bandwagon effect?
5. Are the product and the company brandable?

* * *

> **POKER 101:**
>
> When novices play card games like poker, they often try to emulate the style of others at the table. Betting the same amount or raising before the flop with certain regularity. If you play like the others at your table, you'll chip-off and be "felted" before you can say, "I'm all-in." Be careful not to invest in certain startups because some other person is doing the same. Invest the way you want... on your own terms.

PUTTING THE NEW IN NOTHING NEW

No new problems or overall solutions may exist, but new approaches do. We look for founders with creative, intelligent, and marketable approaches. Travis Kalanick's approach with Uber was to convert a growing reliance on crowdsource models in technical and Internet fields to a new field: transportation. And he started small, in a niche – sedan cars and high-end limousines – and within a community he could manage, San Francisco, California.

GoPro, another of our *former* favorite startups, approached personal video with the knowledge that individuals are more mobile, more discerning, and more connected than ever before. GoPro products build on decades, if not centuries, of photography and video solutions, but the company does so with an eye toward professional image capture and fewer limits on camera person mobility. The company also has created a culture, community, and zealous following of consumers, which no doubt helps brand loyalty – even with a recycled idea.

How do you know something offers a new, or better, approach? We look at four major qualities of a product: efficiency, economics, sustainability, and convenience.

A product or service is more efficient if it saves time or resources; time or resource savings is a reason people choose to buy one product over another. The growing trend in hybrid car sales points to this premise: Despite a number of factors that might turn buyers away–such as higher price point–many consumers choose the vehicle that is presented as most efficient.

The efficiency win with Uber is obvious: With a few clicks on a device pulled from their pocket, consumers can hitch a ride. No more fighting on street corners for the next cab or standing in the rain on a muddy curb. Not only does the app provide ride booking within a few screen taps, but it also makes the process more efficient and satisfying–riders can scan ratings and reviews before making a service decision.

Economics deals with the cost–or perceived cost–to–value ratio–of a product. Beating the competition on cost is an obvious step to a better solution, but we don't need to see lowest–price products to believe that something's a good investment. GoPro is a perfect example.

GoPro cameras are more expensive than other consumer video cameras on the market; for that matter, anyone with a smartphone can capture video without investing in additional equipment at all. The perceived cost–to–value ratio for GoPro cameras is high, however. Consumers get versatile video camera products capable of semi–pro-to-pro quality output at a fraction of the cost of traditional professional equipment. In fact, GoPro can even boast that its performance is Emmy–Award–winning, building on the value.

Sustainability has become a growing factor in investment decisions, because it's a growing factor in consumer buying decisions. Studies have shown that modern consumers are more likely to purchase items–and even pay a bit more for them–if the brand, product, or service is somehow inclined toward environmental solutions. This drive from consumers explains why the green packaging market in America is trending to pass $178 billion by 2018. When selecting investments, we are always cognizant of consumer behaviors, which is why sustainability is a consideration.

Founders and products can bring a more sustainable approach to solutions by using recyclable, recycled, or eco-friendly materials; they can also create processes that are, themselves, sustainable. Uber's crowdsourced taxi model is inherently sustainable: It takes vehicles that are already on the road and puts them to greater use, potentially conserving a great deal of fuel in the process.

Finally, we come to convenience. We love to see a founder with an intelligent idea that makes life easier for the target audience. Drive-thru windows, toss-away plastic storage containers, and a proliferation of frozen pizzas in the cooler aisle of any grocery store illustrate the point that convenience sells, making it a good investment.

Both Uber and GoPro capitalize on convenience. In fact, both companies use convenience to drive increasing values that exceed that of the primary product. GoPro delivers a better solution through the convenience of its many accessories. Filmmakers can strap a camera to just about anything, from helmets to pets. GoPro does hands-free filmmaking better than previous solutions.

Uber's take on convenience is supplying it to both parties in every transaction. The customer gets mobile access to ride apps and anytime capability to book a ride. The driver gets access to a consumer market he wouldn't otherwise have without spending time and money on marketing.

To determine whether a founder has brought you another version of a tired solution or the next better thing, ask yourself:

1. Does the solution do it faster than others do?
2. Is it more affordable than others are?
3. If not affordable, does it provide more value?
4. Can the solution be marketed as green?
5. Is the solution more sustainable than others are?
6. Is the solution easier than others are?

7. Does the solution make some action or need easier on the consumer?
8. Is this a clone of an existing company, or a ground breaking new, and potential monopoly over all others?

* * *

Is the product wallet-worthy?

Before we invest in any idea, we ask ourselves if consumers are going to invest in the product. In short, would you, as a consumer, shell out money for the service or product?

Sometimes, the answer is easy. Evaluating the startup that was Uber likely would have been easy: People across the world were already paying for taxi services. Would they pay for rideshare-style transport? Angel investors considering Uber had a similar industry to look at in that regard–people were already paying for accommodations at residences through numerous websites that let travelers book an extra room, bed, or sofa with those willing to provide the accommodation. If people were willing to pay to sleep in a stranger's bedroom, surely they'd pay for a quick ride in a qualified, vetted stranger's car.

The "would you pay question" is harder for some products. Would you have paid for a GoPro camera when the company was starting out? If you had no interest in video photography, certainly not–bringing up a good point about angel investing. Investing in products–and people–you are passionate about enhances the nonfinancial rewards. You'll be more excited to watch the idea, person, or company grow. It's not the primary reason we invest, but it makes the endeavor more worthwhile all around.

At Angel Kings, we always consider the pay question, but since we're selecting founders and ideas for a wider investing audience, our approach is broader. At an individual level, we might not be willing to pay for a product because of personal preferences or needs. Instead, we consider whether if the needs and wants are there, does the service or product inspire opening the wallet?

With GoPro, the initial branding coincided heavily with a market that has been trending up–sports and high-energy activities. Though the cameras have found homes in a variety of other settings, the fact that they–along with accessories and mounts–could be marketed to the fitness and extreme sports audience gives investors an idea of whether the product would be wallet-worthy. Even a brief glance into the niche sports and fitness market shows that participants are often middle-class or well off, willing to travel, and willing to pay for goods and services that are deemed high quality or specialty. From special clothing to extreme accessories, wallets open when marketing is done right in the sports market, which is only one of the reasons GoPro's product would have appeared to investors to have a high likelihood of meeting the "would you buy it" test.

When considering the "would you pay" factor as an angel investor, ask yourself:

1. Would *you* pay for the product?
2. If you wouldn't, can you imagine a scenario in which someone else would?
3. Does that scenario encompass a large enough group of people to sustain the product successfully?

* * *

Does the product meet a need or create a strong want?

Successful products–particularly those that connect with target audiences quickly–meet a specific need or create a strong want in the consumer. As an investor, need and want considerations should be framed by an understanding of economic status and current trends within a given industry.

Meeting a need is often the fastest way to product success, especially in a down economy. Consumers watching pennies are still going to spend on products that meet essential needs–particularly if those products meet needs in a new, less expensive, or more efficient manner. Part of Uber's success is that it managed to meet a need *and* create a want.

Uber services aren't always less expensive than traditional taxi services, especially in slower-moving environments such as downtown Manhattan. In other cities, including Detroit, Chicago, and Atlanta, Uber services are significantly less expensive than hailing a cab, especially when you factor in a tip to the traditional taxi driver. Immediately, Uber has a win: It meets a common, essential transportation need at a lower cost than the competition.

But Uber also creates a want. Uber services are seen as trendy and fancy–in many cases, the ride itself is more comfortable and luxurious than that experienced in a traditional taxi. Uber's services are also on demand. Users don't need to stand in the weather or a crowded street to hail a cab. They don't need to call a taxi service that could be miles away and wait for the car to show up. Instead, they take action via an app, from the comfort of their home, workplace, or any location they happen to be, and Uber can connect them with the most convenient transport options. Based on Uber's success, modern city dwellers want these conveniences.

When need isn't a driving factor, then strong desire for a product has to push consumers to buy it. Often, what creates that desire is a product that is considered premium or luxury. Let's face it. Shoppers don't buy flat screen televisions because of their need to keep up with news or entertainment. Basic televisions are more than capable of providing the solution for that need. But shoppers *desire* more than a basic television. They want the latest in flat screen technology. That's part of what made GoPro a strong startup. Perhaps you could argue that families *need* a way to capture memories, but most investors would never say consumers needed the products offered by GoPro.

Instead, GoPro, through a strong brand, created a desire for its products. Even consumers outside of niches and hobbies that required GoPro's active camera technology have a want for the products. Today, people are even recommending and purchasing GoPro cameras as first models for young filmmakers because the brand is perceived to be "the best," "reliable," and "premium."

To figure out if a product idea is likely to meet a need or create a strong want, ask:

1. What problem does the product solve, and does that problem require a solution?
2. Is the service or product essential to the daily life of some group of consumers?
3. Does the product have potential for creating or becoming a trend?
4. Does the product or service offer a premium or luxury option that consumers will desire?
5. Could the brand position itself as "the best"?

***

THE BANDWAGON EFFECT

We alluded to the bandwagon effect a bit with GoPro, but successful bandwagon marketing relies on more than creating a product with trend impact or any likelihood that consumers will develop strong want for the item. The product also has to be conducive to the marketing approaches that create bandwagon impact in today's market–television marketing is powerful, but so are social media, online marketing, blogging, and creative PR campaigns. Reviews, ratings, and fan bases all contribute to the ability of an idea to generate bandwagon impact.

Think about it. Nowadays, every product and professional service that can be found on the Internet will have a page solely dedicated to reviews and ratings. If you see that a product or service has amassed thousands of five-star reviews using organic referrals (not paid), you've found a winner and possible billion-dollar startup – as long as this growth is sustainable.

The *Bandwagon effect* requires:

1. That the idea–the use of the product, the benefit of the service, the brand–is communicable.
2. That communication is likely to spread a desire to use the product or service among peer networks.

The bandwagon effect is so valuable that businesses create products to cater to its development. Organizations can purchase fake social media followers to make them look valuable or interesting to the crowd, which entices real users to follow suit. According to news reports, even famous brands and people, such as Justin Bieber, have padded social media accounts.

As an investor, you have to consider the *organic* potential that a brand or idea has for bandwagon impact. Organic means that the brand–the group of fans, followers, or consumers–is real and was developed through organic means such as marketing, customer satisfaction, and word of mouth. To do that, the idea–or part of the idea–must be condensed to bite-sized chunks that are interesting and relevant enough to catch the attention of modern consumers.

Uber is an example of a communicable idea and a company's ability to leverage outside interest to drive continued marketing expansion through others. First, the idea of Uber is interesting: People like to hear stories that put small businesses in the driver's seat, and Uber does this in literal fashion. Second, the idea is not without controversy: Taxi companies still fight against Uber expansion into cities. The result was, and still is, a snowball effect for populating the Uber bandwagon.

Not only did Uber use social media to create buzz, but it also issued press releases nationally and within the areas where it launched. Bloggers, content curated sites, and news media picked up the interesting, somewhat controversial news. Today, Uber is available as a service in hundreds of cities; perhaps more important, the brand has become a household name even in locations where the service isn't yet available.

Communicating an idea isn't enough–the idea has to be relevant and desirable. Peers of those already on the bandwagon must want to join in. As a camera product, GoPro could leverage several communication methods that enticed others to join in. One of those methods, used by other camera companies as well, was to create a reason for using the product. GoPro encouraged users to create their own content and share it, along with hash tags or links, letting user-generated content handle some sharing burdens. But one of GoPro's biggest bandwagon successes came through its own videos.

As part of its initial marketing plan, GoPro launched a YouTube channel. The brand captured its first target audience quickly by collaborating with sports and extreme activity stars to capture short films that highlighted product benefits–namely, that the cameras were versatile and fun. An investor considering the GoPro product at the founding stage might have seen the potential here: Couple an interesting visual product with the world's biggest Internet video site, and creating a fan base becomes easier.

GoPro's plan had enormous bandwagon impact. Not only did the videos garner hundreds of thousands of views, but also they created that want we keep talking about. People wanted GoPro products *and* they wanted to be featured in GoPro's videos. The result was that individual consumers made–and still make–videos with GoPro products, and mentioned the products when videos were shared online. Consumers hope to catch GoPro's attention; GoPro benefits from free marketing.

As an angel investor presented with an idea that may not even be in production yet, determining the potential for bandwagon effect is much harder than considering whether the product meets needs or is likely to encourage consumers to open wallets. That's one reason we, at Angel Kings, do what we do–we combine our experience to analyze potential investments so you don't have to worry about things like bandwagon effect.

If you *are* considering investing in an individual founder, brand, or product, some ways to estimate a potential for bandwagon impact include:

1. Looking at the founder's marketing plan–does it use the product or service in a way that fosters communication?
2. Is the product likely to catch on with a niche market of some type?
3. Would news media care about the product?
4. Does the product–or something closely related to the product–lead to social media content creation?
5. Will consumers be able to easily explain or share the idea?
6. If the idea or product is too complex for sharing in small bits, can it be broken into chunks for sharing?

* * *

A DISTINCT BRAND IMAGE

Branding is so essential that we've touched on it in almost every section so far in this chapter. Strong brand capability means a product or company has the ability to create and instill a distinct image that adds value and helps develop a relationship between the brand and the consumer. Strong branding means a single purchase turns into a relationship: Consumers come back for more or engage with the brand to become influencers and promoters on behalf of the product.

For branding to succeed, a startup must be able to develop loyalty within its consumer base.

Loyalty works for the brand in two ways:

1. It supports return customers.
2. It encourages customers to promote the brand.

Bandwagon impact is a jumpstart to branding, but the company has to continue to encourage loyalty *and* create a unique image. Uber does this well. The name itself is brandable-short and to the point: "uber" means something is a supreme example of what it is. By calling the company Uber, Travis Kalanick announced, "We are offering the supreme taxi service, the outstanding option for both riders and drivers."

GoPro is an even stronger example of brandability, and we covered the startup's video branding experience in the last chapter. One of the things that made GoPro so successful is that Nick Woodman and his team understood whom to reach out to first. Instead of peppering saturated general markets with the camera and tools, they went to the people who would be most likely to use the versatile options to the fullest-the people most likely to show off GoPro in the finest way. Branding GoPro as an active, versatile camera captured a niche market and let the brand move into more general markets later. Consumers of all types noticed GoPro because of the unique branding.

As with the bandwagon effect, evaluating brandability is difficult. You'll need to look at the hype around the startup, the concentration of a potential customer base, ability to address niche needs, and the potential for expanding into other markets without losing what makes the brand unique. In the end, however, brandability comes down to how much customer-perceived value a product or organization can bank. Investors can look at startup plans, interview the founder to ascertain charisma, and make best guesses on how the product will perform with consumers. It's a hit-and-miss evaluation, which is why you must combine it with all the other approaches in this chapter for the best chance at picking products that will go on to perform.

* * *

INVESTING IN THE IDEA

We talked a lot about products in this chapter, but remember that the idea is crucial. Angel investors don't invest in products–young companies rarely have a perfect product yet, which is why they need investors. Founders have ideas, and your job is to evaluate the idea of the product against all the items covered in this chapter and summarized in the checklist below. At the angel investing stage, startups are still in early development; perfecting the product comes in the Seed and Series A investment rounds.

CHECKLIST FOR EVALUATING PRODUCTS

1. Product solves a problem in an innovative way.
    - Less expensive
    - More efficient
    - Sustainable
    - Convenient
2. Someone would pay for the product.
    - It's something you would pay for
    - You can see an audience that would pay for the item
3. The item addresses a need or creates a want.
4. The product has potential for bandwagon impact.
    - It is communicable
    - Communication is likely to create want among peer groups
5. The product is brandable.

4

HOW TO KNOW A COMPANY WILL EXECUTE

"The way to get started is to quit talking and begin doing."
– Walt Disney

As an investor, you need to know that the founder has a plan that moves her from talking about her idea to executing her idea. It can't be just any old plan, which is where a lot of startups fall flat–the plan is often "develop a thing people want and make it available." The problem with the "if you build it, they will come" mentality is that it only works in fantasy sports movies...and in a few rare cases with actual products. As an angel investor, you can't count on your investment choice being one of those rare cases.

Steve Jobs is quoted as saying, "You can't just ask customers what they want and then try to give that to them." You've got to let customers know that they need and want your product before they even know it themselves. Startups need more than a plan for the product–they need marketing and branding plans; the actions laid out by those plans must have potential for engaging consumers and building loyalty.

Evaluating the founder's plans involves strategy and experience, and it's not enough to be able to recognize that a product idea is solid. It goes back to our poker metaphor from chapter two. You might know enough about poker to recognize a royal flush when it's dealt to you, but do you have the skill and experience to play the hand for maximum profit?

One of the benefits of investing through Angel Kings is that we not only help you recognize when a strong hand is being dealt, but we also help you play the hand for maximum potential. We use both a checklist and a points approach when evaluating a founder's execution plan, coupling that evaluation with the considerations detailed in other chapters of this book.

TWO APPROACHES TO EXECUTION

When executing the creation and marketing of a product, most successful entrepreneurs make use of either a Lean Startup or a Novel Startup.

A "Lean Startup" (popularized by Eric Ries) begins with a minimum viable product. The product is simple, often inexpensive or involving a low capital requirement at the start, and can be tested on consumers. Consumer testing–often in the form of a beta distribution–lets startups create multiple reiterations of a product until it meets the needs of the market, at which point distribution usually takes off.

Pinterest is a prime example of a Lean Startup. First, the product itself is virtual, which is less expensive to distribute than a tangible good. Second, Pinterest made use of beta testers for free research and development to perfect its product. The site launched in March 2010 as a closed beta, limiting users to facilitate a tight communication process that allowed for efficient troubleshooting and product tweaking. Even after the closed beta, Pinterest operated as an open beta product for some time, which meant users could invite others to the platform but were still reporting bugs as necessary to product developers.

A Novel Startup is one that involves a very distinct or new product–something that reinvents the wheel. The product may meet needs already being met, but it does it through a new method. In some cases, a startup may fall into both categories–Pinterest, while a Lean Startup, was also a Novel Startup.

Another prototypical Novel Startup was Peter Thiel's vision for what became PayPal. In fact, we highly recommend the book "Zero to One," in which Thiel outlines his vision for homerun startups. The product began as a fraud detection system, as fraud transactions became a bigger concern for consumers. The novel idea–that online and other transactions could be safe, efficient, and easy–resulted in the PayPal money transfer service of today. Money transfer needs were already being met with services such as Western Union, but no one was meeting them in the convenient, mobile manner that PayPal manages.

FIVE CONSIDERATIONS FOR EXECUTION

At Angel Kings, we look at five major considerations when evaluating a founder's execution plan or the potential for a product to be executed. In this chapter, we'll walk you through each of these considerations by looking at Pinterest and Apple as main examples.

1. Does the plan encourage or make use of user execution?
2. Does the plan use product or marketing to create conversation?
3. Is there a potential for memorable marketing?

4. How likely is the brand to spark its own culture?
5. Does the product, service, or brand meet a psychological need?

USER EXECUTION

Successful startups put users and consumers to work. Nowhere is this principle of user execution and marketing more apparent than online, and Pinterest user numbers for the first three years illustrate the power of the user. The platform, which began in closed beta in early 2010, had 10,000 users that year. By 2011, the user number ballooned to an astounding 11,700,000; the user number almost doubled by 2012, coming in at 25 million. For those three years, Pinterest experienced a Compound Annual Growth Rate ("CAGR") that was more than four times that of other platforms, including Google, Facebook, LinkedIn, or Twitter.

Pinterest relies on user-generated content in a heavy visual setting to drive conversion of other users. While the startup had to do some work to get the word out initially, a use increase of 1,170 fold in a single year didn't come solely from online banner ads and resourceful PR. Instead, Pinterest gave users the ability to create one or more online bulletin boards; users pin images from across the web to each bulletin board, and other users can interact with the images by repinning them to other boards or leaving comments.

Because social sharing is a proven means to get marketing messages out, what better way to execute a social sharing platform? Pinterest began with a closed beta–not only a good move from a functionality and control standpoint, but also a smart marketing strategy. As beta users discussed this new site via social media pages and blogs, friends and followers became aware that a nifty online tool existed, and *they did not have access*. The build-up was small at first, but slow growth was short-lived as

Pinterest quickly moved to an open beta that allowed users to invite others to the platform. Suddenly, the have-nots could become the haves; this was a powerful strategy to create user execution.

While some Pinterest users create private boards for their own research or use, most are excited to share her Internet finds with others. Users began linking to their boards, bringing in additional viewers, many of who became users too. Within a year, marketing experts were touting Pinterest as the next big thing in online advertising, and blogs, brands, and websites were sporting "Pin this" links on every page with an image. No longer a startup, Pinterest still relies heavily on user execution for stability-a strategy that led to $764 million in funding as of late 2014.

Today's technology makes it easier for startups to take advantage of user execution, which is why Pinterest initially had more success in this area than an organization such as Apple, which launched in the mid-1980s. But Apple continues to take advantage of the user execution premise with every product it releases. We'll talk about the culture Apple built in a bit, but that culture is what drives the brand's loyal consumers to market for the company. Just pull out a non-Apple device in eyesight of an avid Mac user, and you'll see what we mean.

It's easy to look back and see how brands have used user execution to launch, but how could investors in the early days of Pinterest have known that it would take off? Some things to look for in an execution plan include:

1. Strategy for immediate user engagement on some level.
2. Ability to create a "have and have not" situation to drive user desire.
3. Willingness of the founder to put a certain amount of control in user hands.
4. Capability of the brand to manage that control in a positive or productive fashion.

CREATING CONVERSATION

User execution falls flat if no one's talking about a product–conversation, whether digital or otherwise, is the fuel that drives user execution. Conversation can happen spontaneously among consumers, but one of the best ways to drive it is to start with the product or brand. Investors should look to startup plans for an understanding of brand/consumer relations in the Internet age. The new "consumer" of our techie generation wants:

1. To have input into the product.
2. A continued conversation with participation on both sides.
3. To deal with transparent or open companies.

Brands that invest in conversation starters benefit as the conversation continues–think of it like a cocktail party, where the brand is a single guest. The guest only needs to gather two others and offer a question, comment, or story that sparks an entertaining conversation. As the conversation goes on, others will join. The guest can stop working as hard to sustain the conversation–it will grow and change organically from that point.

The same is true of a startup or established company. Coca-Cola used this idea in a campaign recently, asking its social media followers to publish suggestions for making the world happier. Millions of users generated content and shared the messages; millions of others voted. Coca-Cola benefited from all that conversation; in turn, it funded a winning idea.

Another way brands can encourage conversation is through catchy, shocking, or controversial messaging. Apple's advertising today is staid compared with one ad from its early days–a 1984 Super Bowl ad that still holds a place on the shelf as the best of the best. In fact, most experts as late as 2012 considered the Apple "1984" ad spot to be the best Super Bowl ad ever aired.

The ad, which played on both the year 1984 and George Orwell's novel of that name, answered consumer fear of growing technology in the 1980s. No, Apple said in the ad, technology wasn't for control–it was for freedom. The ad featured a Big Brother style indoctrination meeting being interrupted by a brightly clad woman wielding a sledgehammer; it was also full of glimpses of technology. Consumers wanted that technology and freedom so much that shoppers inundated stores when the Macintosh computer debuted the same week. The resulting conversation was strong enough to drive $155 million in Macintosh sales within three months.

Controversial advertising isn't without its own risks, but the point is, brands have to generate *something* to talk about if they want to benefit from consumer conversation. Sometimes, the conversation is about the product itself–also something Apple has done well from the beginning. The brand has always stepped away from the competition in design or function; since the 1980s, Apple has been the sleek, luxury computer. It brought the first tablet to market, bringing a prop from past science fiction movies to functional use in modern life. Its phones and other devices are packaged in sleek, elegant fashion–all of these things drive user conversation. Even the Apple versus PC debate drives continued conversation.

It's not enough for the product or the message to be interesting or controversial. It also has to get people talking about it once they've used it. The fact that Pinterest users talked about the product *as part of the product's function* is brilliant. Users created boards and then shared those boards with other people–after clicking a few links to user boards and being encouraged to create their own, most visitors couldn't help but join in. Pinterest users began blogging about their Pinterest habit, news media picked up stories about the up-and-coming social media platform, and industry sites such as Forbes started publishing articles about how site owners and businesses could use Pinterest for marketing. Remember the guest at the cocktail party? Talk of Pinterest started with a small group of beta users and became an international conversation in less than a year. In fact, Pinterest even capitalized on the "cocktail" party by inviting early users to events and conventions–or joining users at existing events–to facilitate increased conversation.

You can't always tell what will catch consumer fancy, but investors should always look for signs that a founder understands the need to be the conversation starter and that she includes strategies to drive conversation in her execution plan. Look for:

1. Social media plans for engaging users.
2. Marketing or advertising ideas likely to strike chords with consumers.
3. Products, packaging, and branding that are worth taking about.

MEMORABLE MARKETING

Marketing that sticks is valuable, which is why companies go out of their way to create legendary Super Bowl commercials. When you're spending up to $4.5 million for 30 seconds of airtime, your marketing better be memorable. Apple's 1984 spot aside, most startups aren't likely to be aiming for Super Bowl stardom anytime soon. Still, memorable campaigns on any level are important because they drive all the other things we're talking about. Memorable marketing sparks user conversation, which drives user execution that, in turn, helps to create a brand culture.

As we previously mentioned, memorable marketing isn't without risks–but neither is angel investing. Part of the angel investor's job is to evaluate the planned execution in light of simultaneous evaluations of the people and product–do you trust the people you're investing in to make the right choices about marketing risks? You do need to look at the execution plan, but at the end of the day, the cards you're funding belong in the founder's hand.

Unknown to many, the 1984 Apple advertisement was a big risk. On a 43-point ASI Marketing Research scale, the ad initially tested as a 5 in focus groups. Apple's ad manager at the time kept that news from his superiors, and the one-minute spot aired only once during the Super Bowl. The gamble paid off in the $155 million in sales over the next 90 days.

Startups don't have to invest millions–or even buy television ad space–to create memorable marketing. Just as technology made it easier for Pinterest to leverage user execution today, the Internet offers a sandbox for entrepreneurs looking to draw attention. One example of a small-budget campaign that took off is the GoldieBox "Girls" video. The gaming company, which most people had never heard of, launched an online video calling for increased female interest in technology fields. The video featured girls dressed in various work outfits and rewritten lyrics to the Beastie Boys' song "Girls." Within two days, the video was viewed three million times. It also caused a lawsuit between the company and the Beastie Boys, illustrating the point about risk.

Marketing that is memorable and drives conversation doesn't have to be in the form of content or video. Uber, which we talked about in the previous chapter, regularly uses actionable marketing strategies–such as delivering roses on Valentine's Day, providing on-demand ice cream trucks, or showing up at conferences to entice users in launch cities with free rides.

Some of the best memorable marketing campaigns actually incorporate other components of strong execution. In 1996, Hotmail launched its email service and said no to traditional marketing in favor of user execution. The brand integrated a signature line into every email sent by existing Hotmail users. " P.S.: we love you. Get your free email at Hotmail," read the signature. Hotmail put the advertising burden on users without impacting user experience–the result was a million new members in half a year.

For the most part, memorable marketing is:

1. Clever, shocking, touching, or useful.
2. Strikes a chord with consumers.
3. Provides a starting point for user execution or conversation.
4. Speaks in some way to the culture the brand desires to establish.

BRAND CULTURE

Throwing shocking marketing campaigns at the audience or slipping free advertising into the product isn't enough to ensure long-term success. As we evaluate execution plans from startups at Angel Kings, we look for a complete package of memorable marketing, consumer conversation, and the potential for product loyalty that creates what is known as brand culture. Brand culture is essential to success for many companies. In fact, the author of *Emotional Branding*, Marc Gobe, opines that branding is behind Apple's continued success, particularly after the company's 1990s struggles.

Apple's brand goes beyond a marketing image–it reaches into the consumer audience to create a community. Consumers aren't loyal to Apple–they are in love with it. Apple plays to this brand culture with sleek products that let its users differentiate themselves from the crowd. When Steve Jobs was at Apple, he played to the culture on a personal level, speaking to consumers through advertising and announcements as if he was a friend passing on a secret he'd come up with.

Apple continually positions itself as a bastion of innovation, design and imagination, and that comes across in the consumer culture. Talk to a group of people about which computer to buy, and even people from the PC crowd may tell you that creative endeavors, such as filmmaking or graphic design, call for a Mac.

Apple's product- and marketing-driven brand culture is very different from Pinterest's community-driven culture. Pinterest stepped out of the way and let users drive the culture, just as they drove the early product expansion. The culture is so pervasive online now that it spawned its own language, groups, games, and blogs dedicated solely to recreating things seen on Pinterest. The brand created this culture by meeting the growing social media need with a product that didn't look anything like Facebook or Twitter. In fact, consumers touted Pinterest as "*not* the next Facebook or Twitter." Pinterest cofounder Ben Silbermann is quoted as saying "There's a lot of pressure to look like the last company that was successful." But looking like the last company makes it harder to position a brand or product for a unique culture.

Culture can be seen with all the successful startups we're highlighting throughout this book. The users are different. The companies are varied. The products range from social media sites to transportation services. Still, each success is due in part to a consumer audience that identifies with the culture exemplified by the brand and products.

SATISFYING A PSYCHOLOGICAL NEED

Probably the easiest way to drive brand culture is to satisfy a psychological need with the product or brand. What drives people to want to belong to the culture? With Apple, it might be association–people want to be associated with this culture that displays itself as sophisticated, successful, and always next-gen.

Other psychological needs include entitlement, belonging, and recognition. For early Pinterest users, belonging drove many to embrace the brand. People were using a new social media outlet, and they were having a lot of fun. They were talking about their Pinterest habit and the adorable sweater or awesome party favor idea they just saw. Others just wanted in to get early access to such a hot network.

When evaluating a product or startup idea, ask yourself whether the product can create a psychological need in people that the product can then meet?

* * *

THE ANGEL KINGS EVALUATION SYSTEM

Your poker hand may look good, but can you read the competitions'? Knowing when to hold and fold is similar to knowing when to invest, and evaluating an execution plan in conjunction with the other elements covered in this book can be complicated. That's why we at Angel Kings employ a Point System. Using all five of the components covered in this section, we rate each startup's execution plan on five things.

- **Advertising return on investment.** Think of Hotmail's marketing campaign–millions of text advertisements for free. We'd score that high when it comes to return on investment, but free or low-cost advertising isn't always required. With the right plan, a pricy gamble like Apple's 1984 Super Bowl ad is also promising.

- **Efficiency of product distribution mechanism.** Pinterest drove distribution through users. Early on, it created a "Pin it forward" campaign that let bloggers invite new users. The more invites that bloggers sent, the more invites they were offered, letting bloggers increase readership or reward readers with Pinterest invites.

- **Scalability of model.** Not everything Pinterest did was scalable, but the model itself can scale almost infinitely. For investors, that means an ever-growing revenue potential should the startup be successful.

- **Three- to five-year plan or road map.** Perhaps no company is as savvy when it comes to branding as Apple, and the company has always operated on an extensive road map. As a startup, that let Apple take advantage of opportunities others couldn't; as an established organization, a consistent plan means Apple is always in a leadership position in the industry.

- **Stumbling blocks to date.** When investors can see how startups have dealt with stumbling blocks, they can get a better idea of success. Pinterest stalled out early with only a few thousand users, but it launched the open beta and invitation campaigns to overcome that issue.

Both Apple and Pinterest would score high on Angel Kings' point system for execution if they were being evaluated as startups today. It's easy to see that in hindsight but much more difficult to see when looking at the plans a founder has put down on paper or in a PowerPoint presentation.

CHECKLIST FOR EVALUATING STARTUP EXECUTION PLANS:

1. The plan makes use of user execution.
   - To physically or virtually distribute product.
   - For marketing.
   - To create a community around the brand or product.
2. The product or brand is capable of creating conversation.
   - The execution plan includes communication between brand and consumer.
   - Planned marketing is likely to drive communication or conversation.
   - The product itself is worthy of conversation.
3. The brand has plans for a memorable marketing campaign.
4. The brand or product has potential for creating culture.
   - It creates a psychological need.
   - It can meet the psychological need.
   - The product or brand features significant differences from similar solutions.

ROSS' STARTUP POKER RULES
Find Your Information Advantage

1. Founders must be all-in. | People

Never invest in a founder or founding team, unless every person is all-in with the venture. If anyone is "part-time" or consulting on the side, stay away. You must make sure that they've already taken risks — and believe — in the company. If they haven't, they don't trust their plan, and likewise you shouldn't trust putting your money in that team.

2. Play the people, read the player. | People

In poker, you win or lose by having meaningful information about your opponent. Gain an information advantage by taking notes, as I did, about a person's habits, movements and even physical appearance. Using our startup investing formula, you should probe into every facet of your founders' lives: their background, financial history, education and their work experience. After all, an LLC and Corporation (C-Corp) are both fictional entities backed by human beings, and you are, at its core, investing in people. So know your founders well before handing over a check.

3. The Law of Large Numbers is always true. | Product

When you play poker for an extended time period rather than a quick session, you depend less on luck and utilize more skills (information gathering & reading opponents). Assuming the card deck is shuffled properly, you have the same probability of being dealt pocket Aces as anyone at the table. But you have to be able to "grind."

Likewise, with startup investing, you'll receive an equal amount of bad pitches from companies that stand zero chance of becoming billion-dollar company, aka, "The next Royal Flushes." In order to mitigate your risk profile, you need to be more patient; say "No" to more startups and "Yes" to fewer hands. Venture Capital isn't a get-rich quick industry. Startup investing is a long-term investment philosophy that requires your patience. But you can, and will succeed.

4. Raise or fold. | Execution

Never just call a bet. If you're playing poker and someone bets before you, it's imperative that you either raise or fold. Why? If you just call a bet, you won't know if your hand is better, worse, or if that player is bluffing. Likewise, when investing in startups, you should be all-in or not in the hand. You cannot be perfunctory. Ask tough questions, follow our formula, and don't do anything half-ass. Raise the stakes when you believe the startup is strong by investing more than the crowd, but walk away if the startup doesn't meet all of our criteria.

5. Never play scared. | Execution

Never show up to the poker table with less than the minimum buy-in. If the minimum is a $1,000, bring that amount. I've seen way too many people lose their chips (money) at a poker table because they came with less than the minimum, played like scared little fish and made bad decisions. You must sit at that table like that shark ready to crush your opponents. Scared money never makes real money. In venture capital and startup investing, you should be able to lose on an investment and still be financially sound. If you start investing in startups without the requisite bank account, you won't be willing to execute and make sound decisions.

6. The House always wins. | Execution

Invest in startups where they are the main supply chain, the wholesaler, and the indispensable source of a customer's needs. If a startup relies on one distributor, is vulnerable to supply issues, or in the software world is "just another app" built on someone's platform, you shouldn't invest. Just like Standard Oil and Trust in the 19th century, you should invest in a startup that maintains control of every process and could eventually become the monopoly. The house always wins. Find the startups that want to be the house where every customer goes to eat.

7. Last position is best. | Timing

In poker, the last person to act has the information advantage at the table. This person can see what other bets have been made and can decide whether his or her cards are suitable to play. Example: someone's holding pocket Aces ahead of you and decides to raise pre-flop. If you're holding Kings, and re-raise the bettor, and then they instantly call you, there's little doubt they are bluffing. Similarly, you want to look for startups that are entering industries later. The first mover advantage doesn't equal success. If a startup is pitching you, but has not shown how their product sells relative to peers, you won't have enough information to know whether it'll be a roaring success or a disappointing flop. A company can still create something revolutionary that hasn't been done before, but they must be able to point to competitors who are emulating them or give you sales numbers that justify need.

5

HOW TO KNOW WHEN THE TIMING IS RIGHT

"Audaces fortuna iuvat."
– Virgil, The Aeneid

There's a time for everything–and not just one time. We've already talked about the fact that the same problems are solved repeatedly throughout history, albeit via different products and services. Because of this, timing is an essential concept for investors to consider when evaluating an idea, product, or a startup's potential for success.

At Angel Kings, timing is a pillar of our evaluation and investment process. Using our poker analogy from previous chapters, a good hand doesn't always win the round–how and when you play on that hand is essential when you're dealing with experienced players. Going all-in on a first round of betting tips your hand, making it likely other players fold or bet less; folding early because someone else bets strong forfeits your chance at winning.

It's always best to be the last at the table to bet, because then you can evaluate the actions of all other players before making a decision. The same logic is true when entering the market with a product: The early bird might get the worm, but what if the worm is defective? The last to enter the market benefits from the challenges and mistakes of those who went before, and we'll discuss this more in a later section.

Perhaps the biggest timing factor we at Angel Kings look at–a make or break factor–is whether the founder has either a long-term plan to scale, or an exit strategy appropriate for the current market (or both!). We'll cover this consideration more in the following sections, but it's important enough to repeat: Angel Kings will never invest in a company that doesn't have a solid exit strategy, such as a sale or IPO, planned. As an angel investor, you should always look for the exit strategy before you invest, as it's the only real safety net you'll have and can be the difference between stagnation and profit.

As we enter the evaluation of a product's timing, we ask ourselves some basic questions before moving on to more in-depth considerations. Let's look at these three questions with regard to one of our model startups: Dropbox.

Will the product–or a version of the product–be around in 10 years?

Dropbox is a cloud-storage provider that offers both free and paid virtual storage for anyone who wants to sign up. A little research into the data-storage niche shows us that data storage problems and solutions have been around for years and are just increasing. Numerous concepts are driving individuals and businesses to virtual storage, including:

1. The hard-to-manage growth of big data.
2. A constant need to share documents and ideas with virtual teams and groups.
3. Greater consumer understanding regarding the need to back up documents in a safe environment.
4. A sustainability drive to reduce paper in both the home and business.

With just that much information, someone looking at the Dropbox idea as a startup would have been able to decide that the product–or something similar–would be around and necessary in a decade.

Can a lasting brand be built around the product or startup?

As stated in chapter 3, predicting branding is difficult, but two components tell you a lot about a product's brandability. Remember, products should support return customers and encourage customers to promote the brand. Dropbox supports return customers by offering options for expanding storage space; everyone gets a few gigs free, and customers pay for more storage, as they need it. The brand encourages customer-based promotion through easy-to-use forms and an incentive plan–when you refer someone to Dropbox, you and the person who signs up get a 500MB increase in storage capacity for free. According to Dropbox founder Drew Houston, the referral program increased signups by as much as 60 percent.

Will people still want to use this solution to a problem over other new solutions that might come out later on?

As an investor, you want the idea behind the product you've invested in to have sustainability and competitive staying power. That means the product has to offer something that is going to be timeless and competitive, but it also means the founder must be able to deal with changes in market trends accordingly.

Dropbox has demonstrated its staying power even in the face of competition from strong competitors. In fact, after Dropbox launched, Apple launched iCloud. According to reports, Houston, who believed in his company so much that he had turned down a nine-figure buyout offer from Steve Jobs, had a moment of concern over the iCloud launch. Because Dropbox offered a solution that is simple and accessible on almost any device, however, his worries were short-lived.

The above questions touch on some of the basics to consider when investing in a startup. At Angel Kings, we also apply a checklist to evaluate timing concerns in-depth.

1. The solution must be timeless in some way.
2. The product must be time-relevant and match current tech trends.
3. The product should never be first to market.
4. The product is timed to hit as a new solution is developing or can be pushed to customers.
5. The startup has an exit strategy and long term-plan to scale.

A TIMELESS SOLUTION

How do you know something is timeless? A quick glance at the fashion world illustrates how quickly fads come and go. What may seem like a timeless design to fashion elites today, might be scorned by them tomorrow. One key in evaluating a product's timelessness is not looking at the details of the design, but looking at the overall problem or solution. Z. Cavaricci and hammer pants may be relics of the 1980s, but *pants* themselves are still around-and have been for centuries. To generalize further, the need to clothe the human body has been around since Adam and Eve donned the proverbial ivy leaves.

No product is timeless. Even something as basic as the toothbrush has evolved over time. But solutions can be timeless–must be timeless to ensure a smart investment. There must have been a desire to solve the problem in the past, and you should have a strong conviction that the desire to solve the problem will continue forever. Otherwise, you risk investing in a one-hit wonder.

When considering Dropbox, the timeless solution is communication. We talked briefly about Dropbox as a data storage solution, but it's also a communication solution. One reporter covering the rise of Dropbox discussed how his wife used it to manage PTA fundraisers–it made complex communication among all of the involved parties easy.

Communication is a timeless solution. Before the advent of handwriting, indigenous tribes used paintings to communicate–and store–ideas. Some of the most renowned and celebrated inventions in history have met the communication need. Ask any school-age child about important inventions, and you'll probably get a list that includes Gutenberg's printing press. Other notable communication solutions include the telegraph, Morse code, telephones, radio, and cell phones. Today, communication solutions are endless, with new ideas hitting the market daily. From basic Internet connections evolved email, chat rooms, and video chatting. From smartphones we get more video chatting, texting, and applications such as Snapchat that offer unique ways to communicate. Communications solutions existed already, but technological advances allowed companies to meet needs and wants in different ways.

Once you establish that the solution is timeless, you just need to ensure that the product correlates to the solution. Dropbox lets users communicate by sharing almost any type of file–text documents, PDFs, images, PowerPoints, and videos–with other users. Not only can users share, but they can do so with ease. Dropbox doesn't require a lot of technical know–how or special software, and it reduces the strain on email and other systems. Users can even share files via Dropbox that are too large to share via email.

Dropbox wasn't just solving any old problem; the founders identified a big problem – inconsistency and lethargy in corporate sharing and communications.

THE PRODUCT MESHES WITH CURRENT TECH

Investors should never evaluate a product or startup in a vacuum–the outside market plays an important part in your decision, particularly when considering timing. A top concern is whether existing technology will support the product or idea. There are certainly cases where a startup company has had to create the infrastructure and technology to launch and support its product; however, it will take a lot of resources, cash, and support structures to continually adapt the product to meet the market's changing needs. As an angel investor, bankrolling a startup with such changing needs and expenses certainly is not where you want to be.

Instead, look for ideas and products that can integrate into existing technology–even better if the idea utilizes existing technology. Snapchat is a great example of this–the app combines texting and pictures, letting individuals share time-limited photographs. Snapchat is only possible because of the existing technology–smartphones with cameras, as well as wireless networks capable of transmitting photographs and text in almost instantaneous fashion. Even better, the support technology was widely popular before Snapchat entered the market, which probably accounts for the immediate acceptance of the app among users.

Looking at Dropbox, you can see the same development. The foundational requirements were all in place: personal computers and mobile devices, the Internet, capable technology users, and software to create and read all the information that would be stored and shared using its services.

When considering whether technology aligns with a product or idea, ask yourself and the founder:

1. How will the product or service reach users?
2. How will consumers use it?
3. Does anything have to be built before the product can be used?
4. Does anything have to be built before the product can be marketed?
5. Does anything have to be built before the product can be disseminated?

You're looking for ideas that have existing answers to the first two questions and minimal requirements–if any–for the last three.

DON'T BE FIRST OUT OF THE GATE

It might seem promising to be the innovator–the Henry Ford of whatever industry is represented by the particular startup you're evaluating. Despite common belief, however, Ford didn't invent the assembly line. He also didn't invent the modern automobile, interchangeable parts, mass production, or the combustible engine that made his Model T possible. In short, Ford wasn't the first mover. He was the mover we remember, in part because he studied what came before and he used that information to meet a market need with a solution that didn't have many of the problems of previous solutions.

The first-mover is always at a disadvantage. Consider our poker game–or any other game, for that matter. The person who moves first has not seen anyone else move. The person who moves first moves blindly. The person who moves first has nothing to build on. In poker, the last to act has the advantage; the same is true in product launches.

> **POKER 101:**
>
> The last to act is always at an advantage. In fact, within Texas Hold em' being "Under the Gun," or first to act after the dealer is a terrible position. You always want to be later in position to bet, raise or fold. If you're a founder launching a product, doing so after someone else has, is a major advantage. Launch second. Not first. Learn from the others who have failed in the industry, before making the same mistakes.

Although many of the startups in our list of seven are now considered innovators in their own space, like Henry Ford, they didn't move first. All seven startups verified that the solution they were providing was something that consumers desired and were willing to pay for. All seven studied the market, watched competitors, and learned from the mistakes and challenges of those competitors. Each company used that information to create a better product when it did enter the market.

Dropbox was far from the first to market digital storage space. Something as simple as the flash drive had been around for years. Google Drive didn't yet exist in its current form, but Gmail and other online email systems provided a rudimentary form of file storage and communication. You could Gmail yourself a document and then access it from any location where Gmail access is possible; you could also email some files to others, though file size and type were limited. These are just a few of the storage and communications solutions that came before Dropbox, letting Drew Houston learn from previous solutions.

It was because of a failure of one of these previous solutions that Houston came up with the idea for Dropbox. While on a four-hour bus ride from Boston to New York, Houston realized he'd left behind his USB drive and didn't have the files he planned to work on. His frustration with existing limitations drove him to begin working on the code for Dropbox.

As an angel investor, it's okay to consider something exciting and innovating. Dropbox was innovative enough to catch the attention of top CEOs in the industry, including Steve Jobs. But look for founders with ideas that build on existing solutions, offer solutions to existing limitations, and make use of information about previous challenges and failures.

THE PRODUCT LAUNCH IS IN LINE WITH A DEVELOPING SOLUTION

The most successful startups enter the market at a point when desire for a solution is emerging and the infrastructure or platform for the solution is also developing.

Consider streaming devices, such as the Roku. These devices hit the market with impeccable timing, because the platform driving them was developing quickly. More and more people were turning from traditional entertainment options, such as cable television, to streaming services such as Netflix or Hulu. While streaming services could be accessed via technology like smart televisions and BluRay players, or by connecting Apple or Google devices to televisions, these solutions could be complex and were often limited by brand. Consumers often found they needed multiple solutions to meet their needs.

Roku combines almost all common streaming options in a single box, catering to a growing consumer desire for both simplicity and on-demand entertainment. The desire was there; the driving factors were there. Roku simply needed to capitalize on them.

Dropbox entered the market in much the same way. Consumers desired a simple solution for sharing and storing files. The Internet, devices, and wireless plans were already there–someone just needed to write the right code and present the product in the right fashion. When that happened, the result was 3,900 percent growth over fifteen months. Dropbox's timing, along with its referral plan, brought in four million users in that time span.

One notable timing factor with the Dropbox launch is the development of cloud storage.

During the first decade of the 21st century, cloud computing was a science-fiction concept that was blossoming in real life. As late as 2012, surveys indicated that many Americans didn't fully understand what cloud computing was; many responded that the cloud didn't exist, even though there were transparent cloud applications that they were using. Still, cloud computing was a buzzword, even outside of the tech industry. People everywhere were interested in this new concept, which sounded almost magical. When Dropbox arrived on the scene, offering free cloud storage and communication to anyone, people flocked to the site to catch a glimpse of the technology. When the functionality turned out to be easy to use, they told their friends. Suddenly, Dropbox boasted millions of users.

LOOK FOR AN EXIT STRATEGY

Why invest in something if you think there's a chance it might fail? The truth is, there is always a chance something won't work out. You, as an investor, cannot predict everything with 100 percent accuracy. The founder you are investing in can't, either. People make mistakes. Before founding Dropbox, Drew Houston worked on a startup dealing with SAT preparation that he would eventually abandon. As it turned out, it wasn't the right idea for him at the right time.

At Angel Kings, we never invest in anything without seeing a solid exit strategy. Exit strategies don't offer 100 percent protection for either the founder or the investor, but they can lighten the blow if a startup doesn't work out. The existence of an exit strategy also tells you something about a founder: He or she understands that things aren't going to come easy, and has thought carefully about many possible eventualities.

Exit strategies are also not all about picking up the pieces. For an angel investor, funding only those startups that have plans to continue as successful companies with modest growth isn't a good financial strategy. You want a mixed bag of investments–as you do with any type of portfolio. In angel investing, that means buying into startups that have planned exit strategies to cash in after reaching initial success–usually by selling to another company after proving the product can drive revenue.

POKER 101:

In poker you should never just call a player's bet. Always raise or fold. Why? By raising or folding your hand, you will be able to see how great your hand is relative to your opponent; if your opponent calls your raise or re-raise, they are signaling they have a decent hand – maybe even better than yours.

Likewise, in startups, an equivalent strategy is raising or folding once you have enough data to determine your likelihood for success: product traction and momentum. On the one hand, don't continue building a company or spending investor money for the sake of it. If you're trying to build a billion dollar company and you're not seeing 10% month-to-month user growth or revenue growth after the first year your product is launched, something's not right. Fold your hand and try something new. On the other hand, if you are seeing massive growth in a certain vertical, niche or new category position, raise the stakes – capital – and continue to scale to your IPO.

To evaluate exit strategies, look for information in the pitch about similar startups that were able to sell to larger companies. Exit strategies require that:

1. The startup can provide something of value, whether or not the product itself is seen as a success. Sometimes, the research or idea alone is valuable to competitors.
2. Possible buyers exist-usually larger companies that are established in the niche. With Dropbox, possible buyers might have included Apple, Google, or Microsoft.
3. The market is big enough to support a purchase.

SKILL, LUCK, AND PEOPLE

The successful poker game requires more skill than luck. You can only play the cards you are dealt, after all. Success when investing in people and products requires a similar mix of skill and luck. You can make all the right observations about people, products, execution, and timing, but some factors–such as how the market will react–are out of your control.

That's not to say you can't get lucky occasionally with a random investment. Plenty of people lucked out by investing in Apple–a truth that was used in the fictional investment of Forrest Gump. Others in the 80s and 90s got lucky with random investments in new concepts such as Yahoo or Amazon, but those aren't repeatable successes. How well you do as an angel investor depends for the most part on how well you utilize the information–minimal though it may be–you are given beforehand.

Concentrate on the founders and the products when you consider investing. What the competition is doing right now isn't essential. The right product in the hands of the right people will outperform others with the same idea, which is one reason Drew Houston was confident enough in his company to not sell to Apple. Even if the market seems primed for a certain product or solution, the wrong product or the wrong people are likely to fail.

* * *

HOW WE EVALUATE TIMING

At Angel Kings, our decisions are always based on a desire to seek a return on investment. As such, we carefully consider all aspects of our evaluation through a point scale. The same part of our scale that covers execution, which we summarized in the last chapter, also covers timing. Here's a breakdown of how that point scale might apply to Dropbox.

- **Advertising ROI.** While Dropbox has used some traditional online advertising, much of its initial success came from the referral program. Dropbox put users in charge of recruiting, paying up with 500MB of space for each new member–a minimal cost for a marketing campaign that saw enormous success.

- **Efficiency of product distribution mechanism.** Users access the product in minutes via an email address and/or a download. Dropbox also delivers its product via apps on multiple mobile platforms.

- **Scalability of model.** With an ability to scale from a few thousand to four million users in less than a year and a half, Dropbox is one of the most scalable companies on our list.

- **Three- to Five-Year Plan/Roadmap.** Drew Houston had a strong plan with Dropbox, and he knew where he wanted to go with it. He was committed to building the company into a major player, and he regularly turned down offers and mergers that would have prevented him from completing his mission. Since Houston successfully pitched multiple investors throughout the first years of Dropbox, it's likely his plan was evident in those pitches.

- **Stumbling blocks to date.** When Houston pitched one of the original investors on the Dropbox concept, the investor required that Houston find a co-founder. Houston looked to his own network for a co-founder, thus quickly landing $15,000 in initial funding while demonstrating his ability to meet stumbling blocks with flexibility and action.

POKER 101:

There's a difference between a gambler and a poker player, though they're not always mutually exclusive. As an investor, you should put capital in startups led by poker players, not gamblers– these poker players are founders who know when to get up from the table and walk away. A gambler, like a Pavlovian dog, is conditioned to keep losing with the faux sounds of a slot machine. A poker player however, can get up from a table and walk away for years before returning without any sense of win or loss. Invest in the poker player, the calculated risk taker, and not the gambler who doesn't know when to cut off or break free from losing hands. Almost every Icon had a losing or mediocre business before striking it big. And they wouldn't have been able to strike it big but for the fact they knew when to walk away.

A CHECKLIST FOR EVALUATING TIMING

1. The solution is timeless.
   - There was a past need.
   - There is a current need.
   - You can envision the need extending into the future.
2. The product matches current technology.
   - There is no need to create infrastructure.
   - Consumers are able to use the technology.
   - The product integrates with existing solutions, product, or needs.
3. The product is not the first to market.
   - The founder demonstrates an understanding of what went before.
   - The plan uses the mistakes or challenges of others.
4. The product is part of a new solution that is developing.
5. The founder has an exit strategy.

6

FINANCIAL CASE STUDY OF STARTUPS

At a high level, when evaluating the financials of a startup, you can generally group it into one of the following buckets:

1. Pre-revenue
2. Breakeven
3. Profitable

Unicorns are companies that are given a $1 billion valuation by investors and venture capitalists, and potential unicorns exist in each of these buckets. Unicorns are not always easy to spot, so how do you know what to look for? Let's start with the "unprofitable" bucket.

Three key questions to ask when analyzing an unprofitable startup are:

1. Is the startup growing sustainably?
2. Is there a clear path to breakeven?
3. In order to earn investors a strong return, what does this startup need to accomplish before its next round of financing, and how realistic are those goals?

DISCOVER THE NEXT UNICORN

HOW TO USE THE ANGEL KINGS' STARTUP FORMULA TO FIND THE NEXT BILLION-DOLLAR STARTUP.

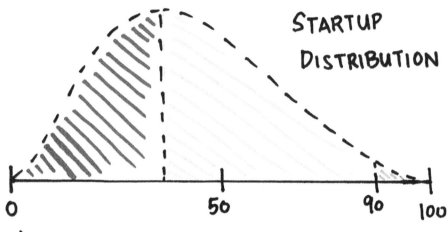

ANGELKINGS STARTUP RATING SCALE

- ▨ = LOW SCORE ON PEOPLE, PRODUCT, EXECUTION & TIMING
- ▨ = MEDIUM SCORE ON PEOPLE, PRODUCT, EXECUTION & TIMING
- ▨ = HIGH SCORE ON PEOPLE, PRODUCT, EXECUTION & TIMING → POTENTIAL UNICORN

· See page 28 for the full outline of the Angel Kings' Startup Formula

FAB, A CAUTIONARY TALE

Round	Date	Amount ($M)	Cumulative
Seed	7/11/11	$1.0M	$1.0M
Series A	8/11/11	$7.7M	$8.7M
Series B	12/7/11	$40.0M	$48.7M
Series C	7/18/12	$105.0M	$153.7M
Series C (Ext)	11/1/12	$15.0M	$168.7M
Series D	6/19/13	$150.0M	$318.7M
Series D (Ext)	7/31/13	$10.0M	$328.7M
Series D (Ext)	8/12/13	$5.0M	$333.7M

Over the past four years, Fab, a former unicorn startup, has raised over a quarter of a billion dollars of venture capital and pretty much burned through all of it.

For anyone not directly involved, this was an Icarus-like tale of a startup that flew too close to the sun. For Fab's investors, however, this was a complete debacle. Investors, who at one point thought they held golden tickets, now find those golden tickets to be completely worthless.

So how can you avoid that fate? Let's look at some of the telltale signs that Fab's financials exhibited that should have thrown up red flags.

THE BIG MONEY

In mid-2012, Fab raised $105 million in a Series C round of financing based on a $500 million valuation. As mentioned, Fab was one of the hottest startups at the time, and some of Silicon Valley's smartest investors lined up to get in.

TRACK RECORD OF UNSUSTAINABILITY

	Amazon (1997)	**Fab (2012)**
Revenue	$148M	$115M
Gross Margin	19%	43%
Operating Margin	(21%)	(78%)

Was growth sustainable? There were a couple of red flags indicating that it was not. Fab CEO Jason Goldberg's prior startup, Jobster, had lost its investors in the neighborhood of $50 million, and it should have been clear that Fab was going down a similar path.

For starters, Fab's $105 million Series C financing in mid-2012 came less than *seven months* after raising $40 million in a Series B round! Show me a startup that raises back-to-back massive rounds of financing, and I'll show you a startup that's burning cash like it's 1999. (Note: It was later confirmed that Fab was burning a mind-boggling $14 million a month before it imploded.)

NEITHER HERE NOR THERE

Fab's CEO openly admired Amazon, and its CEO boasted about the fact that the company had increased gross margins from ~30% to > 40% in 2013, which he stated made Fab's unit economics excellent (compared with Amazon's ~20% gross margins).

The only problem is that Fab occupied a "no man's land" in terms of demonstrating a sustainable financial model. Amazon's low gross margins reflected its distinct competitive advantage in pricing power. Amazon, as an ultra-efficient, high-volume, low-cost provider, had the ability to set rock-bottom pricing.

A quick comparison of Amazon's financials when it was at a similar scale to Fab (see exhibit above) shows that Amazon's operating losses were a fraction of Fab's. While Amazon had low gross margins, it also had lower operating expenses.

Fab: Financial Snapshot	2011	2012
Revenue	$20.0M	$115.0M
Gross Margin	29%	43%
Marketing Expenses	-	$40.0M
Operating Loss	-	($90.0)

Fab had to spend inordinately more on sales and marketing to achieve similar scale. For example, in 2012, Fab spent $40 million on sales and marketing to generate $115 million in revenue. While we don't have the exact numbers, it's safe to assume that Fab spent all, or close to all, of its gross profit on marketing alone.

After paying salaries to its 700 employees, and other operating expenses, it ended the year $90 million in the red.

CLEAR PATH TO PROFITABILITY?

One other very quick, but extremely effective tactic when evaluating unprofitable startups is to figure out how much an unprofitable startup would have to grow revenue and gross profit, while holding operating expenses flat, just to break even.

	2012	2015P
Revenue	$115M	$325M
Gross Margin	43%	43%
OpEx (Est)	$140M	$140M
Op. Inc. / Loss	($90.0)	$0.0

Fab had a 40% gross profit margin and a $90 million operating loss. So even if you had made the unrealistic assumption that Fab could keep operating expenses flat, Fab would have had to *triple* revenue from $115 million to ~$325 million just to break even (i.e. every $100 million in additional sales would add $40 million, or 40%, in gross profit).

The conclusion? Fab had a not-so-fabulous path to profitability.

FAB'S MISSION IMPOSSIBLE

You may be wondering how Fab, a startup that was up to its eyeballs in operating losses, was able to raise $105 million in venture capital at a $500 million valuation for its 2012 Series C financing. According to sources, Fab's CEO "delivered flawlessly" the pitch that there were only four e-commerce companies (including Amazon and eBay) worth more than $10 billion, and that not only would Fab be the fifth, but it would achieve that goal quicker than the other four.

In addition, Fab's Board approved a plan in 2013 to double its burn rate to $200 million, relying on the company to grow its revenue target by over 100% to $250 million and to raise another $300 million in yet another round of financing, ideally at a valuation of $1 billion or more (up from the $500M Series C valuation).

I wasn't present for those pitch meetings, but those Board-approved targets seem like the equivalent of handing someone a bow and arrow and asking him or her to shoot a bulls-eye, while riding on a horse backward and blindfolded.

It's hard to build a billion-dollar business, let alone a $10 billion business. Asking a startup to more than double revenues to a quarter billion dollars in one year, while burning $200 million, and in such a short-time frame, seems nearly impossible.

All in all, Fab's business model, track record, and financial metrics had some clear (albeit hard to spot amid the hype) red flags, and these lessons are valuable ones for angel investors to learn.

* * *

SHOW ME THE BREAKEVEN!

Investors often have to evaluate startups that are at or near breakeven, and figure out if that startup can not only turn the corner, but how far that ensuing momentum might take them.

Three key questions to ask when analyzing a startup when it's at breakeven are:

a. Are unit economics sustainable?

b. Can profitability scale asymmetrically?

c. What are my hurdle rates (required growth) to hit my target returns?

In mid–2012, Etsy raised $40 million in Series F financing. At the time (May 2012), Etsy was a fraction of its current size (around $500 million in gross merchandise revenue and $40 million in revenue), but astute investors would have spotted the green-light indicators that Etsy was onto something big.

Round	Date	Amount ($M)	Cumulative
Seed	6/1/05	$0.4M	$0.4M
Series A	11/1/06	$1.0M	$1.4M
Series B	1/1/07	NA	$1.4M
Series C	7/1/07	$3.3M	$4.7M
Series D	1/1/08	$27.0M	$31.7M
Series E	8/26/10	$20.0M	$51.7M
Series F	5/9/12	$40.0M	$91.7M
Series F (Ext)	5/22/14	$5.6M	$97.3M

Source: Crunchbase

TRACK RECORD

Startups usually become less, not more efficient after you write them a huge check. The reason is pretty simple: In the early days, founders are cash-strapped and watch every penny. But when you have millions of dollars in the bank, things tend to get a little looser.

So if the founders you're investing in haven't demonstrated that they can take your hard-earned cash and not only make that cash last, but build something valuable with it, then you're probably in trouble.

Prior to its Series F financing, Etsy had raised about $50 million, and with that cash, it had built a $40 million revenue business (year-over-year growth rate of 70%), with healthy 60% gross margins, and also a business running at virtually breakeven. In other words, by almost any measure, Etsy was worth a lot more than the capital that investors had put in to-date.

SUSTAINABLE UNIT ECONOMICS

For every dollar of merchandising volume that flows through its platform, Etsy generates 8-9 cents of revenue (i.e., its take rate). Given the valuable role Etsy plays as the largest platform (in its niche, with 60 million unique monthly visitors) in a two-sided market, it's unlikely that a competitor would be able to undercut its pricing.

In contrast (to provide an example of a less sustainable business model), "flash sale" startups that rely on suppliers not only heavily discounting their merchandise, but also giving up a huge cut of the remaining revenue, haven't fared as well.

Etsy Financials ($ in 000s)	2012	2013	2014
Marketplace	$55,330	$78,544	$108,732
Seller Services	15,863	42,817	82,502
Other	3,409	3,661	4,357
Total revenue	**74,602**	**125,022**	**195,591**
Cost of revenue(1)	24,493	47,779	73,633
Gross profit	**50,109**	**77,243**	**121,958**
Operating expenses:			
Marketing	10,902	17,850	39,655
Product development	18,653	27,548	36,634
General and administrative	21,909	31,112	51,920
Total operating expenses	51,464	76,510	128,209
Operating Income / (Loss)	**$(1,355)**	**$733**	**$(6,251)**

GROWTH/PROFITABILITY SCALABILITY

Another huge green light was that in 2012, Etsy spent a mere $11 million on sales and marketing to generate $75 million in revenue (i.e., 15% of revenues spent on sales and marketing, compared with Fab at over 35%). This indicated that there was further potential for rapid growth.

In fact, that's exactly what happened. Between 2012 and 2014, Etsy increased its marketing spend by $30 million, and in return it grew revenue from $75 million to $200 million. That growth has turned the company into an attractive IPO candidate and what should be a home run for investors.

In contrast, a startup that is already investing a bundle in sales and marketing (i.e. Fab) has probably exhausted its best growth channels. At that point, your VC dollars might be going to less productive attempts at gaining traction.

REASONABLE HURDLE RATES

When you invest in a startup, it's usually not a good thing if you have to make crazy assumptions to pencil out a good return. When Series F investors put $40 million into Etsy, they were betting that Etsy would continue its strong growth, but they weren't counting on a miracle.

Etsy is currently worth a reported $2 billion (in early 2015). In order to achieve that valuation, the company grew revenue at a 40% annualized rate from 2012–2014, and didn't require any significant additional financing or dilution.

Was this outcome predictable? Given that the startup had demonstrated 70% growth in 2011, was already running near break-even thanks to its healthy 60% gross margins, and had seemingly untapped growth potential from its low historical expenditures for sales and marketing, investors who made the decision to invest in Etsy in its 2012 Series F made a good and somewhat predictable bet that the company would continue its trend of growth without burning excessive capital.

***

SHOW ME THE MONEY!

There's nothing better than a startup that is already in the black. They don't need your money, which makes you want to give it to them all the more!

But profitable startups are a different animal. In this case, the unicorn (or potential unicorn) isn't hard to spot – the company is *already* throwing off cash, and you and every other investor is fighting to get in!

Instead, the key risk is whether or not you're overpaying for the unicorn, and how hard and fast the unicorn can run.

Three key questions to ask when analyzing a profitable startup are:

1. Why is this company able to achieve profitability?
2. Where are the untapped areas of growth, and why would a capital infusion not only increase, but turbocharge growth?
3. What metrics do you need to hit to give investors a return of three to ten times capital?

OK, GIVE ME AN EXAMPLE...

Buffer is a great example of a promising startup that is already profitable. In late 2014, Buffer raised $3.5 million in Series A financing at a healthy $60 million valuation. Even to the casual observer, Buffer had great financials, but what were the underlying indicators that it had a strong chance of providing venture-sized returns for investors?

Round	Date	Amount ($M)	Cumulative
Seed	10/1/11	NA	NA
Angel	12/20/11	$0.4M	$0.4M
Series A	10/27/14	$3.5M	$3.9M

LOW COST GROWTH

Buffer grew monthly revenue 140% –from $180,000 in October of 2013 to $440,000 in October 2014. It did this without the assistance of any external financing, as the last round it did (prior to the Series A) was back in 2011.

As a social media SaaS provider, Buffer's business model is extremely lucrative: For every $100 in revenue, about 15% goes to payment processing, servers, and other software / tools. The rest goes to gross profit, and Buffer's 85% gross margin gives it a lot of, well, buffer to pay salaries and other operating expenses, grow the team, invest in growth initiatives, and still clear a small but healthy profit.

Buffer Financials (2014)	Monthly	Annualized	% of Rev
Total Revenue	$341,203	$4,094,431	100.0%
Team Member Salaries	223,940	2,687,277	65.6%
Servers	22,891	274,689	6.7%
Fees to Stripe	13,885	166,625	4.1%
The Tools We Use	14,162	169,941	4.2%
Advertising & Marketing	6,302	75,629	1.8%
Retreat	17,588	211,058	5.2%
Health Insurance / Workers	6,636	79,631	1.9%
Office Rent	7,176	86,106	2.1%
Payroll, Legal, Accounting	5,883	70,597	1.7%
Computer and Equipment	2,578	30,934	0.8%
Kindle books & Culture	1,594	19,122	0.5%
Internet	1,293	15,511	0.4%
Office Supplies & Communit	1,120	13,446	0.3%
Other	489	5,865	0.1%
Operating Income	**$15,667**	**$188,000**	**4.6%**

One of the key signs that Buffer is onto something big is that it spends a paltry 1.8% of revenue on sales and marketing. In other words, the product pretty much sells itself. Investors can take comfort in knowing that any additional capital investment in sales and marketing will be targeting extremely low-hanging fruit.

One other key aspect of Buffer's profitability is that most of its revenues are "fixed" – in other words, as Buffer scales revenues, its largest expense (salaries) probably won't grow as fast. As a result, Buffer's net income margin should improve asymmetrically over time.

IT LOOKS LIKE A UNICORN. IS IT A UNICORN?

As mentioned, Buffer raised its Series A at a ~$65 million post-money valuation. Is it possible, without making crazy assumptions, for Buffer to "grow into" a $200 million to $1 billion valuation over the next five years, thus providing its investors with a 3-10x venture return?

At the time of the Series A financing, Buffer's run-rate revenue was $5 million and it was growing by 140 percent.

For Buffer to achieve target returns for its investors, let's assume that it will need to grow into a $40 million to $80 million revenue company (fast-growing SaaS startups are typically valued at five to ten times revenue), with no additional financing. In order to do this, Buffer will need to grow 50-70% over the next five years.

While growing 50-70% won't be a walk in the park, Buffer has a few things going for it:

- It already demonstrated 140% (compared to the prior year, in 2014), and achieved this without any financing.
- As a small startup ($6 million in ARR as of March 2015), Buffer has the ability to engineer a paradigm shift upward in revenue growth. For example, a single

business development deal with the right partner could conceivably double (or more) revenue.
- Buffer has spent little money on sales and marketing, so any capital infusion should be extremely productive
- Buffer's product team and engineers can reasonably be expected to introduce new features that significantly increase value to the user, and significant additional sources of revenue.

So will Buffer's Series A investors earn a venture-like 10x return? Time will tell, but the indicators are all flashing green.

PART TWO

The Official Angel Kings Rankings

The Next Billion Dollar Startups

7

THE NEXT BILLION DOLLAR STARTUPS

"To win without risk is to triumph without glory."
— Corneille

Great success doesn't come without risks, and that is certainly true in angel investing. Risk is inherent in the process, but you don't have to take unnecessary or uneducated risks to succeed. In fact, that's something we avoid at Angel Kings by applying our checklists and point system during evaluations of every startup we consider for our portfolio.

Learning to apply rigorous evaluation to the information presented by founders can be difficult, and one of the best ways to enhance your ability to pick winning products and ideas is to research startups that have experienced success. To that end, we're providing our exclusive list of top startups. We have ranked the best startups in various categories using our proprietary formula, as well as interviews and research on founding teams, products, and visions for future liquidity events such as mergers, acquisitions, and IPOs.

Our first list covers what we consider the top 25 startups; we'll also cover some successful startups in niches such as cyber security, biotechnology, fintech, mobile to consumer, vice, and enterprise. For each listing, we'll provide a brief summary of what the startup does, and we'll go into more detail on a few focus startups from each list to give you an idea of how they relate to our checklist.

Any company herein with an asterisk* is an Angel Kings Portfolio investment.

ANGEL KINGS' RANKINGS OF THE NEXT BILLION DOLLAR STARTUPS

1. **Dropbox**

    Covered in depth in the last chapter, Dropbox offers cloud-based storage and file sharing. New users can open a Dropbox account for free; paid services are offered, as users require more space for data. As of 2015, this former startup boasted 300 million users from around the world. We expect Dropbox to go public (IPO) by 2016.

2. **Buffer - A Focus Startup* (Now Buffer.com)**

    Buffer is a social media management product that lets companies and users publish and analyze social media performance with convenience on a large scale. Buffer and its founders meet a number of the criteria in our evaluation checklist.

    When it comes to people, Buffer has a strong set of founders. Joel Gascoigne, the co-founder and CEO, was able to take the idea for the product to revenue in just seven weeks, probably due to extensive experience as an investor, advisor, and developer. Gascoigne is financially stable, investing between $5,000 and $10,000 in other companies, and he works hard to make his endeavors successful. Gascoigne's co-founder, Leo Widrich, has a similar background with startup experience prior to BufferApp.

    Like the startups covered in the previous chapters, Buffer doesn't solve a new problem. As soon as social media sites attracted users, marketers and companies have been attempting to leverage profiles and content to drive conversions. The growing number of platforms to handle, as well as increasing competition across the board, means companies must manage accounts in efficient, cost-effective manners. Solutions such as HootSuite and Klout already offer services to help brands manage content, but Buffer offers a service that is more scalable than its competitors.

While the brand hasn't yet made the cultural connections that products such as HootSuite have, Buffer is brandable. The startup is already creating a culture through blog posts and social media shares offering tips and guides for using the solution. The brand looks for proven needs or growth areas and strives to fill those needs with integrated products. For example, Buffer looked at the fact that social media and blog posts with images perform much better than those without pictures. Recognizing a need, Buffer created the Pablo app, which lets users create sharable images in as little as 30 seconds. This new offering is in line with the streamlined, convenient approach of the overall brand.

Buffer makes use of a unique marketing approach to entice users. On the website, a streamlined page offers few links to explore, and one of them immediately draws the eye. It's titled "the Awesome Plan." Clicking on the link brings you to a landing page encouraging you to sign up for a free BufferApp account. The page says, "Take your social sharing to the next level. It's magical." The page also gives some basic details about the Awesome Plan, saying users can unlock access to the plan by signing up for the free account. Effectively, Buffer uses game theory to drive signups: Users are given a quest and can get a chance at the next level by signing up. It creates a psychological need in the user to open the door to see what's on the other side.

Buffer is an excellent example of great startup timing. We've already covered how it's not first to market, which allowed the founders to identify specific challenges that weren't being met by other solutions. The capabilities of Buffer match current technology, but the app also makes that technology easier to use. Paying users can manage up to fifteen RSS feeds and ten social profiles from a single dashboard, and business accounts offer even more functionality.

Overall, BufferApp scores high across all our checklists, which is why it's both a focus startup and part of the Angel Kings portfolio. They are also the most transparent company in America – even going so far as to publish revenue numbers online for the public to see. We are proud to have invested in Buffer and could easily see a big IPO one day from this great team.

3. **inDinero***

We are proud to call this an Angel Kings investment company. Having started several companies in the past, I realize how painful bookkeeping and accounting are for a business owner. The inDinero platform has absolutely revolutionized the way small and mid-sized companies in America keep track of their books. Jessica Mah and her team are on-track to become a bigger acquisition than Mint.com. Every company in America should be – and might someday – be using inDinero to replace the headaches of dealing with QuickBooks and Intuit's platform. The future holds big things ahead for inDinero.

4. **Github**

Leveraging the ongoing growth and popularity of open source collaboration, Github delivers a Windows-based collaboration platform. Teams from disparate locations can create code together via the downloadable, cloud-based application, which is free. Github offers cost-effective upgrades for teams that want to work in private environments.

5. **Boosted Boards**

Boosted Boards delivers lightweight long boards with a literal boost-they operate on a battery and offer adjustable speed and power. A Bluetooth remote provides control, and the boards are popular in urban areas for running small errands or reducing travel times to and from work. Boosted Boards offers test rides to convert consumers to its unique concept.

6. **Authy - A Focus Startup***

Like BufferApp, Authy is a startup that rings many of the bells on our checklist, and it's also in the Angel Kings portfolio. The company offers a two-factor authentication security solution for individuals and organizations working in cloud environments. Founded by a software engineer, Authy especially meets our criteria for timing.

First, Authy offers a timeless solution: data security. Solutions for securing information have been around as long as information has-which is to say, practically forever. Centuries ago, codes were used to protect information as it traveled from one area to another, and locked boxes have secured documents for almost as long. More recently, filing cabinets, passwords, and biosecurity have all protected data.

As information moves increasingly to virtual environments, security is a growing concern, and organizations across the globe have invested millions in security programming. Authy was not the first company in this space, which let founder Daniel Palacio see where other solutions were falling short. Problems with existing solutions included prohibitive cost and a need for multiple products to protect each device or computer.

Authy offers solutions for individuals, small businesses, and enterprises, so it's able to provide affordable options for each type of user. A single app offers multi-account protection, including data backups and multi-step verification. Users can protect computers, tablets, and smartphones with easy downloads through all the major platforms. Authy checks Angel Kings' boxes for product matching current technology, offering a timeless solution, and not being the first to market.

Remember, we said the most essential part of our timing checklist was the exit strategy. Authy recently announced that it had been acquired by Twilio (2015). While we do respect this acquisition, we do believe they sold too early and could have continued to scale 10 to 20 times greater than before exiting.

7. **Zapier**

Supporting more than 300 existing apps, Zapier's workflow system connects events and tasks from various platforms. Users can automate tedious tasks and keep social media, email, productivity, and other apps in synch without constant work. The low-cost solution meets an enormous need for small businesses, which can use Zapier in lieu of hiring developers to integrate tasks.

8. **Firebase**

Firebase offers an API for app developers, reducing app-building requirements to frontend code. Within three years, the product attracted more than 100,000 developers and caught the eye of Google. Today, Firebase is part of the Google umbrella–a notable and validating achievement for any tech startup.

9. **Zenefits**

Zenefits took a function that is notoriously difficult, particularly for small businesses, and created a free online platform to automate 99 percent of the work associated with the task. The HR app lets businesses handle payroll, taxes, insurance, benefits, and reporting. Zenefits is able to offer its service to small businesses free by working with benefits providers, such as insurance companies, to cover program costs.

10. **AngelList**

AngelList is a portal to angel investing opportunities, connecting founders and investors. Investors can research trending startups, get to know the people behind the ideas, and see what other investments a startup has attracted. AngelList has developed such a brand within the niche that news and business sites often reference it when discussing startups. Naval Ravikant has brilliantly demonstrated just how important opening investing up to the masses can be. We applaud him for his continued innovation and look forward to partnering Angel List with Angel Kings.

11. Stripe

An entire suite of APIs lets developers create customized commerce solutions such as mobile payments and shopping carts. Developers can work in numerous coding languages, including Java, PHP, Python, and curl. Stripe lets businesses develop systems that can accept more than 100 global currencies, so companies of any size can go global.

12. Pebble Technology

Originally launched with a Kickstarter campaign, Pebble Technology makes smart watches. The 2012 Kickstarter campaign brought in over $10 million in crowd funding, breaking records and proving that the product met numerous requirements from our checklists for branding and timing. The original product was introduced a year later.

13. Hello Inc.

Hello Inc. is the second startup from James Proud, who previously sold a music-based company. The first product from Hello Inc. is a sleep monitor that goes beyond wearable devices, such as Fitbit, to monitor sleep patterns. The device is meant to provide data to let users improve sleep without distractions, and it launched after a $2.4 million Kickstarter campaign.

14. Airware

Cashing in on a growing commercial interest in drones-fueled by statements from notable CEOs such as Jeff Bezos-Airware's Aerial Information Platform walks the line between cost-prohibitive military tech and hobby projects that don't comply with commercial needs. The platform lets commercial enterprises customize drone programs to meet specific needs.

15. Medium

Co-founded by Twitter notables Biz Stone and Ev Williams, Medium is a crowd-publishing site that lets writers publish content and be found. It offers an alternative to blogging, particularly for those who don't want to publish constantly. Launched in 2012, part of Medium's brand has been built around the inability of industry experts to completely define the platform.

16. ZenPayroll – *A Focus Startup

ZenPayroll markets itself as a "modern, delightful payroll product." This tagline contributes to unique and memorable marketing, because anyone who has ever worked with payroll would likely not call it delightful. Traditionally, payroll is a tedious task involving numerous manual processes, even in an "automated" environment. In fact, payroll is one of the areas a small business owner is likely to make an accounting error in, particularly when you consider complications such as benefits and taxes.

ZenPayroll, therefore, works to meet the needs and wants of the user. Those responsible for payroll want a solution that makes their job easier without risking accuracy. An investor evaluating ZenPayroll can be reasonably certain users will pay for the service, given the more expensive products seeing success on the market. Because so much risk is involved in the payroll process, organizations are willing to pay for products that reduce those risks. Tax audits or payroll tax mistakes can cost a company much more than the cost of the payroll product itself.

Features of ZenPayroll include automated W-2 and 1099 generation, virtual paystubs for employees who receive direct deposit, and secure access to personal payroll information for every employee. Users can manage a variety of complex payroll transactions, including bonuses and benefits deductions, and the cloud-based functions are protected by 256-bit SSL encryption and two-step authentication–an illustration of how ZenPayroll integrates with and meets current technology needs.

ZenPayroll realizes it's not the first to market, and it makes use of that fact in marketing materials that compare its functions to both self-service and full-service providers. The brand even uses a landing page for a memorable "Payroll of your dreams" presentation, where it lists reasons the product is right for you using dating language. With statements such as, "We're easy on the eyes," and "We're great listeners," ZenPayroll positions itself as the attractive, friendly option in a niche full of unwieldy, tedious competitors.

17. Shopify[1]

The team at Shopify originally developed their product to meet the needs of their own e-commerce business before realizing that other companies probably had the same need. The product lets retailers manage in-store and online sales, orders, and customers. Launched in 2006, Shopify now supports 150,000 stores and helps manage $7 billion in sales.

---

[1] On May 2015, Shopify priced its initial public offering at $17 per share. Kokalitcheva, Kia. "This Is the Latest $1 Billion Tech Company to IPO."*Time*. Time, 20 May 2015. Web. 07 July 2015.

18. Percolate

Percolate takes the project management software concept and applies it to a specific niche: marketing. Every marketing need and task can be planned, recorded, and tracked in a single location, increasing productivity for businesses and teams. Project management solutions have been around for some time, but Percolate combines the best of marketing without the manual hassles.

19. Shyp

In a twist on Uber's app-based ride concept, Shyp launched a shipping return service in San Francisco in 2014. Looking to the growing number of Internet shoppers as a market, Shyp makes one of the disadvantages of online shipping more palatable: The company picks up return orders and ships them to businesses such as Amazon via the most appropriate or lowest-cost service. Shyp is following Uber's lead, launching in one city after another as it sees success. Traditional players such as FedEx and UPS should be aware of this startup.

20. Hullabalu

Calling itself "Disney for the next generation," Hullabalu is a digital media brand for kids that uses interactive story apps created through proprietary software. The apps and eBooks certainly hit on a specific want and need in the market; within a year of launching the first products, Hullabalu saw its titles hit number one on lists in 38 countries. We could see The Walt Disney Company or DreamWorks acquiring this company.

21. Postmates

Available in select cities, Postmates uses bike- and vehicle-based delivery drivers to deliver products, including groceries, food, and specialty goods, in less than one hour. The service works through an app, letting users in select cities access delivery options around the clock. Like Uber, Postmates brings together users who desire convenience with drivers looking for profitable work. Postmates also announced a major partnership in 2015 with the Starbucks Coffee Company to serve as the delivery platform for its thousands of stores across America. This will be a major revenue catalyst. And we can expect Postmates to be acquired either by a traditional player like UPS, FedEx, or eventually become a standalone IPO that trades publicly.

22. Instacart

Another service capitalizing on modern consumers' constant search for convenience, Instacart facilitates the delivery of grocery orders in select locations. The service uses local personal shoppers who handle grocery pickup and delivery, but the brand streamlines processes by publishing its own product and pricing lists. With partnerships at Whole Foods Market and other major groceries, Instacart will continue to grow rapidly.

23. Treehouse Island

Treehouse Island combines two rapidly trending ideas in a single product: online education and the need for web development in small business environments. Thousands of videos walk users through CSS, HTML, and iPhone app development, among other subjects. Both basic and pro packages are offered at an affordable monthly fee. Unlike its boring counterpart, Lynda.com, this site is more interactive and engaging for employees looking to expand their career skills.

24. Asana

Over the past few years, numerous business publications have reported on the time that teams waste reading and managing internal email–sometimes as much as 40 to 50 percent. Asana stepped in to solve that problem while increasing overall efficiency for teams and projects. Its product offers an all-inclusive project or team management platform that keeps communication out of tedious email threads.

25. HandyBook (now Handy.com)

HandyBook is another company taking the Uber concept to a new niche. This time, it's home cleaning and repair services. Residents can book services with the ease of ordering a pizza online, and they don't have to worry about checking into companies or reading multiple service reviews. HandyBook verifies its professionals and offers a money-back guarantee. The problem with sites like Angie's List and Yelp is that you read reviews but can't act upon anything. HandyBook controls the entire process from reviews to order services.

OFFICIAL ANGEL KINGS RANKINGS TOP CYBERSECURITY STARTUPS

1. **Authy***

Covered as one of our top 25, Authy tops the list of cyber security startups due in part to its wide-ranging authentication services and the fact that it's already been acquired. We invested in Authy because we realized its growth trajectory, and its integration within websites was unmatched.

2. **Lookout**

Lookout customizes cyber defense for the mobile market by using predictive analysis tools to plan for threats before they become a problem for users. The company now boasts more than 60 million users, including organizations such as AT&T and Sprint. Mobile security is the next frontier for cyber security expansion.

3. **Blockscore**

In 2014, Blockscore landed $2.4 million in funding for its identification verification product. Marketed as an anti-fraud and compliance product, Blockscore enters the market at a time when newsworthy hacks have made it obvious that simple password protection is fruitless against modern cyber criminals. While Blockscore is competing with dozens-if not hundreds-of security products, it markets itself as the simple, convenient, and effective option. On its landing page, the brand cleverly shows that users can sign up and use the service in the time it would take to read the competition's contracts.

4. **SiftScience – A Focus Startup**

With more than 191 million digital shoppers in the United States alone, e-commerce sites across all niches are seeing growing business. Along with the increasing revenue comes a growing problem: fraud. In 2012, online retailers lost $3.5 billion to fraud, so it's not surprising that companies are cautious about potentially fraudulent orders. The problem is that setting the bar too high for "clean" orders means retailers either deny real orders–and lose out on that profit–or they manually review a high percentage of orders and pay out more than is necessary in labor costs.

All of that information creates a perfect stepping-stone for SiftScience, which provides an automated service to sift through orders more efficiently than most basic e-commerce solutions or manual processes. The product uses a rules and data engine to process every transaction against a databank of known patterns, identifying problems such as fake accounts or fraudulent payments. The results are that companies identify fraud accurately, reduce false positives on fraud detection, and reduce manual reviews.

Founded by Brandon Ballinger and Jason Tan, Sift Science checks our boxes for the people evaluation. Brandon Ballinger came to the startup after time at Google, which is a historical proving ground for young technical entrepreneurs. Jason Tan has experience in a number of technical markets and has invested in multiple successful startups.

The product itself covers all of our evaluation requirements. It solves a known problem for e-commerce shops, and does so with the convenience of an automated solution. Because Sift Science can save retailers on both front-end review costs and fraud-related costs-in addition to ensuring that more genuine orders are processed-we don't doubt retailers will be willing to pay for the service. According to Lexis Nexis, retailers spend as much as 10 cents on the dollar to protect or handle fraud losses, and Sift Science's pricing ranges from free to 2 cents per order.

E-commerce fraud protection services may seem more difficult to brand, and you might not see a bandwagon potential at first. But consider the need to keep up with competition. Eventually, more retailers will have to buy in to the Sift Science product or risk the loss of consumers whose orders have been incorrectly denied.

We also like that Sift Science is integrated within thousands of websites. Once you're able to build dependency, similar to CloudFlare, you're on your way to becoming a billion dollar company.

5. **True Link Financial**

True Link Financial offers monitoring and education tools for older adults and caregivers to help seniors avoid fraud and scams. Few cyber security companies dared to tackle this niche for the older generation Americans. We are fascinated by the potential here.

6. **BugCrowd**

Applying crowdsourcing concepts to software security, BugCrowd brings more than 15,000 freelance programmers and IT experts to software testing and reviews. With several levels of service, the company provides penetration testing, glitch sourcing, and vulnerability testing. By delivering its services in a more cost-effective, faster manner than in-house resources, BugCrowd hits home with organizations of all sizes.

7. **Disconnect.me**

Even savvy Internet users today can fall prey to the lack of privacy in the online world-search for something once or view a product, and suddenly Facebook ads are showing you similar items, for example. Disconnect.me help users cut through the invisible web of trackers. Users see what is being tracked and can take advantage of extra layers of protection against identity theft and security issues.

8. **Trulioo**

Trulioo checks a number of our boxes, so we aren't surprised that it's been able to obtain millions in funding from various sources. The company offers identity verification solutions for web and site masters, helping users determine what traffic is from real people and what is from bots. In 2012, Trulioo hired a former Google executive and launched a product that sorted real Facebook accounts from spoof accounts-a move that would have scored high on our people, products, and execution lists.

9. **Spotflux**

At a time when Internet users are growing increasingly worried about tracking and monitoring, Spotflux provides a free tool that keeps ISPs, marketing companies, and even Google from tracking online movements. The tool is an encrypted VPN client, and it routes your traffic and queries through a series of services. The activity masks your IP address so bots can't follow your movements for marketing and other purposes.

10. ZeroFox – *A Focus Startup

ZeroFox is a cyber security development firm, which doesn't sound impressive given the influx of security companies in today's market. However, what places ZeroFox on our list are the people and the product, which touch on almost every aspect of our evaluation checklist and *are* impressive.

ZeroFox was started by James C. Foster, Evan Blair, and Rob Francis. Combined, they bring cyber entrepreneurship, investment, technical engineering, and project leadership to the table. Add in Blair's experience with previous startups and multimillion-dollar solutions and Foster's speaker and author background, and the group has everything required to launch a startup, manage a business, and inspire engagement from investors and consumers. Not to mention, the founders have put together an impressive team to help them. The team at ZeroFox has:

- Written books about their industry.
- Spoken on Capitol Hill and at major security conferences about cyber security, thus becoming thought leaders.
- Built previous high-level, military-grade technologies.
- Appeared in leading industry publications, including Cyber Defense Magazine and Wired.

The founding group and core team are brandable in their niche, a fact they've continued to take advantage of as their startup sees massive success.

The flagship product for the startup is ZeroFox Enterprise, a risk management platform that addresses a growing need for organizations across the globe: social media security. With social networks taking up a growing piece of the Internet pie, organizations can't avoid interacting with them or on them. As ZeroFox points out, "if your organization has people, social media makes you vulnerable."

Social media is a frustrating problem for many enterprises. Locking down social sites can inhibit workflow for departments such as customer service and marketing. Many companies don't want to block employees from their own personal networks, either–allowing access during break times is an easy perk to offer. The increasing sophistication of phishing scams and other social media frauds means that even individuals well versed in Internet attacks can fall prey, though.

ZeroFox enters this market with what it calls cyber security's first social media risk management platform. The company isn't the first to market–other platforms offer defensive security tools for organizations, such as block management. ZeroFox offers a solution that goes beyond other tools, however. The platform uses both technical and behavioral indicators across social platforms to create a proactive approach to security.

Users build a database of what matters to the organization–including people and brands–as well as what should be monitored, such as keywords, accounts, and pages. ZeroFox uses that information, along with the overwhelming data associated with social media, to create user-friendly dashboards and alert systems. Alerts are launched when activity appears to impersonate profiles, violate PCI or HIPAA requirements, or include phishing links, among other warning signs. We love this company's potential.

11. Signifyd

With a number of plugin and API solutions for online retailers, Signifyd helps Internet stores boost and protect sales through fraud prevention. Retailers enter custom rule sets for credit card and other transactions, and Signifyd applies those rules in a real-time data review and automated decision process. The goal is to save businesses millions on chargebacks and incorrect payment denials while catching potential fraudulent transactions on the front end.

12. LaunchKey

LaunchKey puts security in the palm of the user's hand by moving authentication processes from centralized servers and password processes to mobile devices. Users can create multilevel authentication, including fingerprint requirements, for software or hardware. The product increases security and convenience and lets users customize authentication requirements.

13. Trustev

Trustev is fraud analysis software that reviews real-time transaction data for retailers to ensure purchases are on the up and up. One of the things we like about Trustev is the way it markets its concept. Instead of concentrating solely on the protection factor, which a number of companies already do, Trustev points out that two percent of revenues are lost when fraud software catches real customers inadvertently, and Trustev claims to be better at identifying the real fraudsters than the competition.

14. Synack - *A Focus Startup

Take two former NSA employees, give them the problem of enterprise technical security, and they do something surprising. Jay Kaplan and Mark Kuhr of Synack are solving a problem that certainly isn't new, but they are taking a different approach that generates a more convenient and less expensive product for clients.

Synack is another company that applies a crowd worker concept to a space where vendors, contractors, and in-house employees formerly reigned. Synack vets its entire crowd workers to ensure teams are educated, experienced, and possess appropriate skills. It sells security services as a subscription, and clients pay a single monthly fee based on their needs. With a global crowd to pull from, Synack can customize security services for each enterprise without excessive expense. In a crowd environment, chances are there are experts available for every system, platform, and industry challenge.

Our product evaluation checklist asks whether the product solves a solution in a more convenient fashion. Synack's services do away with the need for cumbersome vendor contracts, tedious statements of work, and ongoing budgeting for license fees or per-service fee structures.

We've touched on how Synack's product meets our evaluation requirements, but the people behind the solution are also impressive. Jay Kaplan brought experience from the Department of Defense and NSA; Mark Kuhr's experience includes time at the NSA, and he holds a Ph.D. in computer science. Kuhr has published a number of papers on security and worked on high-level research projects within the industry. The founders were more than entrepreneurs with a sound-good idea: they were established professionals with likely connections in the industry–always a good thing for a startup.

We're not the only ones impressed with Synack's cloud-based service model. The company raised $1.5 million in the Seed phase and $7.5 million in the Series A phase and boasts investor interest from organizations such as Google Ventures and Allegis Capital. Get ready for a future IPO.

15. Shape Security

At a time when cyber attacks are evolving quicker than the ability to prevent them, Shape Security offers a product that eliminates the impact of malware on websites altogether. The technology disables malware capabilities on a site, so it can protect even against new and unknown automated attacks. The product meets an existing–and growing–need in an inimitable, convenient way, so we aren't surprised that organizations such as Fast Company are calling it ingenious.

OFFICIAL ANGEL KINGS RANKINGS TOP BIOTECHNOLOGY STARTUPS

1. **TuteGenomics – *A Focus Startup**

Like several of the biotech startups in our list, TuteGenomics is a company in the genome research space. It's both a focus startup and a company within Angel Kings' portfolio for a number of reasons, starting with the founders. TuteGenomics (Tute) was founded by Reid Robinson and Kai Wang. Both men have experience in the industry–Robinson began as a physician and moved into data science; Wang has a PhD and a post-doctorate degree and works as a professor in the niche.

Although we like to see experience and knowledge of the industry, Robinson also has startup experience. He was a cofounder for Anolinx and Clinical Methods, both startups that were later acquired. That tells us that Robinson doesn't just know his industry–he also knows how to manage a successful startup to an exit.

The product–which is referred to on the startup's website as Tute–lets genome and DNA researchers collaborate, research, and access existing knowledge via a fast, low-cost platform. Tute markets itself has having the largest genetic knowledge library available and provides access to 200 relevant genomic knowledge sources in real-time. Users can also access secure patient portals and clinical reports and advanced analysis tools.

Tute isn't the first to market, and it capitalizes on this fact by building on previous technology. Tute uses ANNOVAR, a recognized genome annotation and interpretation technology, to deliver efficient, accurate results for labs and patients. Vendors and providers can further build on the technology by using Tute APIs in existing pipelines.

TuteGenomics recently partnered with Google to publicly release DNA/Genomic data. We look forward to Tute's massive growth.

2. **Theranos**

Healthcare lab testing has been around for decades, and for-cash online testing options have existed for several years. Yet what is the major problem for many people with both of these options? It is the need for a phlebotomist to fill an entire vial with your blood for a simple test. Elizabeth Holmes, a young pioneer in healthcare, founded Theranos. She is bringing a fascinating solution to this market: affordable testing with minimal amounts of blood or pain. A drop or two are all that's needed for hundreds of common tests, which makes life easier for healthcare providers, lab workers, and patients. I've also been fortunate enough to get to know Elizabeth's parents while living in Washington DC. They're great people, who no doubt inspired Elizabeth to make an impact on humanity.

3. **Benchling**

Benchling is a cloud-based platform for scientists and research teams. The platform offers complex DNA and other research tools, as well as a chance for global research teams to collaborate on projects. The platform tracks work, letting researchers revert to previous versions of DNA sequences if desired, and teams can download high-quality images for reports and presentations. Public access is free, and labs and research teams can take advantage of affordable monthly subscription options.

4. **Science Exchange**

Science Exchange offers organizations access to researchers and experts across the globe in a market-based format that keeps pricing fair and opens doors for R&D in companies of all sizes. Users can order experiments from a lab that specifically meets the technical requirements of the experiment, regardless of the location of that lab. One benefit of the service is that companies can access specialty equipment and staff that may only exist in a few places in the world.

5. **Kaggle**

Kaggle caters specifically to the data science niche. It bills itself as the world's largest data science community and boasts over a quarter million users as of 2015. The site includes a job board. It also hosts student competitions and engages with prestigious universities across the world to support science education. Kaggle competitions include participation by professionals who are working to solve real solutions for customers–the results often beat benchmarks by weeks.

6. **Counsyl – *A Focus Startup**

Counsyl enters the healthcare market with a product that answers a specific patient and individual concern: Worry. Counsyl's web-portal lets individuals access several medical screenings, including genetic screens that help reassure women that their pregnancy is not at increased risks for DNA abnormalities and a DNA screening that lets couples understand their chance of passing issues on to children. The business also offers cancer screening so families can understand inherited cancer risks.

While public access to these screenings is a strong product, Counsyl goes even further by working with clinicians to provide web-based consulting sessions with patients. Patients who use the screening services are connected with an appropriate clinician, who can explain what the results of the test might mean for individuals and families. The result is a better-informed individual who can make life choices while weighing risks appropriately.

One of the things we like about Counsyl as a startup is that it enters a market that is already prepared for its services. Just a few years ago, these services might have sounded extreme or frightening to layperson. With more medical professionals ordering such screenings in a practice or clinic environment and explaining the usefulness and purpose to patients, more people are hearing about the screenings. What Counsyl does is offer these useful screenings to people who haven't yet gone to the doctor with cancer or a pregnancy. The screenings do have to be ordered by healthcare providers, but Counsyl opens the door for discussions about these issues.

From first-hand experience, my wife and I used Counsyl during our first pregnancy. It was quite reassuring to learn our baby would be okay after using Counsyl's simple, informative tests.

7. **DNAnexus**

DNAnexus offers a cloud storage and work platform for labs, researchers, and clinics working with DNA and genome projects. The platform offers robust, secure storage with simple upload and download procedures. Users can take advantage of automatic checks to verify data uploads and integrity, reducing tedious manual reviews when something goes wrong. The platform offers a number of integration and collaboration tools, letting organizations expand DNA work to offsite teams or real use cases without risking compliance issues.

8. **TrueVault**

Healthcare developers are dealing with a growing web of compliance requirements, which makes designing the data-storage capabilities of software time-consuming. TrueVault offers APIs that are HIPAA-compliant so developers can concentrate on the unique functionality of their products. Designed to support startups in the healthcare software space, TrueVault works with traditional, web, and mobile apps.

9. **Cambrian Genomics**

Cambrian Genomics does something that excites our evaluation process. It takes two solutions and combines them to meet a growing need in a niche industry. The solutions are DNA cloning and 3D printing. The industry is DNA research, which requires over a billion dollars' worth of DNA each year. Cambrian Genomics uses 3D laser printing to create DNA to order for researchers, reducing expenses and the time it takes to receive viable samples.

10. **Experiment.com – *A Focus Startup**

Experiment.com takes a model that has proven itself and applies it to a niche in great need of a solution. The model is one made popular by sites like Kickstarter–funding sites where the crowd picks the winner. With Experiment.com, though, funding requests are limited to scientific research needs.

At a time when scientific funding is increasingly political and when many researchers can no longer rely on the availability of grants, Experiment.com lets interested organizations and philanthropists drive innovation. The startup points out that researchers in the past five years have spent more time seeking funding by writing grant proposals than doing the work to solve major problems. The product, then, meets a need that people can get behind-supporters who want to see results can impact the efficiency of research through their funding.

Researchers in categories ranging from biology to mathematics can seek funding for a variety of projects. Funders can support their preferred industry or choose projects in which researchers promise to release results in open access formats.

One thing we like about Experiment.com is that the startup partnered with other organizations, including a number of universities known for quality research. Founders Cindy Wu and Denny Luan did have their own research experience, but partnerships with academic programs supported the legitimacy of their product. Experiment.com is currently part of the Angel Kings portfolio.

11. Transcriptic

One of the biggest challenges to small and midsized businesses in the biotechnology space is the prohibitive cost of equipment. Transcriptic answers that challenge with a remote life science research lab which users can access via the web. The lab is powered by robotic automation, and users can access a variety of testing environments and equipment at hourly rates. By offering hourly rates, Transcriptic delivers as-needed technology that works with a wide range of organization budgets.

12. **Iodine**

Iodine delivers expert information about drugs and medications, including side effects, expectations of the drug, comparisons with other medications, and reviews from thousands of users. Almost a quarter of American consumers search for in-depth drug information online, often finding sketchy or unclear information. By providing user-friendly and accurate information, Iodine hopes to improve consumer health by putting patients in a better position to ask questions and reducing the chance of incompatible prescriptions. We regrettably missed the opportunity to invest in this one.

13. **PillPack**

Healthcare providers and caregivers have been trying to organize medications for years. When someone is on multiple medications–particularly someone who is elderly–taking the right pills at the right time can be difficult. Taking the wrong pill, however, can be disastrous. PillPack steps in to meet a timeless problem with a clever solution: preprinted, sealed packs that contain one dose of pills. The pack tells users what day and time to take the pills, and lists all the medications enclosed, making life easier for patients, caregivers, and providers.

14. **Cake Health**

Growing out-of-pocket medical expenses mean more Americans are dealing with medical bills. Tracking spending and benefits statements can be tedious. Cake Health offers a web-based solution that imports medical statements directly from your insurance company. Benefits to consumers include a better understanding of medical bills, the ability to ensure claims are being paid properly, an understanding of when deductibles will be met, and simplified tracking and reporting for tax purposes.

15. Fitbit[2] (now publicly traded, as "FIT")

Fitbit hits a homerun on our product checklist. The physical fitness bracelet entered a market already primed for branding–loyal fitness audiences quickly attach to any device that makes workouts more fun or convenient. Before wearable devices, individuals were strapping bulkier mobile units to arms and chests before walking, biking, or running. Fitbit tracks and manages multiple data points, but is more comfortable and convenient to wear when working out. Even though Fitbit is now publicly traded, we kept Fitbit in our rankings because other hardware startups should aspire to similar success.

---

[2] FitBit has since gone public and priced its initial public offering at $20/share – the third largest U.S. IPO in 2015. Driebusch, Corrie. "Fitbit IPO Prices at $20 a Share, Above Expectations."WSJ. Wall Street Journal, 17 June 2015. Web. 7 July 2015.

OFFICIAL ANGEL KINGS RANKINGS
TOP FINTECH STARTUPS

1. inDinero – A Focus Startup*

Both a focus startup and part of the Angel Kings portfolio, inDinero illustrates the principle from Chapter 3 that there's nothing new under the sun–particularly when you're talking about accounting services. The startup's cloud-based accounting services offer payroll, tax, and other bookkeeping options, which are all available through other companies or software. Remember, though, that a product that offers less expensive or more convenient services has a good chance at succeeding, and that's what inDinero delivers.

The startup offers all-in-one back office accounting so businesses of all sizes can concentrate on revenue-generating activity instead of tedious accounting functions. InDinero also charges clients based on monthly pricing that is easy to predict, which may not always be the case with traditional accountants and bookkeepers. One thing that excites us about inDinero is that its product is designed for small and mid-sized business, but the product scales with business growth to support organizations with eight-figure revenues and 100 or more employees.

inDinero's startup story is interesting, as it provides a different outlook than some of the other companies we've covered in depth. The startup launched in 2010 and was successful at seeking seed funding. The product in 2010 was a self-service, small business, financial tracking tool–not what inDinero is today. While pursuing the first version of its product, inDinero faced challenges. It almost ran out of money and had to lay off all its employees before revamping the product; at relaunch in 2013, inDinero was able to land $7 million in funding and has since seen more success.

The story is important, because it speaks to our point in a previous chapter: As an angel investor, you are not investing in a perfect product. You're investing in people and ideas, and some ideas take more tweaking than others to achieve success. We are proud to have inserted capital with InDinero.

2. **Recurly**

Recurly's platform makes it easy for businesses of any size to set up, manage, and automate recurring bills. An increase in subscription services in all types of niches has made recurring bills a big business opportunity, and a secure, customized platform is a product that generates substantial interest among small and midsized businesses. Recurly entered the market just as this need was rapidly increasing following the success of subscription services such as Netflix and Ipsy.

3. **BillGuard**

In a world where no retailer or bank seems capable of guaranteeing protection of your account information with 100 percent assurance, BillGuard makes it easy for you to do the monitoring yourself. The startup partnered with Experian and offers an app that displays all your account information in a single dashboard. A few glances throughout the day provide peace of mind about account status, and the app also provides security notifications. BillGuard scores high as a startup due in part to its entry into a consumer market that is frightened by growing virtual threats and has a psychological need to do something to protect itself.

4. **Wealthfront**

   Wealthfront delivers on-demand investment advice and services without high account minimums and fees that keep many people from building wealth through investing. One thing that makes Wealthfront a top fintech is that it takes an existing solution-investment services- and makes it available to a new market. We talked before about creating a have situation for the have-nots, and this product does that. Deeply entrenched companies like Charles Schwab are now copying these auto-investing platforms. When the big boys copy your clothing, you know you're onto something big.

5. **Acorn Investing (Acorns)**

   Acorn investing has opened investing and financial management up for the masses. Their seamless interface allows for auto-investing and saving for millions of investors who want to get in the stock market game. This platform is groundbreaking. Of course, they do run the risk of being copied or cloned by companies like Rocket Internet, but if they do hit scale fast enough, we expect this one could be a billion dollar company in no time.

6. **FreshBooks**

   In a niche previously dominated by complex options such as Peachtree or QuickBooks, FreshBooks offers web-based accounting software that doesn't require an accounting degree. The application meets a specific need: billing and tracking. Since inception, the startup has garnered over 5 million customers, speaking to the need and desire for a simple invoicing software. We were one of the first customers of FreshBooks, and as a continuing customer, we can see FreshBooks growing into a billion dollar company.

7. **Lenda – *A Focus Startup**

Launched by cofounders Elijah Murray and Jason van den Brand, Lenda is both a focus startup and one of the companies in Angel Kings' portfolio. Both of the founders had previous startup experience, and van den Brand was involved with Urban Escapes, which was eventually acquired by Living Social. With two strong founders who tick the boxes on our people checklist, Lenda's quick traction with investors was no surprise to us.

The startup has gone through three phases of seed financing, with the last phase netting $1.54 million in investments. One reason for strong interest in the project is that Lenda is one of the first companies to bring a disruptive approach to the mortgage industry. Companies with disruptive technology enter an industry with processes that run against traditional methodologies. In the case of Lenda, it takes the middlemen and lead generation out of the mortgage refinance market.

The product is an obvious high score on our checklist. First, it saves people money–you'll always find someone willing to buy in to a product that generates savings. Second, it lets users seek mortgage refinancing without the inconvenience and unpleasantness of going through a sales process. Generally, when users search online for mortgage refinance options, they arrive on landing pages that require them to enter contact information. At that point, they either are put into a specific sales process or are entered into lead-generation databases that are sold to multiple entities. Either way, the result is phone calls, emails, and physical mail that the customer may not want.

Lenda cuts to the chase by assuming that a homeowner will enter accurate information into a short form. Using that information, Lenda generates a quote for refinancing. When the original information is accurate, the quote will be accurate, too. Homeowners can then decide if the quote is desirable before moving on to a lengthier official application form. By minimizing human interaction during the early stages of the process, Lenda allows customers to explore its services on their own without scaring them off.

Lenda also offers a less expensive alternative to traditional refinancing processes, because it is a lender and not a broker. The startup removes the middleman, which means homeowners benefit from interest rates that are on average an eighth of a point to a quarter-point below the competition. It might sound like a small advantage, but over the life of a mortgage, the difference can be worth thousands of dollars. Lenda also says its closing costs are generally lower than those quoted by the competition.

As of 2015, Lenda is the only company handling refinance loans in this way, though it wasn't the forerunner of the idea. Lending Club, for example, handles personal loans in a similar manner, and there are several companies in the subprime market that handle direct lending online. We are happy to have invested alongside the Winklevoss twins, who led a syndicate for Lenda.

8. **Stripe**

Included in our top 25 list, Stripe offers developer solutions that let businesses customize secure shopping carts and payment structures for both physical and online retail environments. This has the potential to be the next PayPal. Get ready for this to soar.

9. WePay

WePay offers a series of APIs that let developers create custom, brandable payment options. Its service is an alternative to common existing options such as placing a PayPal button on your webpage. The benefit of WePay is that you can integrate functionality into your own software, increasing your opportunities for branding during the payment and billing process.

10. Standard Treasury

Standard Treasury began, like several of the fintech companies on our list, by offering technical assistance in the virtual finance world. Its services include payment systems, fraud detection, integrations and APIs, and role-based delegation management. Today, Standard Treasury is seeking independent banking status in the United Kingdom and intends to couple its technical solutions with banking products, cutting out the middleman to provide efficient, cost-effective banking services.

11. Kickstarter

Kickstarter has combined existing social media structures with psychological need to create a successful product. Kickstarter began with a principle associated with social media–the crowd is powerful. It added the psychological desire within all individuals to belong and matter–to be a part of something bigger. Kickstarter lets individuals be a part of launching companies, funding charities, and helping others, all through easy-to-navigate technology that has the feel of familiar social media.

12. Bitcoin's "Blockchain" technology

Like many people, we're skeptical of personally using bitcoin for payment processing. However, underneath the bitcoin concept is technology with even bigger implications: the blockchain. We labeled this as our #12 ranked startup, not a specific company, but rather the technology infrastructure that will allow for billions of disenfranchised people to bank smarter and faster, one day. We expect the first mover advantage her to be huge and see current companies like Kraken, BitPagos and BitPay to run to the top of this new industry.

13. SumZero – *A Focus Startup

SumZero is another startup that would have scored well on the Angel Kings' rating. The company was founded by Divya Narendra, who is not only established, but also has experience with other startups. Narendra is also responsible for launching ConnectU, and he has ample professional background in finance (he technically helped create the first version of Facebook). He worked as an analyst at Credit Suisse, so he understands how to review and rate the financial status of an organization, which is part of what SumZero does.

The SumZero product combines several existing ideas to create a unique solution in a targeted niche. The website acts as a professional community–along the lines of LinkedIn, but without the broad scope. The target audience includes professional investors, advisors, and money managers. The audience can participate in an online community, sharing resources or promoting themselves, but SumZero's masterstroke is its detailed research database. Members of the community can share proprietary research or access data regarding top investment opportunities for vetting purposes.

SumZero offers its product at several levels. Basic access lets anyone read white papers written by the SumZero community or access free research. Elite access provides more premium content and industry research access. Professionals and money managers can choose from allocator or buy side subscriptions, which provide in-depth access to databases and networks, including job listings.

By providing information in a single location that helps fund managers achieve more success for clients, SumZero offers a product that professionals are willing to pay for. The targeted product also increases opportunities for successful branding and word-of-mouth marketing: Industry professionals are likely to subscribe when information is appropriate and easy to find, even if they already have subscriptions to other professional services, such as LinkedIn. I also went to Cornell University with Nicholas Kapur, the current Chief Operations Officer at SumZero. I rowed on the Cornell crew team with Kapur and can confidently tell you that he pulls his weight and always goes above and beyond; SumZero is lucky to have him on board. We expect SumZero to continue to grow and become the thought leaders in its space.

14. Regalii

Regalii created a service that lets immigrants to the U.S. send money to family and friends in home countries in secure, safe, and almost instantaneous fashion. The mobile app lets user send credits–similar to gift cards–to family members. The credits can then be used to buy a variety of items, including groceries. Beginning with a beta test involving transfers between the U.S. and the Dominican Republic, Regalii has branched into other Latin American countries and successfully sought investors for numerous seed rounds to expand further.

15. NarrativeScience

NarrativeScience is a prime example of a startup bringing a product to market at a time when a need is growing. The company creates software that converts data into narratives so business managers and others can simply read the story that the data tells. In an environment where data analysis is a growing challenge for organizations, and dashboards and spreadsheets are often misinterpreted by non-analytical staff, adding narration increases cross–departmental communication and enhances organizational productivity.

THE OFFICIAL ANGEL KINGS RANKINGS OF TOP MOBILE TO CONSUMER STARTUPS

1. **SendHub - *A Focus Startup**

   The founders of SendHub are a well-rounded group with strong professional and education backgrounds. Ash Rust worked for Klout and has a computer science degree from Oxford; Garret Johnson led billion-dollar projects as an aide in the U.S. Senate and was a Rhodes Scholar-twice. Ryan Pfeffer also has a computer science degree and worked as a senior engineer for Intuit. This strong founding team is only one reason SendHub is both a focus startup and part of the Angel Kings portfolio. The product also meets a variety of our requirements for investment.

   SendHub is a business communications application that provides simple, all-in-one phone solutions at a time when telecom decisions are growing more challenging for organizations of all sizes. The solution, which doesn't include hardware leasing or purchase, is relevant in a world where small and mid-sized businesses are exploring outsource, contract, and work-at-home methodologies. With resources across the globe-or, at least, across town-easy communication is an essential need.

   It's not that SendHub enters a market where telecom product offerings are scarce. It's that SendHub offers a product that is more convenient-and possibly affordable-than many others. SendHub works through a downloadable app, which means companies can use existing mobile technologies and hardware to run the solution. The app combines voice, SMS, and conference call functions with essential management functions such as call transferring, company directories, voicemail transcription, message forwarding, and use analytics.

From 2012 through 2014, the company was able to attract investors for three rounds and a total of $10 million. At a time when residential consumers are converting to all-mobile phone communications, SendHub is taking advantage of that mindset to brand itself as a solution among business consumers. It is reinventing how businesses communicate around the world.

2. **Life360**

Life360 automates and makes more convenient many of the functions families now rely on mobile phones for. You can build a circle of family or friends in the app, which provides map technology to let you know where everyone is. The app lets you automate check-ins, so teens don't have to remember to text home when arriving at a destination, and families can communicate in-group texts about their plans. But Life360 is far from being a one-off app idea. Life360 is a platform connecting families with each other.

3. **Dropcam (now part of Google's Nest Labs)**

Dropcam offers an easy, affordable solution for monitoring homes and businesses from mobile devices. Taking advantage of a growing market for home security solutions, Dropcam delivers a device that doesn't require contracting with a monitoring network. With almost plug-and-play ease, users can set up the camera to check in on babysitters, kids, empty homes, or pets from any location. Yes, Google's Nest Labs acquired this company, but it still remains a startup in the sense that they're continuing to innovate and could easily be spun off in new ways.

4. Flipboard – *A Focus Startup

As one of our focus startups, Flipboard scored high in the people, product, and timing areas of our evaluation. The current Flipboard team includes a number of individuals with wide-ranging startup and technical experience, such as Craig Mod, who is an advisor and investor in a number of other successful endeavors. The original launch team included Evan Doll, an Apple engineer, and Mike McCue, the former CEO of Tellme. The team and product inspired immediate confidence among investors, and was able to achieve a Series A investment of $10.5 million in 2010 and another round of investments in 2011 that totaled $50 million.

What is the product that inspired so much investing confidence? It's an app that curates customized content for each user, creating a personal virtual magazine. Available on almost all mobile devices and platforms, Flipboard lets users set up social media accounts and website subscriptions and browse top-level content without visiting each site or downloading multiple apps on their device.

Doll and McCue reportedly designed the original Flipboard product after a discussion about what the web would look like if it was designed from scratch with what designers know today. The two realized social web would play an enormous role in that process, and a graphical user interface, they thought, would be most appealing to users. The resulting product delivers user-specific content in a graphical manner.

One of the reasons we like this startup is that the product builds on what came before in such a clever way. The solution is not new–connecting users with content is something hundreds of sites and companies do. But connecting users with all of their preferred content in an easy-to-manage format adds a unique spin to an existing solution.

5. **Paper by FiftyThree**

   Paper is a platform that brings the simplicity of paper brainstorming and doodling to mobile devices. Users can create sketches, design products, or write to-do lists-anything they might normally do on paper. The benefit is that Paper keeps things more organized than random scraps in your pocketbook or desk drawer, and it also integrates with collaboration application, Mix. Paper connects everyone, from kids designing at school to architects making blueprints for buildings.

6. **Instacart**

   Listed as one of our Top 25 startups, Instacart makes the Mobile to Consumer list for its integration of growing mobile capabilities with a long-term demand among modern consumers for convenience. People have been able to order pizza and other takeout items on mobile devices for several years; Instacart expands that capability to groceries.

7. **Imgur**

   The idea behind Imgur is deceptively simple: The platform provides one-stop image-sharing solutions for the entire web. Users can upload images to either public or private galleries and then use links to share images on blogs, via email, or on other forums. With millions of users launching simple sites and social media profiles, easy access to image sharing is an obvious product win. But Imgur goes a step further by bolstering its product with a viral-sharing platform, which has become one of the most popular hangouts on the Internet.

8. **Rdio**

   Rdio is a streaming music application along the lines of Pandora or Spotify. Unlike some of the other streaming options, Rdio offers a low-cost subscription option that is completely free of advertising, meeting a growing want of consumers in this market. The solution also integrates with most social platforms and works on most mobile device platforms, making it easier to share music suggestions and playlists.

9. **Snapchat**

   Mentioned in a previous chapter, Snapchat offers mobile-to-mobile picture texting. What makes it different from other solutions on the market is that pictures last only a short time before disappearing. While users originally touted the app as a safer way to send pictures, due to privacy concerns, the lasting brand impression of the product is that it's a fun way to share silly, instantaneous picture messages that tell a quicker story than tedious words of text.

10. **Spotify**

    Spotify is a paid or free music streaming app. Users can subscribe free via email or Facebook, but music experiences are occasionally interrupted by ads, which prompts many users to buy in to the paid Spotify product. The solution also includes third-party applications for song suggestions and one of the larger listening libraries among applications of this type. The artist Jay-Z introduced "Tidal", which should heat up the music industry space even more.

11. **Uber**

    Covered in-depth in our product chapter, Uber makes the Mobile to

Consumer list because of its innovative, consumer-facing product and strong brandability. The company lets users score rides via a crowdsourced taxi service, which is accessed from mobile devices.

12. ZocDoc – *A Focus Startup

With almost $98 million in investments over five years, ZocDoc is one of the most successful startups on our list from a capital-raised standpoint. One of the main reasons for ZocDoc's success may be that it meets a deep psychological need in almost every consumer.

ZocDoc operates on a similar principle as sites such as Angie's List, but it does so in the healthcare niche. Users can search for physicians and other healthcare providers in their area, read reviews, view certification and education information, and determine whether the provider meets a particular need. Once all the research is done, users can click a button to schedule an appointment or access office contact information if the provider doesn't offer appointments through ZocDoc.

The psychological need met by ZocDoc is a reduction in stress regarding something that gives many people anxiety: finding a physician and making an appointment. Individuals who are concerned about finding a solid practitioner can vet choices through ZocDoc's reviews, reading about previous patient experience on things such as bedside manner or friendliness of staff. For many, the ability to schedule the appointment with a few clicks of the mouse makes the entire process less stressful.

There's also a convenience factor. Individuals can generate a list of physicians in any area by specialty, find out if insurance is covered, and peruse open appointment times – all in one location. ZocDoc adds to convenience by offering a telephone and email helpline and covering hospitals and clinics as well as single providers.

ZocDoc also meets our checklist item for pricing. Since the service is free to patient-side users, it's more likely people will use it. ZocDoc can then monetize on the provider and business sides. The knowledge that ZocDoc can bring patients to the site via its free services persuades businesses to buy in to the concept. ZocDoc has profound implications on the future of healthcare in America.

13. Pocket

Social media and Internet users have been searching for years for ways to save everything from keystrokes to their browsing history. Pocket isn't the first solution to the problem-saved tabs and favorite websites have been around almost as long as the Internet browser. But Pocket delivers a solution that is more scalable and convenient than previous options. The app works on all major platforms and integrates into social apps such as Twitter and Flipboard, so users can save anything from statuses and images to full articles for later perusal.

14. **RobinHood**

RobinHood is a stock trading app, where customers can buy and sell their stocks with their iPhone. It allows customers to skip the hassle and intimidation of dealing with stockbrokers and their commission fees by providing a simple and accessible method for anyone to participate in the financial market. RobinHood allows customers to take charge of investing their money, and thus, making stock trading more appealing and approachable to the masses.

15. Lyft

Lyft was developed from the founders', Logan Green and John Zimmer, original company, Zimride. Similar to Uber, Lyft is an app that connects passengers and drivers, where each party establishes a trustworthy reputation on the app's user network through a 5-star-rating scale. Lyft originally branded their drivers' cars with pink mustaches on their grills until 2015, and continues to market itself with the tagline, "your friend with a car."

OFFICIAL ANGEL KINGS RANKINGS THE TOP VICE STARTUPS

1. **DraftKings**

   DraftKings takes the cult following of fantasy sports leagues and turns it into a profitable venture...for some. Meant to increase the competition and interest of fantasy sports, DraftKings lets users put money on the line while they compete for high-level prizes. While many applications are limited to specific sports, DraftKings offers access to events in baseball, football, basketball, soccer, golf, hockey, and more. As even more validation for this vice startup, The Walt Disney Company just announced a major investment of $250,000,000 at a $900 million dollar valuation. Draft Kings is set to soar even higher, and you can expect a future IPO.

2. **Vice.com and Vice Media**

   What "Vice" list would be complete without including the ultimate Vice – a TV, content, and internet sensation called Vice Media ("Vice"). Vice is penetrating mundane media with insightful and forward-thinking reporting. We are absolute addicts of this media distribution network; from stories about the African drug trade funding terrorist networks abroad, to groundbreaking looks at vaccinations to cure cancer, Shane Smith and his brilliant team continue to innovate and disrupt the boring media networks. As absolute validation: A&E Networks and 21st Century Fox have both invested at greater than $2 Billion dollar valuations. This one is a winner.

3. **Massroots**

Massroots also provides a service for cannabis users. The mobile app, which boasts semi-anonymous use, doesn't limit itself to dispensaries. It's a social app that brings cannabis users together for discussions, shared information, and real-life connections.

4. **Ploom - *A Focus Startup**

Ploom is an interesting startup, because its product and brand score high on the Angel Kings' point system, but the company faced challenges because of regulations within its industry. Ploom, which makes sleek vape products for tobacco, marijuana, and other products, launched a few years ago at a time when the e-cigarette market was heating up and the vape market hadn't yet reached the cult status it has in 2015. Take a quick peek at our chapter on timing, and you'll see that Ploom fits the bill. The market was heating up, consumers were interested, several companies had already entered products, and there was a growing consumer need for a healthier smoking option.

Ploom's sophisticated and simple products, which come in elegant packaging, have been called the iPods or iPhones of the vape market-an obvious branding strength. The devices are more attractive-more desirable-than some of the bulkier items on the market. One interesting thing to note about Ploom and its Pox devices is that the startup didn't see immediate success. The small company knew it had a good idea, but it didn't have the expertise or resources to bring it to a mass market. By teaming up with Japanese Tobacco International, through a minority stake investment by JTI, Ploom gained access to industry scientists, research, and development departments-proof that people and planning matter for startup success.

Ploom's devices let users retain almost all the nicotine and taste properties of tobacco without inhaling any of the smoke. One of the startup's major challenges was how to compete and brand itself in a growing and competitive field when, by law, it couldn't make health benefit claims. In the end, Ploom capitalized on its other benefits: small, discreet devices that offered optimal convenience. Ploom will continue to deliver and expand on a seamless experience.

5. **Youbet.me**

Youbet.me brings the office football pool–along with anything else social groups might like to bet on–to social media. From sporting events to the due date on the latest family addition, friends can add betting interest to any event. Youbet.me lets users create events and invite people to bet, and it keeps track of winners.

6. **Virtuix Omni VR**

Virtuix launched via Kickstarter in a similar way that Oculus VR (acquired by Microsoft) had been. Unlike the other startups on our Vice list however, Virtuix is part Vice, part productive tool ... with billion dollar implications. Virtuix is a platform for gamers to immerse themselves within the multi-billion dollar gaming industry. Beyond gaming, Virtuix could easily become a platform for exercise, movies, entertainment and the broader social networking tools like Facebook and Twitter. We expect big things from this company.

7. **Leafly**

You might look at Leafly as the "WebMD" of cannabis. The site lets you find doctors willing to prescribe medical marijuana and dispensaries, but it also offers a growing databank of information for both recreational and medical users. You can access articles, read about popular strains, and peruse reviews of facilities and marijuana types. The startup enters a growing market at a time when users have a psychological need for legitimacy, and by framing marijuana information in an authoritative way, Leafly delivers on that need. There are also some major investors behind this one.

8. **Betable - *A Focus Startup**

Betable enters a market that is already flush with startups, since open app development makes it possible for anyone with basic technical skills to develop mobile-based games. At first glance, that might make it seem like Betable faced a big handicap on the timing and product fronts, but because it brought a solution to market that worked with other developers' products, the growing competition among online and mobile game developers works in Betable's favor.

Betable's consumer audience is developers. Developers, who make games of any type, may want to add the ability for users to integrate real-money gambling, but anytime users add currency to a development process, they run into headaches. Money transactions require security and compliance protocols–something individual developers can spend countless hours working on. In an environment of hackers and cyber threats, money apps also have to be as perfect as possible, making it tedious for developers who are trying to create games. These complications make it impossible for many organizations and individuals to launch games with a gambling component.

That's where Betable's product comes in. The startup does the work for developers, offering APIs that developers can integrate into games and apps. Betable's product is the only solution that allows developers to offer legal gambling in a variety of games. The reason is that Betable itself keeps a current gambling license.

Mobile gameplay is already extremely popular among users of all ages, and games such as Candy Crush illustrate that people are willing to add money to game accounts for extra access, perks, or winnings. Developers are willing to pay for Betable, because the product is likely to increase revenues for them through the gambling stream.

9. **Cashbet**

Like Betable, Cashbet holds its own gaming licenses that cover any developer that uses its platform. The startup targets mobile gaming and is available on a variety of platforms. Developers don't have to rely on Flash-based desktop games, opening their revenue streams to social media and other mobile-heavy platforms. Cashbet also lets game developers create marketing campaigns through email and push notifications to bolster revenues.

10. **Junglee Games**

Unlike Cashbet and Betable, which cater to developers, Junglee Games seems to be keeping its software to itself, and with a good outcome. The startup projects its 2015 revenue at $80 million, ten times its projected 2013 revenue. The reason for quick growth is that the online casino gaming company uses proprietary software to launch new games up to five times faster than the competition, letting the company capitalize on novelty games before markets are saturated.

11. Drync – *A Focus Startup

From 2009 to 2012, wine consumption in the United States saw a per capita increase of over 14 percent. Wine continues to grow in popularity among almost every social and cultural group, with wine bars and vineyards opening throughout the country. Historically, however, wine has been a connoisseur's beverage, until Drync came along.

Many wine newcomers have been stuck browsing wine shelves at random or poring through books on wine to try to determine what vintage might be best or how to pair a wine with dinner. Seeing a need for consumer education, Drync stepped in with a half-authoritative, half-crowdsourced product. The app, which is available on all major devices, lets users access information about hundreds of thousands of wines. Information includes images, reviews, ratings, and databases of ingredients and flavors. From the site, users can purchase wine from more than 40,000 U.S. stores, providing consumers in smaller areas with increased wine choices.

The app lets users track favorite wines, view label photographs to make shopping easier, and order wine for direct home delivery. Startup founders Brad Rosen and Bill Kirtley wanted the brand to become the official wine authority. We like the branding possibilities for this startup, both because of its plans for the future and the fact that it targets such a wide range of users with a real psychological need. No one wants to be the host or hostess who serves a poor bottle of wine, and many users choose wine because of the sophistication associated with the bottle, the glass, and the sipping. By allowing consumers to increase their proficiency in wine service and enjoyment, Drync meets their desire to appear more sophisticated and cultured.

12. Drizly

We talked about the importance of convenience to consumers in several previous chapters, and that's something Drizly capitalizes on. The startup's app lets users order beer, wine, and liquor for home delivery in a variety of locations. Like Uber, it isn't operational in all cities, though it is expanding.

13. Flaviar

Flaviar delivers curated liquor samples on a monthly subscription basis. It also offers the ability to organize the liquor that subscribers have on hand, the liquor they have tasted, and the liquor they want to try in the future. Tasting parties can be organized, and suggestions for tasting packs can be created. Their popular blog offers recipes, reviews, suggestions, and pairings. For those who don't want a monthly subscription, the sample pack can be purchased as a one-off option. The company primarily provides a small sample of each liquor, but has also moved into full-bottle service.

14. Reddit

Reddit provides entertainment, news, and social networking, based around topics of interest. Reddit is an online bulletin board that anyone can use. People register for the community, and then they can submit content. Direct links are allowed, as are text posts. Submissions from Reddit users are voted up or down by other users, which determines where a post falls on the site's pages. Areas of interest are called "subreddits," and are used to organize content. As of November 2014, Reddit boasted 174 million users. Why do we call Reddit a vice? Well, it's only a vice to the millions of companies whose employees spend hours each day browsing its fascinating pages. I guess, we would add Facebook and Twitter to this list if they were still startups!

15. Buzzfeed

Traditional media is dead. Print, radio and the old methods of communicating news are just out of style (maybe just for now). Now websites like Buzzfeed are taking productivity time away from millions of employees working each day, Buzzfeed is just that. Buzzfeed articles are link bait. They serve little purpose other than getting the user to share something they find interesting. It's sort of like the bored-networking tool for people during the day. This isn't to say I haven't read or shared articles myself using Buzzfeed; admittedly, I have shared volumes are articles from Buzzfeed with friends and colleagues, only to realize later that I'll never be able to get back that 10 minutes I spent doing just that. We commend the Buzzfeed team for building a quite humorous and entertaining network. In fact, there are several other companies, like *Business Insider*, who have followed suit and are doing quite well. Both companies will either IPO someday or be a major acquisition target.

Admittedly, a couple of the companies mentioned above aren't startups in the traditional sense-neither bootstrapper nor pre-Series A-but we believe they continue to innovate similar to how startups should. These companies also have not found an exit yet, but we do expect them to become billion dollar companies.

OFFICIAL ANGEL KINGS RANKINGS
TOP ENTERPRISE STARTUPS

1. **Dropbox**

Dropbox provides both cloud-based storage and file sharing for individuals and businesses that need the space or the capabilities of sharing files rapidly and conveniently. New users are able to open a Dropbox account for free, and paid services are available for users who need more data space. In 2015, Dropbox had 300 million users from all over the world. The former startup facilitates the sharing and storing of files to enable creation and completion of projects that involve people who may not be geographically near one another.

2. **Optimizely**

Optimizely creates software that optimizes the experience customers have with companies. That lets businesses conduct A/B, multivariate, and multipage testing so they can make decisions based on the data they receive. Optimizely has testing solutions for websites and iOS apps. The Software as a Service (SaaS) model used by Optimizely can be used by any size business. The company is headquartered in San Francisco, and has launched its platform in nine languages in addition to English, cornering more of the market for online customer experience testing.

3. **Sendwithus**

   Sendwithus is a Y combinator-incubated startup. It provides A/B testing and optimization options for marketers and others who send out targeted emails that are promotional in nature. Customers who use the service are able to choose pre-made email templates, or they can upload their own. Then they log into the email provider they normally use, and are able to set up drip campaigns and A/B testing. To understand how campaigns and variants are doing, customers can access analytics. The company focuses on transactional emails, as opposed to broad campaigns or newsletters.

4. **Codementor.io – A Focus Startup***

   Codementor.io is a company that functions as an online marketplace. Located in Mountain View, California, the company connects experts and developers for one-on-one help through an on-demand model. This help is offered through text and video chat and through screen sharing. For those who want to move beyond the on-demand model, there are options for dedicated mentorship on a long-term basis... The mentoring provided through the marketplace can help businesses overcome the key challenges that they face, speeding up the project development process. The Codementor platform can save businesses thousands of dollars by avoiding the necessity to call in professionals to handle urgent issues that developers cannot solve.

   Codementor.io was founded by Weiting Liu, a graduate of Stanford University with a master's degree in engineering. Before founding Codementor, Liu started companies such as SocialPicks and bootstrapped other startups until they reached 50 employees. Liu's goal with the founding of Codementor was for people to feel as though they have a developer there beside them. Often, just knowing that help is available if needed can make a significant difference in the confidence of a coder to accomplish the task at hand.

The culture of Codementor is all about helping people succeed. In a time when many businesspeople look for ways to get ahead and sabotage others, Codementor is focused on ensuring that people can move forward with the projects that are important to them. That makes the Codementor brand one that carries a good connotation, one associated with improving the lives of people and the goals of their businesses. Because it is an online marketplace that brings coders and mentors together, it fosters a sense of connectedness and camaraderie that is not often seen at other sites.

Having an on-demand model means people can get one-off help when they need it. They won't need to sign up for a monthly subscription or pay a retainer fee to keep someone available at all times. If they desire a more long-term relationship with their mentor, that choice is available to them.

The company's mentors receive the satisfaction of helping others, which can go a long way for those who are retired or simply want to give back to other people who are trying to build their businesses. There are currently 300 mentors based in the U.S., Asia, and Europe, and they continue to expand this community.

The most urgent questions are answered within two hours, while other questions have a 24-hour turn-around time. The goal of Codementor, though, is to have mentors available in real time, so questions can get answered right away. As more mentors come on board, this goal is expected to become a reality.

The startup timing of Codementor could not be better. The number of people building businesses today continues to grow, as does the need for websites, mobile applications, and other technology. With that in mind, Codementor is getting into the market just when it is needed most. Founder Liu has stated that he wishes something like Codementor existed when he was learning to code. It is not just about solving urgent issues, but also about helping coders train themselves to work through the problems that come up during creation of their projects.

5. **Slack App – A Focus Startup**

Slack App offers chatting and communication with a business focus. Unlike apps that are more targeted to social media, Slack is about helping employees and businesses communicate with one another. As of March 2015, the company was valued at $2.76 billion, and it continues to grow. In the course of six months, the company has more than doubled its valuation. The explosive growth of the company has come from the addition of an average of $1 million in new contracts every 11 days, and from $12 million in recurring revenue from the previous year.

In just one year, Slack App has grown to hundreds of thousands of daily users. It has been deemed the fastest-growing business app ever. The reason Slack has experienced such phenomenal growth is because it did something the other app companies did not: It worked with the business app as though it was a consumer app. The gap traditionally seen between business and consumer apps has been shrinking, and Slack has taken advantage of this opportunity.

Slack's timing was impeccable. Many businesses were disenchanted with the options they had for connecting with co-workers on a business level. With the Slack app, smaller teams throughout various companies discovered it in the cloud and started to use it. Quickly, Slack has become many companies' first line of communication.

In the beginning, there was almost no marketing done by Slack. The app sold itself, as people discovered it and word-of-mouth advertising caused more people to start using it. Because it provided employees with exactly what they needed and wanted in a business communication app, they told everyone they knew about it. That meant a more organic adoption of the service, and a higher level of loyalty from the user base. What made Slack so popular, though, was Twitter.

Businesspeople who used and loved the app would make mention of Slack on Twitter, where all their followers would see it. That led many more people to try the app, to see what the buzz was all about. CEO Stewart Butterfield believes that the app may not have seen such a high level of success so quickly if it was not for Twitter and all the people mentioning Slack on the social media platform. That was not the only reason the Slack app became so popular so quickly, though. Another reason was its ease of use, which is important to businesspeople who don't have a lot of time to learn yet another new piece of technology.

The layout of the Slack app is intuitive, and it integrates seamlessly with hundreds of other apps, so the information from them can be pulled into Slack. There is no training needed to start using the app, and the ease of customization makes the app a hit with people in all different types of businesses. If they need communication that's fast, easy, and well-prepared to work with other apps and technology, they need Slack – and thanks to the buzz around the app, they know it. Will Slack be acquired by LinkedIn, Microsoft, or Google? Only time will tell.

6. **Mixpanel**

    Mixpanel is a Y combinator-incubated startup. It has a focus on analytics, and has moved into providing testing for mobile developers who have several different versions of an app. This type of testing can show which version of the app is the best choice based on user input. Mixpanel has a unique approach that makes changing an app fast and easy. That allows more people to feel comfortable using the product, and being an engineer is not required. The A/B testing service offered by the company is tied to analytics, making it easy to see what changes are best for users.

7. **Huddle**

    Huddle offers users the opportunity for cloud-based collaboration. Government and enterprise organizations use Huddle to store, share, sync, access, and work on files with anyone who needs to be involved in the project, securely and safely. That includes those who are located outside of the organizations' firewalls. It provides its software for free to registered charities throughout the world, and has headquarters in San Francisco and London. New York and Washington, D.C., are also home to Huddle offices.

8. **Zenefits**[3]

    Zenefits is a human resource platform that is based in the cloud. Businesses that use the service can manage a number of services related to human resources from the convenience of one dashboard. This streamlines the process of hiring and on-boarding new employees and of ensuring that they are set up with benefits and payroll. It also

---

[3] On May 6 2015, Zenefits raised $500 million at a $4.5 billion valuation. Lynley, Matthew. "Zenefits Just Raised $500 Million At A $4.5 Billion Valuation." *TechCrunch*. TechCrunch, 6 May 2015. Web. 07 July 2015.

allows them to be removed easily if they choose to leave the company or if their employment is terminated. The service is free for businesses to use. Clients that change their plans after signing with the company pay a commission.

9. **DigitalOcean**

Based in New York City, DigitalOcean provides virtual private server options. Capacity is leased from existing data centers in Amsterdam, Singapore, London, New York, and San Francisco. In October of 2014, DigitalOcean was #4 on the list of the world's largest hosting providers. Its cloud servers are fast and reliable, providing companies that use the service with quality that they may not be able to access from other companies. Growth in 2014 was almost 850%. DigitalOcean now has more than 160,000 users, with 1,000 new users added every day.

10. **Couchbase**

Couchbase is a data management and data processing company. It is expanding its research and development opportunities and has plans to expand on an international level. Based in Mountain View, California, the company is focused on data management and recovery. It is a distributed database, which allows it to handle more users and their requests in a way that centralized databases cannot. Scaling up a distributed database is much faster. Couchbase can also allow apps to work on mobile devices even when they lack an Internet connection.

11. **Docker**

Docker is virtualization software. It is an open-source project that permits deployment of applications inside software containers through an automated process. By using additional layers of automation and abstraction on a Linux platform, Docker avoids a lot of overhead, making it easier to run apps efficiently. By packing an application that can be run on any Linux server, Docker provides both portability and flexibility for the application and those who wish to run that application on bare metal, public cloud, and private cloud.

12. **CoreOS**

CoreOS is a lightweight operating system based on Linux that provides an infrastructure to clustered deployments. It focuses on automation and ease of application deployment, along with reliability, security, and scalability. Only minimal deployment functionality is offered for applications, as that is all that is needed to deploy them inside of software containers. Configuration sharing and service discovery are also built-in mechanisms. It uses source code from Chrome OS as its base, and adds functionality and other customization to support server hardware.

13. **Nutanix**

Nutanix is a company focused on storage and enterprise visualization. It offers the Nutanix Virtual Computing Platform, which provides storage and computing power through deploying commodity computing servers (or "nodes"). Each of these nodes runs the Nutanix OS and a standard hypervisor. Both Nutanix and Dell sell the NOS. The company is headquartered in San Jose, California. It has sales offices in Europe, Australia, Asia Pacific, North America, Latin America, and Japan. Just four years after its launch date, it reached a $1 billion in valuation.

14. **Asana**

Asana is all about employee productivity. It is designed to enable team collaboration without the need to use email. It is both a mobile and web application, allowing it to be used anywhere. As of 2014, Asana was being used by tens of thousands of different companies and teams in need of collaborative efforts and options. Every industry and every continent–with the exception of Antarctica–has companies that use Asana to raise productivity and allow their employees to more easily work with one another. As a "post-email application," Asana is gaining popularity in more industries every day. Will it be in Antarctica one day? Only time will tell.

15. **Illumio**

Headquartered in Sunnyvale, California, Illumio is a cloud computing security company that works as an enterprise data center. The security model used by the company is able to adapt to changes in application and infrastructure. By decoupling the security features from the infrastructure underneath them, this approach to security can be used across a number of different types of platforms. These include both public and private clouds, along with private data centers. The service is based on security in real time, with current assessment of risk through declarative programming instead of the imperative programming used by firewalls and other security options.

16. **Anaplan**

For operations, sales, and finance, Anaplan is the choice of many businesses. It is cloud-based and focused on business modeling and planning, providing a platform for businesses to plot their futures. The single hub design of the service was created to allow business users to create, deploy, maintain, and share their ideas and models without the need for IT support. Headquartered in San Francisco, Anaplan has offices in France, England, Sweden and Singapore. The company is growing rapidly. In 2012, revenues grew 800% and the company base grew 500%.

17. **CloudFlare – *A Focus Startup**

CloudFlare offers both a distributed domain name server system and a content delivery network. The company acts as a type of reverse proxy for websites, and improves the speed, security, and availability of a mobile application or website through changes in the DNS. Founded in 2009, the San Francisco-based company was created by Lee Holloway, Matthew Prince, and Michelle Zatlyn, who had past experience with Project Honey Pot. It also has an overseas office in London.

In 2014 CloudFlare acquired CryptoSeal, which was designed to help extend security services across the web. It also acquired StopTheHacker, adding to its ability to provide malware detection and removal, as well as blacklist and reputation monitoring. CloudFlare's goal is to make sure that malicious traffic never reaches the apps and websites of its customers, even though hackers and other individuals attempt to send such traffic. Because CloudFlare intercepts so much hacker traffic, the FBI and other law enforcement agencies have paid the company a compliment by at times requesting information as to who is using its servers. The difference between CloudFlare and other security and protection companies is that CloudFlare's protection is all in the cloud. There is no software for a customer to install, and no firewall settings that have to be adjusted.

There are 28 data centers throughout the world that house the company's servers and routers. These are designed to reroute visitors to its customers' sites to the closest CloudFlare server. Any traffic that is deemed to be a threat is turned away instead of being rerouted. With its business model, the company is going up against big names in the security and rerouting industries, such as 16-year veteran Akamai. CloudFlare speeds up websites in the same way Akamai does, but it also emphasizes the protection it provides against botnets and other malicious agents.

CloudFlare could not have come onto the scene at a better time. While the company initially focused on smaller businesses that Akamai was not interested in, larger companies have since come on board. This is in direct correlation to the number of distributed denial of service (DDoS) attacks that have been seen in recent years. These attacks have been on the rise, and have jumped tenfold just since 2009. CloudFlare guards more than 2 million websites, with the majority of them taking advantage of the free option the company offers. Of its many customers, 4 to 5% pay between $20 and $5,000 a month for a higher level of protection.

CEO Prince doesn't mind that the majority of customers use his free service, because the algorithms that protect every site learn from every bit of traffic that comes through the company's data centers. That means he is getting a benefit from the non-paying customers as well as the paying ones. Every customer is helping to make his business and its ability to protect websites stronger. Those who pay for the service get firewalls, encryption, and stronger DDoS protection. Some of the largest clients pay more than $1 million annually to ensure their sites are kept safe and customers can access them when they want. Each year, CloudFlare has grown around 450%; it had its first cash-flow-positive quarter with actual revenue in 2014.

Prince is a lawyer, law professor, businessman, and computer enthusiast. His service often defends and protects sites that may be deemed unpopular, but he believes in the right to free expression. Despite the fact that Prince and his employees have been the victims of personal hacking and attacks, he sees what his company is doing as much like soldiers protecting the front lines. With a careful mix of transparency and discretion, CloudFlare has made a name for itself in the security and protection sphere. That name will continue to be used in more businesses and households, as the company grows and more people need the protection it can provide. I also was lucky enough to get to know Matthew when my first company was a TechCrunch Finalist in San Francisco. He's a great guy and someone to look out for in the future; a potential icon in the cloud and software industry.

PART THREE

The Best Articles on Angel and VC Investing

8

ARTICLES FOR THE INVESTOR

MEET THE TOP 5 DORM ROOM FOUNDERS

Many impressive companies have been founded in dorm rooms. These companies have re-defined society, technology and cultural movements in America. Here are some of the most impressive dorm room founders:

1. MARK ZUCKERBERG

The name that comes to mind most often when mentioning founders who were in college when they created their big idea is Mark Zuckerberg, a co-founder of Facebook. The other four co-founders were Andrew McCollum, Chris Hughes, Dustin Moskovitz, and

Eduardo Saverin. Originally, the site was called theFacebook, and it was created just for fellow Harvard classmates. It was an online place where classmates could find information on one another, and where they could connect with people who were sharing their classrooms and hallways.

It brought students together, and allowed them to learn about one another's lives at a time when the Internet was still getting a good foothold in the minds of many people and the term "social media" wasn't something everyone had heard of. While there were social media sites available before Facebook (MySpace, anyone?), Zuckerberg and his co-founders created something inimitable. It was so different that it captured the interest of a high number of Harvard students – and people outside of Harvard begin complaining that they didn't have anything like that to use.

Over time, Zuckerberg and his co-founders became aware that other schools were jealous of what he was offering to the students of Harvard. The site was expanded to allow students from other schools to connect with Harvard and with one another, and the popularity of that option grew until a number of schools had high percentages of their students logging on and linking up to see what others were doing. What started out as a small idea to keep students at one school connected had become something much greater than that.

When the popularity of "theFacebook" began to soar, Zuckerberg realized its massive potential. Rather than remain in college and focus on his studies in computer science and psychology, he dropped out and focused the majority of his time and attention on the development of the site. The site was renamed Facebook and opened up to others outside of educational circles. As of 2015, use of the site had grown to more than one billion people worldwide. It's the largest social media site in the world, and all indications are that it will remain that way indefinitely. It has changed throughout the years, but its popularity remains high.

2. LARRY PAGE AND SERGEY BRIN

While Zuckerberg may be one of the most famous dorm room founders, he's far from the only one who took what he learned in the classroom and coupled it with real life to make something amazing. Other dorm room founders who created companies with household names include the duo of Larry Page and Sergey Brin, the creators of Google. They were Ph.D. students at the time they started developing the search engine, which started out as a part of Stanford's Digital Library Project. They wanted to see a more powerful search engine that was also effective.

While searching was already possible, it often did not work well, and its lack of power meant that much was missed during a large number of searches. Navigating the Internet was clunky, at best, and other search sites gave results that could often be considered questionable. A targeted, proper search engine was needed, but it had to be easy to use and it had to be comprehensive. One of the main complaints with previous search engines was that they did not return enough results – and much of what they *did* return was not relevant to what the searcher was actually looking for.

A better way had to be out there somewhere, and Page and Brin discovered it as they were trying to catalog the digital library and make it searchable. When they saw what they had, they knew they were on the cusp of something that could change the Internet forever. It was then just a matter of continuing to develop what they had already started. That took time and effort. At first, one could not simply type in "Google" and reach the search engine. The original address was google.stanford.edu. That was changed as the site continued to be developed and more capability was added to it.

Today, Google is the world's most dominant search engine. From there, the company evolved into more than just a way to search the Internet. The conglomerate now provides a significant number of Internet-based services and products, including Google+, Blogger, Picasa Web Albums, and more. Most people don't say "search for that." They say "just Google it." The site has become such a common part of daily life for so many people that there is no reason to use a different search engine in most cases. The majority of people who want to find something online know Google will give them the best results, fast. Google has branded itself synonymous with the word "search".

3. BILL GATES AND PAUL ALLEN

Another top company that started out in a dorm room is Microsoft, founded by Bill Gates and Paul Allen during their time at Harvard. While Microsoft took time to develop, Gates and Allen worked together to determine what worked and what did not. That helped them navigate through problems that the company would have and to focus on what they would do in the future. Still, they refrained from actually starting up the company for some time. They did not have the capital, and Gates didn't have the support he needed from his parents, who wanted to see him stay in college and finish his proposed path of study.

As the idea of Microsoft continued to be developed, though, both Gates and Allen discovered that they had stumbled onto something big, and that they could lose out if they didn't take the chance and act on what they had found and what they believed in. Realizing the value of what they had created, Gates made the no-longer-difficult decision to drop out to begin building the software company, following the vision and plan he and Allen had created. While Gates' parents wanted him to pursue a law career, he studied computing and gained their support before dropping out of Harvard to pursue his dreams.

In 2015, Gates was said to be worth more than $82 billion. He is among the best-known people involved in the computer revolution, although some have questioned his business tactics. Those questions haven't stopped Gates from moving forward, and they haven't stopped Microsoft from developing into a multibillion-dollar company that is a household name in most developed countries. Gates has also given billions of dollars away to charity through the Bill & Melinda Gates Foundation and other philanthropic endeavors.

4. FRED SMITH

Fred Smith is the founder of global shipping company FedEx. While the company was not technically founded while Smith was still enrolled in college, it was what he did during college that led to the eventual founding of the company. During his time at Yale, Smith composed a term paper based on the idea that technological advances and changing business needs would lead to a complete revolution in the shipping industry. His detailed analysis of how shipping was done and how it would need to be done got the wheels turning in his brain.

His professor did not find the paper interesting, but Smith didn't let that stop him. The idea of having a new kind of shipping company continued to grow, and Smith eventually founded FedEx, which is now boasting more than $40 billion in yearly revenue. Whether the paper Smith wrote was any good is up for debate, but it's clear that the ideas he had and his willingness to push through negative attitudes to put those ideas into practice were enough to catapult him past the naysayers and into the lead in the global shipping race. FedEx is growing strong, guided by the principles and values Smith used to create it.

5. **MATT MULLENWEG, MIKE LITTLE, AND MICHEL VALDRIGH**

WordPress is another dorm room startup, founded by Matt Mullenweg, Mike Little, and Michel Valdrigh. Mullenweg was just a freshman at the time, but the value of what he and the others had created quickly became obvious. There was no need to finish years of schooling when the opportunity became available to start something that had such large-scale implications. Like many other entrepreneurs who create their companies in college, Mullenweg dropped out to pursue what he could do with his new company. He had a big vision and decided it was worth taking a risk on that vision, to see what would come of it.

WordPress is now one of the top blogging platforms, and a prolific company that continues to grow and develop. The company has become more than just a platform for blogs, as it now allows for creation of entire, multi-page websites with WordPress addresses or purchased domain names. More companies are switching over to WordPress every day, because they see the value the site offers and its ease of use. Anyone can learn to use the platform, which allows for hosting of a free blog or website or the option to purchase paid services and domains. Wordpress now operates close to 20% of the world's websites.

SO, WHAT MAKES AN ENTREPRENEUR?

What led these men to create billion dollar companies, where so many others had failed? Did they have something in common? They came from different backgrounds, and had different ideas about what they wanted from life. They weren't even all in the same college, or interested in pursuing the same type of career. What they *did* have in common was an entrepreneurial spirit and an ability to recognize the value of their ideas – as well as the willingness to push through difficulties until their ideas became reality. They weren't willing to give up on the vision they had for the future, and how they could be part of it.

The value in that can be seen by looking at the success these and many other entrepreneurs have had, and can also be explored by looking at the teachings and knowledge of Peter Thiel, an entrepreneur and venture capitalist who co-founded PayPal and teaches others how to create their own successful startups. He now teaches classes on startup creation at Stanford University, to help others who have big ideas take those ideas and turn them into reality. He tells students that, if he does his job correctly, his class will be the last one they ever need to take, as he will teach them everything they need to know for a successful startup opportunity.

Some of what he teaches regarding startups encourages people to drop out of school, an idea that has been met with mixed reviews. One of the points Thiel makes – and one that can be seen in the lives of those who have gone on to create successful startups – is that complacency and risk aversion discourage people from looking for secrets that are waiting to be found. Those secrets often lead to discoveries of companies that are waiting to be created, and those companies can become the next billion-dollar startup ideas. Entrepreneurs who know that won't back down, and they are the ones who succeed. Refer back to our original investing formula for "People", and you'll notice the shared traits of the entrepreneurs we mentioned.

TOP COLLEGES FOR ENTREPRENEURIAL FOUNDERS

THE TOP 7 SCHOOLS THAT CREATED THE WORLD'S BEST ENTREPRENEURS

Does where an entrepreneur attends school matter? It could. There are several schools throughout the country that consistently turn out the highest number of entrepreneurs and the largest and most lucrative startups. Whether that's by accident or not can be argued, but it's worth investigating, just in case there's a link between location and vocation. Does it matter if the founders of the startups created there stayed in school or dropped out to pursue their passion? Would it have been different if they had attended a different educational institution?

It's hard to say for sure whether attending a particular school would have mattered in the grand scheme of things, but it's easy to see that there are several schools that offer environments that seem to be conducive to the development of ideas and the creation of lucrative businesses. The people at the school at the time, the ways in which the learning environment was structured, and the timing of the person's education can all add up to a good or a bad experience, and that experience can have a lot to do with an entrepreneurial spirit and how strongly someone will pursue his or her goals and dreams.

1. STANFORD UNIVERSITY

When looking for a top-rated school that also turns out plenty of top-notch entrepreneurs, one doesn't have to look any further than Stanford, and its track record of high-quality thinkers who set out to change the world. The creators of Google, Yahoo!, and Snapchat all went there – and they all dropped out. That doesn't mean Stanford isn't a great place to get an education, just that they didn't need any more schooling once their ideas began to soar. They made their own paths in life at that point, but Stanford helped them get their start. The education and opportunities they received there were catalysts toward following their dreams.

Who they met during their college years also played a role in how much success they saw, since many startups have more than one founder. People often form strong bonds with others they meet during their college years, and Stanford's ability to teach others to work together provides even more of an opportunity for people with big ideas and grand dreams to find others who share their interest in making a difference. Because of the ways the school encourages this in its students, Stanford is an excellent choice for people who want to find others to work with as they develop their ideas for the future.

2. HARVARD UNIVERSITY

Of course, Stanford doesn't have a monopoly on entrepreneurs. Many other schools have seen their students create successful startups. Harvard, for example, gave rise to Mark Zuckerberg and Facebook. While Zuckerberg isn't the only founder to come from Harvard, he is one of the most notable when it comes to name recognition and use of his product or service. Part of the reason there have been so many startups created by Harvard students is that the school accepts only the best and the brightest. Students attending the school may already be intellectually ahead of their peers.

That's not the only part of the equation, though. Harvard, like Stanford and other prestigious schools, provides plenty of opportunity for students to work together, and encourages the creativity and free-thinking of those same students. The lack of restrictive teaching and the ways in which expanding on ideas is encouraged goes a long way toward ensuring that Harvard students feel free to consider their ideas and goals as actually attainable. That grows their desire to explore and provides them with the tools and opportunities to do so.

3. MASSACHUSETTS INSTITUTE OF TECHNOLOGY LABS

With all the technology available to them, it makes perfect sense that the students of MIT Labs would have the opportunity to do more with their schooling and their lives. It's not just about the physical technology, though. It's also about the ways in which MIT goes about encouraging students to get involved in the dreams they have, and see if they can make them into reality. Many people have great ideas, but they're too afraid to move those ideas from thoughts to actions. At MIT, large efforts are made to get students moving toward action.

One of the ways the school helps encourage startups is through its $100K Entrepreneurship Competition, which is run by students for students. To date, it has effected the creation of more than 2,500 jobs and 130 companies. Not only is that impressive for the school and the people who have created the companies, but it also shows other students that following their dreams is possible and that they can succeed in their goals. That understanding is one of the main reasons students there are willing to do what it takes to be more successful and are persistent in following their dreams.

4. CORNELL (My Alma Mater)

Like the other schools that seem to bring out the entrepreneurial spirit in their students, Cornell has a curriculum and an atmosphere designed to encourage startups. Students work together in many of their classes, and they focus on larger and more significant ideas, as opposed to rote memorization of facts and figures. By doing this, they allow themselves to expand on ideas they have, and help others do the same. The teamwork and encouragement fostered by this approach can make the difference between pursuing dreams and choosing to stay with the crowd and not attempt to branch out to something more.

Cornell also has a large "Entrepreneur Network" that was founded in 2001. Hundreds of events have been organized by the Network, with more planned in the future. These events are open to students, staff, alumni, parents, and friends. By including so many people, Cornell gives their students the opportunity to get involved in the dreams and ideas of large numbers of people. That can lead to people partnering to create startups or improve on something that already exists, and can help others get jobs at these new companies. The close-knit, family atmosphere of these get-togethers contributes to the value they offer.

5. UNIVERSITY OF CALIFORNIA, BERKELEY (UC-Berkeley)

One of the reasons that UC Berkeley is so popular with students who have an entrepreneurial mindset is that the school offers three distinct "incubators" for startups. The most popular of the three options is SkyDeck, which is designed to help the business and engineering schools at the university work with the research office. By combining different schools of thought and different areas of study, there is a higher chance that great ideas will not only be created, but that they will also be carried out. Coming up with a new business is wonderful, but only if the idea is taken to fruition.

At UC Berkeley, the idea of taking those ideas to fruition is one that is carefully considered and deeply encouraged. That keeps students engaged and shows them that the university they attend believes in the value of the education they're getting and the ideas they have when it comes to improving the world. Startups are about innovation, belief, and value, all of which are needed if students of any university are going to see their ideas come to life. Working with an educational institution that encourages individuality and creativity is among the best ways to get an idea off the ground.

6. CALIFORNIA INSTITUTE OF TECHNOLOGY (Caltech)

Caltech is another school that can boast large numbers of highly successful alumni. Despite that fact that it has a student body of fewer than 2,300, it has 32 Nobel laureates among its faculty and alumni numbers. That's worth noting, because the school is doing something right to produce high-quality, focused, and driven individuals at that level. Much of the success of Caltech comes from the smaller size of the student body at its campus in Pasadena. With small class sizes, students interact more with one another and their instructors. They are also offered more opportunities to work together on projects.

Often, working on a project together gets people thinking, and can help them become more comfortable talking about their ideas, goals, and dreams with others. Having the freedom to express this information is among the best ways to help a student move forward in life and pursue the things that matter most. Those pursuits are generally related to education, but they may also move toward entrepreneurship and startups as students learn more about their world and the ways in which that world can be enriched by the ideas those students have for the future.

7. UNIVERSITY OF CALIFORNIA, LOS ANGELES (UCLA)

It shouldn't be a surprise that UCLA made the list, or that three of the top schools for startups and entrepreneurship are found in California. With Silicon Valley and the tech culture that permeates so much of the state, California is a natural destination for people with big dreams when they want to start something important. UCLA is also focused on helping those dreams come to pass, hosting events like the LA Hacks hackathon for more than 4,000 developers each year. Technology is synonymous with California, and the educational institutions there are aware of it and capitalize on it.

Universities in California focus more on technical pursuits, because that's what their students want and need. There is more to becoming an entrepreneur and launching a successful startup than just having a computer science or other technology background. The ways in which students at these top schools are encouraged to work together and to pursue what matters to them can make a significant difference in how they interact with their peers and instructors, as well as how seriously they take the creation of their ideas and the pursuit of their dreams.

GIVING BACK TO THEIR SCHOOLS

Giving back is important to many entrepreneurs, and those who have created highly successful startups can generally be counted on to provide financial help and other benefits to the schools they attended. People like Bill Gates, Mark Zuckerberg, and Larry Page all give to the schools they attended. In many ways, it was those schools that helped to shape who they were and that encouraged them to follow their dreams and make those dreams come true.

A large number of entrepreneurs also met the people who would become co-founders of their startups while they were enrolled in a university, and would not have had that opportunity were it not for their attendance at that school. There are different ways they can acknowledge that gift, and one of those ways is through providing financial gifts to the university that helped to make them what they are today. While no entrepreneur has any obligation to give back to a school he or she attended, many startup founders see doing that as a worthwhile opportunity and a good business practice.

VENTURE CAPITALIST RECRUITMENT

Attending a school that turns out a high number of entrepreneurs with successful startups can be beneficial in more than just the obvious ways. Another benefit to attendance at these schools is that venture capitalists often recruit from schools where they find large numbers of successful people. For students with great ideas but not enough money to get those ideas off the ground, that can mean the difference between getting funded or being turned down. While it's not a guarantee, coming from a "known" school when it comes to ideas and startups can give an entrepreneur more opportunity.

That is certainly worth considering when looking for a school to attend, especially for those who are committed to getting just the knowledge they need so they can go on to start their own companies. Some schools offer more of a chance to do that than others, and there are also people who view some schools as being much more significant or high quality than others. Because venture capitalists are careful how they use their money, they will focus on valuable ideas that come from known quantities. If the student isn't known but the school is, that may sway their thinking enough to make a difference.

* * *

10 FEATURED IPOS AND RETURNS FOR ANGEL INVESTORS

While most people know that companies like Facebook and Twitter went public through an IPO and became successful public companies, that doesn't mean their road to get there was always easy. Even with the value that was placed on Facebook, for example, its IPO was actually botched. It ended up with an extremely low stock price, and struggled for some time before recovering. Many companies, including Facebook, learned from those crucial mistakes. Other companies that were considering an IPO were paying attention, as well.

A number of these other companies, some that were already going strong and some that were just getting off the ground, waited and avoided going public. If Facebook could have such a hard time with an IPO, what did that say about the likely success of *their* business? As time advanced, though, more companies began to figure out what they needed to do differently. That resulted in their taking the plunge and doing an IPO of their own. While a number of companies were successful in doing this, some failed. It turns out, though, that 2014 was an impressive year for companies going public.

1. ZENDESK (Original investors: estimated 59,135% return)·

This company is focused on revolutionizing customer service, along with improving help desk functions. It does this by taking those services and turning them into ad hoc options that can be purchased and managed via the web. The original opening price was $11.40, with the funding from the IPO at $100 million and an offering price of $9. While Zendesk is not the only company that's focused on the alleviation of fixed costs for other companies, it's by far the most notable, and the one to watch.

The current price of shares is up to more than $24, indicating a successful launch of the IPO. Part of the success of Zendesk is in the timing. Customer service is becoming more important to companies, even as companies work to streamline those processes. With that taking place, Zendesk came on the scene in a big way just as companies were looking for the solutions it offers. Had it waited, another company with similar ideas might have taken its place. Making sure the time is right is important for success with an IPO, no matter what the company offers.

2. TRUECAR (Series A investors: estimated 2,604% return)·

Truecar's funding from its IPO was $70 million, with an opening share price of $9.70 and an offering price of $9. Current share price is more than $21. Truecar provides useful information about what other people have paid for new and used cars, so that those who are interested in buying new or used can compare and see what the true price of the

---

· This calculation is based on the investors' estimated 16.7% equity stake. See image, "How Startup Funding Works", source: paulgraham.com/startupfunding.html.
· This calculation is based on the investors' estimated 33.3% equity stake. See image, "How Startup Funding Works", source: paulgraham.com/startupfunding.html.

vehicle should be. The company also operates online car buying programs for private labels such as Overstock.com, USAA, and AAA.

Shares rose 12 percent the first day of the IPO, and the company remains strong. People want to know how much they should pay for something, and if they find that they are being asked to pay too much, they may purchase their products or services elsewhere. Keeping that in mind, Truecar's business model is designed to ensure that people can find out not what a car *should be* worth, but what people are *actually* paying for cars, both new and used. That can help them decide if they want to pay what a dealer or private party is asking, and helping people save money is always a good business model.

3. COUPONS.COM (Series C investors: estimated 25,385% return)·

Coupons used to be seen as something low-income mothers clipped from the newspaper to save money and would never be used by younger or more affluent people, but that attitude is changing. Young and old, rich and poor, more and more people are using coupons to get great deals on all kinds of things. This company saw that, and took the idea of couponing to a new level by leveraging the power of technology. When people can get their coupons – and information on how to save the most with them – right on their computers, it tends to pique their interest.

The funding from the Coupons.com IPO was $168 million, with an offering price of $16. While its original opening share price was more than $32, prices per share have dropped to under the offering price. Still, the company is strong. The shares were too high originally, but

---

· This calculation is based on the investors' estimated 33.3% equity stake. See image, "How Startup Funding Works", source: paulgraham.com/startupfunding.html.

are at much more realistic levels now. These kinds of price corrections can occur, even when a company times its IPO correctly and has a strong company. The value of couponing is on the rise, and the company will continue to provide quality and value to people who want to get involved in using coupons to save money, which should help improve the share price.

4. **ALIBABA** (Original investors: estimated 678,000% return)[*]

Alibaba, China's biggest Internet company, is somewhat of a hybrid between eBay and Amazon. With all that its marketplace offers to consumers, it's surprising that it didn't create an IPO sooner than it did. The company reportedly looked for every angle or improvement that was needed before the IPO in order to ensure the highest possible level of success. The timing of the IPO and the quality of what the company could offer were a winning combination, and shares were quickly purchased by investors in large quantities.

Approximately 500 million people use Alibaba's site, and the funding from its IPO topped $22 billion. The offering price was $68, with an opening share price of $92.70. Shares have risen slightly since then, to $110 each. There are concerns about the structure of the company, though, as it is owned by Jack Ma and the Chinese government. The level of control they have over the company has been questioned, but it hasn't been enough to stop the success of the IPO or the perceived value of the company overall. Time will tell whether the ownership structure has a negative effect on future share price.

5. ONDECK CAPITAL (Series A investors: estimated 22,682% return)·

The funding from OnDeck Capital's IPO totaled $200 million, with an initial offering price of $20. The opening share price of just over $26 is similar to the current share price – an indication that the price of the shares and the value of the company are holding steady. The company offers small business loans and other opportunities for alternative financing. Using technology that's state of the art, it's possible to get a lending decision within minutes instead of waiting for days or weeks, as one would commonly have to do with a traditional bank.

Being able to get a quick lending decision can affect whether a company can move forward with a project, making it a significant advantage when doing business. In a tight lending market and a time when there are more small businesses getting started than ever before, OnDeck Capital chose the opportune moment to get involved with an IPO and allow investors to support a company they believed in. The helping aspect was also instrumental in the company's success, as people are interested in contributing to companies that are doing good for others.

6. GOPRO (Original investors: estimated 365,976% return)·

With funding from its IPO at $425 million and an offering price of $24, GoPro made its mark on the world. The high-definition, high-performance cameras offered by the company are extremely portable and durable, allowing them to be used in places where a standard camera would be impractical. These cameras can be found in any

---

This calculation is based on the original investors' estimated 16.7% equity stake, and Series A investors' estimated 33.3% equity stake. See image, "How Startup Funding Works", source: paulgraham.com/startupfunding.html.

· This calculation is based on the investors' estimated 16.7% equity stake. See image, "How Startup Funding Works", source: paulgraham.com/startupfunding.html.

number of places, and are used by professionals and laypeople alike. GoPro has done very well since its IPO. The current share price is double the original share price of just over $31.

Some of the buzz surrounding GoPro came about because, as a hardware IPO, it was a refreshing departure from all the software IPOs. Most technology IPOs in any given year are for software. It can be difficult to create a company designed around a new and valuable form of hardware, but GoPro managed to do it, and to do it well. As with a number of other IPOs that have done well, timing was a large part of GoPro's success.

7. GRUBHUB (Series A investors: estimated 104,040% return)[*]

With an initial IPO of $200 million and an offering price of $26, GrubHub is an online and mobile service for ordering food. It connects diners by the thousands with takeout restaurants throughout the country. The share price has been up and down since the IPO. The first few days saw rapidly rising share prices, but in time that tempered. However, GrubHub has strong prospects and an opportunity to continue to monopolize its market, as it has little competition.

Grubhub intends to expand to others cities in the future, raising the value of its stock. Eventually, GrubHub may become an option for people in every major city, and even in smaller towns. Anywhere there are takeout restaurants there is an opportunity for the company to move into the market and provide value to people who want to have a quick, easy meal but who don't want to leave their house. People who are housebound for any reason can also get value from the service, further strengthening its customer base.

8. LENDING CLUB   (Original investors: estimated 54,755% return)·

Almost $870 million was raised by Lending Club's IPO. Like OnDeck Capital, Lending Club offers alternative financing for businesses. Both peer-to-peer and institutional investor lending are available on the site, giving people who need capital for their businesses plenty of options to consider. Since there are a number of people and institutions on the site who are available to lend to others, those who are looking for capital can make their case a single time and get responses from more than one lender.

That allows a person to choose the best lender for his or her needs, and can mean the difference between getting something funded and being turned away in frustration by more traditional lending channels. Shares are only slightly above their offering price, as Lending Club's value has held steady. Many companies still try to go through traditional channels for lending, but as that changes and interest in peer lending broadens, companies like Lending Club may see their market position improve.

9. KING DIGITAL ENTERTAINMENT·

A surprise in the IPO market in 2014 was King Digital Entertainment. It makes the popular Candy Crush Saga game, but investors were concerned that it might not be successful at branching out from that. Currently, the revenue from Candy Crush Saga is 80 percent of King Digital Entertainment's revenue. The concerns were generally pushed aside during the IPO, though, which brought in $500 million with an

---

· This calculation is based on the original investors' estimated 16.7% equity stake, and Series A investors' estimated 33.3% equity stake. See image, "How Startup Funding Works", source: paulgraham.com/startupfunding.html

· This company did not disclose their funding round information.

offering price of $22.50. The current share price is several dollars below the opening share price, but there is still hope that the company's prospects will improve with its expansion potential.

If King Digital Entertainment makes other games that do even a fraction as well as Candy Crush Saga, its value and share price will become and remain strong. At this point, however, it remains to be seen whether the company will branch out, or whether its share price will fall and it will struggle because it did not do enough to ensure that it kept a strong base. Basing so much revenue generation on one product may not be the most productive long-term strategy, but for now it is working for the company and its investors.

10. VIRGIN AMERICA·

Virgin America, the low-cost airline owned by Richard Branson, is doing great. Its IPO brought in $306 million, with an offering price of $23. The current share price is up more than $5 over the opening share price, and the value of the company remains strong. The IPO took place in the face of the crash of Virgin Galactic's space shuttle. Despite that disaster, investors still believe in what Branson and his companies can offer. Since the airline and the space exploration companies are not one and the same, the IPO for Virgin America was a success.

Branson is a charismatic individual, and the sharp dip in oil prices has allowed the company to lower its fares, instilling confidence in investors that the company is a good choice. Additionally, Branson already has a reputation among investors, and most of what he gets involved in does well. The more he focuses on making a company valuable, the more other investors get involved and want to add to

---

· This company did not disclose their funding round information.

that value. This helps Branson in the long run, and also helps investors who put their money on his success.

THE TOP VENTURE CAPITAL FIRMS IN AMERICA

OFFICIAL RANKING OF TOP VC FIRMS

Venture capital firms receive capital from investors who already have wealth and want to grow more of it through non-traditional means. Then, they take that money and invest it into startup companies and other ventures that a traditional bank wouldn't be interested in, based on the risk. Investing in startup companies can be a risky proposition, and not for the faint of heart. Still, many people do it because they know that the rewards for success can be lucrative. Some venture capitalists just take their own money and invest it, but some form firms that use their money and that of others, and then choose where to invest based on consensus.

A number of factors make a great venture capital firm. The success it has with investing is important, but other factors have to be considered in order to determine why a VC firm is successful and what it can offer to investors that other firms may not. What makes a successful VC firm? What do these firms do differently that catapults them to the forefront of their industry? Those are questions both investors and startups want answers for, but those answers may not be as clear-cut as one would expect. Some VC firms stand out, though, and understanding what they do and how they do it can help investors get a handle on what makes a good VC firm and how these firms attain (and retain) their success.

1. NEW ENTERPRISE ASSOCIATES (NEA)

NEA is located in Menlo Park, California. In 2014, its early-stage deal count was 44, and it had just over $690 million in early-stage investments. The company operates in the United States, Asia, and Brazil, and focuses on a number of industries, not restricting itself to just one or two areas in which to invest. Common industries for NEA to invest in include communications, energy services, networking, software, IT services, healthcare supplies and devices, biotechnology, pharmaceuticals, refining, production, and the exploration of energy services.

Throughout 2014, the VC firm worked with a number of different types of startups that showed a great deal of promise. These included Fire1, a developer of therapeutic medical devices. NEA also worked with Jet, a company involved in e-commerce and focused on how to address the logistics of doorstep delivery for online retail companies, along with the distribution of those items. Another deal was with Lumena Pharmaceuticals, which develops oral medications used specifically to treat a rare liver problem in adults and children called cholestatic liver disease.

Branching out into different countries and industries seems to work for NEA, indicating that the focus is not on an industry or region but on something else the startup is offering. A unique business idea – or one that can be executed better than the competition – is important, but there is more to investing than that. The owners of NEA see something in the startups they invest in, whether that's a great idea, a great founder, or something less tangible.

Sometimes, a gut feeling is all that's needed in order to want to invest in a startup, although successful VC firms will analyze that feeling to ensure that it matches with a realistic level of risk and reward.

2. KLEINER PERKINS

Kleiner Perkins, also located in Menlo Park, California, made 33 early-stage deals and $490 million in early-stage investments in 2014. It invests in many of the same types of industries as NEA, including computer hardware, healthcare supplies and devices, biotechnology, pharmaceuticals, and software. The company also focuses on commercial services, financial services, and media. It prefers to do business in the United States and China, and has had recent deals with Farmers Edge Precision Consulting, Chill, and Crossfader.

Kleiner Perkins is investing in almost the identical industries that NEA is targeting, putting the two VC firms in direct competition with one another for the best and the brightest of startups. This competition is good for the startups, too, because they have the opportunity to get more than one investment firm focused on what they have to offer. The more companies that decide to invest in a particular startup, the better off that startup generally is, and the more likely it is to succeed, all other things being equal. Rapid developments and advancements are taking place most frequently in the categories where Kleiner Perkins shows the most interest. That indicates a good strategy on the part of the VC firm, because it is involved where the action is, providing more value for those who provide their money for investment.

Kleiner Perkins did face many headwinds in 2014 and 2015 with litigation from a former associate named Ellen Pao, but you can expect them to rebound.

3. ANDREESSEN HOROWITZ

Another Menlo Park, California, company, Andreessen Horowitz, had 50 early-stage deals in the works in 2014, for a combined total of just over $1 billion in early-stage investments. The company is large and well-established, and wealthy individuals who want to build more wealth into their portfolios know they can come to this VC firm and trust what it provides. It focuses its efforts entirely in the United States, and limits itself to only a few industries, such as software, consumer products and services. CipherCloud, Zenefits Insurance Services, and Optimizely are recipients of recent deals.

The focus of this VC firm is different from some of the others, as it operates only in the United States, and its universe of target industries for startup funding is limited. Still, there doesn't seem to be any shortage of startups for Andreessen Horowitz to fund, and the company has the capital to back up its interest in software, services, and consumer products. One of the reasons it has plenty of investor opportunities is the breadth of the categories on which it focuses. Consumer products and services, for example, offer latitude for investors and good opportunities for funding startups.

While it looks as though this VC firm doesn't have enough options because of its limited geographic area and restricted areas of funding, it has done well for itself and its investors. Becoming one of the top-rated VC firms takes time, and it doesn't happen by making bad decisions or investing in companies that don't perform well. Andreessen Horowitz knows what to look for in a startup, and it shows in its success rate.

4. KHOSLA VENTURES

Founded in Menlo Park, California by Vinod Khosla, Khosla Ventures had 45 early-stage deals and early-stage investments totaling $809 million in 2014. This VC firm focuses on China and the United States as its preferred regions for investing, and sticks to startups in the software industry. Recent deals include Datera, Summon, and Tule Technologies. Sticking to one industry could seem like a bad choice, since it limits opportunities, but that hasn't appeared to slow Khosla Ventures. Instead, the firm has continued to add more deals and more startups to its list.

One of the reasons that sticking to a specific industry works for this VC firm is that it helps Khosla fine-tune its methodologies and or how it plans to move forward. It can learn everything about a particular type of industry and spend its time focused on what that industry is offering in the way of startups, instead of having its hands in many arenas. It is often easier to focus on just one type of industry. Technology, in particular – and especially software – is an industry that is growing with amazing speed. In order to keep up with that industry, it may be necessary to stay out of others.

The founder of Khosla Ventures is why the VC firm is successful. We have met Vinod and admire his ability to make deals happen.

5. SV ANGEL

SV Angel is located in Palo Alto, California, and was founded by investors, Ron Conway and David Lee. It had 47 early-stage deals in 2014 and early-stage investments of $736 million. The company is focused only on commercial services and software and operates only in the United States. It further narrows its market by emphasizing

Silicon Valley, San Francisco, and New York. Harry's (specialty shaving equipment) and Delighted (one-click customer survey tools) are a couple of companies with which it has reached recent investment deals.

That sharpened focus ensures that the VC firm is taking on only the best startups for its investors. Not every investor is comfortable taking risks in multiple sectors, so it's possible to reduce the risk to those investors by ensuring that they receive an opportunity to invest only in specific sectors. By limiting the scope of its investing even further – to certain geographic areas – SV Angel is indicating that it believes the best startup opportunities for investors will come from those areas. That can backfire for some VC firms, as they will miss out on important opportunities for investing. However, this model of limited geography and limited industries appears to be working well for SV Angel. For investors who want to focus only in certain regions, or who see growth as coming from only a specific industry, VC firms like SV Angel are often the right choice. That way, investors won't be asked to put their money into industries in which they don't see a potential for growth and a high level of return on their money. The level of trust that develops can keep investors coming back to the VC firm, and allow that firm to grow larger and fund more startups in the future.

We are a big fan of David Lee, and his ability to invest in startups and master them.

* * *

STARTUP BURN RATE VS. STARTUP PROFIT AND LOSS

DON'T BURN ALL YOUR MONEY

The gross burn rate is the amount that is being spent every month. The net burn rate is the amount of loss. Both are of equal importance. One of the reasons that net burn is such a valuable number to investors is that it provides some idea of how long the business can continue to operate, assuming it doesn't increase its net burn. As such, the net burn can be a way to determine how many more months a startup can stay in business, based on the cash it has in the bank. A company with one million dollars in the bank might sound promising, but if its net burn is $250,000, it can only stay afloat for four more months unless drastic changes are made. So that scenario does not sound like a good investment at all.

The net burn rate can help current investors measure and determine their level of risk, and can also give them an idea of how quickly they will need their teams to focus on fundraising. New investors will also be interested in the net burn of a startup, because they will want to know how quickly they need to raise cash, and how much cash they will be asked to invest.

While it's important that startups keep their net burn as low (or at least as realistic for their company and industry) as possible, having a very low net burn actually can work against them if they're looking to raise a significant amount of money. To illustrate this point, a startup with a net burn of $150,000 wouldn't appear to need to raise millions of dollars right away, and asking for that kind of money might put investors off. Prospective investors could wonder why the company would need that level of capital. So simply seeing if investors will fork over large sums of money isn't a good practice for startups, and can lead to their being overcapitalized.

Here are some tips and questions for you to consider when reviewing a company's net and gross burn rates:

1. IS THE COMPANY RESPONSIBLE WITH MONEY?

Make sure that company founders who are seeking your capital investment articulate why their company needs it. If the company's net burn rate is low, why are they seeking a high-dollar investment? Are there other expenses that are not being disclosed? Be wary of companies who respond with the idea that "more money is always better". These companies tend to develop a bad habit of unnecessary spending.

The burn rate of any startup should be similar to the burn rates of the competition, but the size of the company and its operating expenses will dictate the overall burn rate. It's always best to invest in companies that have 10% month-to-month growth and at least 18 months of burn rate, as these companies have proven to be more viable in the long run.

2. WHO MAKES UP FOR MOST OF THE COMPANY'S REVENUE?

Make sure that the company's revenue is not reliant on a few customer accounts, and there is a varied distribution on where the company makes money. This provides a safety net for investors since market fluctuations cannot be easily foreseen and can happen quickly. Having a wide array of customers allows a company to survive any revenue losses due to unpredictable market fluctuations. SaaS companies are ideal for investors because their biggest customer may account for <5% of their revenue, and their revenue is ongoing and recurring.

3. IS THE COMPANY SPENDING ON GROWTH AND DEVELOPMENT?

Pay attention to where the company does spend its money. A company may have a high gross burn rate due to growth and development expenses. It is a calculated risk that provides investors with longer-term rewards if the company raises the value of its product and broadens its customer base. Stay away from companies that have low burn rates in a stagnating market since these companies will provide little return of investment.

* * *

HOW MUCH SHOULD STARTUPS COMPENSATE THE CEO?

The compensation a startup offers to its founders or CEOs greatly varies. However, paying CEOs and founders–if they get paid too much– can turn investors off. The concern is that everything investors put into the company might go into the pockets of the CEOs or founders via salaries, instead of being invested into the company and its growth. This is a serious concern for investors who want to be sure their money is going to the right causes. When setting up a company and getting a startup off the ground, CEOs and founders may need to work for free (and sometimes for a long period of time) before the company is making enough that they can safely draw a salary without making investors uncomfortable. Whether founders or CEOs should pay themselves is one of those questions that have no easy answers. It works for some companies but will not work for others, making it a complicated decision that should not be taken lightly.

Ross's Rules for Angel Investors:

1. CEOs of startups should make no more than 5% of the ARR.
2. Every employee should be on a 4-year vesting schedule.
3. All companies should look to the previously mentioned, Buffer Company as a model of transparency.

Peter Thiel has made the argument that the top-performing startups generally pay their founders, CEOs, and others very little. There does appear to be a correlation between low pay and the success of a startup. When founders and CEOs take little or no salary, it frees up capital that can be reinvested into the company. By pumping any and all money back into the business, CEOs and founders of startups show that they are serious about growing and developing their company. If they have unwavering, unfailing belief in their companies, and they're willing to back that up with their own money, investors are much more likely to stop and take a look at what they have to offer. Why is the startup so valuable? What does it have to offer to the investor that others don't? If investors see the company's value and potential for growth, they'll be more likely to invest, and provide the much-needed infusion of cash that might otherwise have been missed. While there is no guarantee that investors will flock to startups simply because the CEOs and founders aren't being paid, it does raise the chances of piquing investors' interest.

The link between startup success and not paying founders and CEOs a salary is too strong to ignore. For founders who are committed to their startups, avoiding any salary–especially in the beginning – is worth considering. It may make the difference between success and failure, and can attract investors who appreciate a founder's complete investment to the growth and development of their company. Company first, compensation later.

The same is true with employees. Most people work with the expectation of getting paid, but there are people who will work for free to join a cause in which they believe. Some employees of startups work for free because they have high hopes of substantial compensation when the company has moved beyond the startup phase and is successful. If the company fails to reach profitability, as some startups do, there is no compensation for the employees who stuck with the company. That is a risk that some employees of startups are willing to take.

Companies start paying their CEOs and founders after they have moved out of the startup phase. For some, it is after an IPO has raised significant capital. For others, it is before that takes place – and in some companies an IPO will never take place at all. The decision of whether to pay a CEO or founder – and when – has to be left to the company, because it is a question that doesn't have a right or wrong answer. However, there is more than one way to pay CEOs and founders.

Some startups compensate their CEOs, founders, and even their employees in stock. If the company does well, the stock will have value and everyone who worked for payment in stock will be rewarded. If the company does poorly, the stock will be worthless and that the people with stock will not receive any money. Often, CEOs or founders will work for a "salary" of $1 per year or some other token amount, because they are already wealthy from shares of stock. Founders or CEOs may also have other forms of wealth they have accumulated, depending on what other companies they have been involved with or what types of investments they have. The best option for most companies is to stick close to what their competitors are doing to avoid getting too far outside the compensation norm for their industry.

ROI | THE ALL-TIME BIGGEST ANGEL RETURN ON INVESTMENTS

Angel investing has provided some big returns. Among the most notable are Peter Thiel's investment in Facebook and Marc Andreessen's 312x return on Instagram, but there are others. Each year, angel investors and venture capitalists invest $25 billion in the U.S. and $3 billion in Canada. Though plenty of reliable information exists on how much of a return venture capitalists get, there's almost nothing to be found on angel investors. Fortunately, a recent study has been done on angel investors that can shed some light on the subject. The study was relatively comprehensive, analyzing 86 groups of angel investors throughout the U.S. encompassing 539 actual investors. Results of the study showed that the average angel investor received a return of 2.6 times the capital that was invested over a 3.5-year period. The internal rate of return on an angel investor's investments averaged a comfortable 25%.

Investing early, and making non-monetary contributions as well, can make angel investing an excellent choice for many venture capitalists. Still, having an idea of how well angel investors have performed in the past and anticipating how well any single angel investor will do in the future are two different things. There have certainly been angel investors who have lost money, just as there have been angel investors who have made their money back more than 100 times from a particular startup. It's about the company itself, and how well it will actually perform. Sometimes even the best, most educated assessments fail to be accurate.

1. PETER THIEL AND FACEBOOK

Peter Thiel's return on his Facebook investment is around 6,000 times what he put into the company. That's far more than what the typical angel investor can expect, but it's certainly not out of the realm of possibility. It's been done, and it's provable – it's just not common. Thiel got involved with Facebook in 2005, paying $500,000 and receiving a 10% stake in the company. Facebook was worth over $33 billion in 2010, so his stake would have been in the area of $2 billion to $3 billion at that time. In just a few years, he made a return on his capital that is unparalleled.

While that's one the best investment deals in history, it isn't the only major return that has been seen when an angel investor got involved in a startup that took off.

2. MARC ANDREESSEN AND INSTAGRAM

With numerous filters and editing options that make photos more fun, Instagram changed the picture-taking experience by allowing every cellphone owner to become a professional photographer with a quick tap of a button. With its instant sharing across social media, Instagram created a platform for people to share their pictures across the globe. But the company, like so many others, was once a startup, struggling along and looking for investment money. In swooped angel investor Marc Andreessen, who ended up with an astronomical return on his original $250,000 investment. His return was worth $100 million. He made well above the 2.6x return common to many angel investors.

3. KLEINER PERKINS AND GOOGLE

Another significant angel investing win was Google. Kleiner Perkins and Sequoia acquired a 20% stake in the search engine conglomerate for $25 million. Google's IPO was worth $27 billion, so the 20% stake became worth $5.4 billion. That's a return of 216x the investment. While it can't quite touch Peter Thiel's Facebook deal, it's a return any angel investor would be more than happy to make. These kinds of returns are becoming more common with tech startups, as it can be hard to tell what the next big thing is going to be. It might be something that starts out small, but suddenly snowballs into one of the biggest technological advances in history. Any investor would want to be a part of that.

TOP RETURNS IN TECH

For angel investors today, the question becomes how to get returns like Thiel's, or how to receive the average, anticipated return, with little risk. Any startup, in the early stage, has equal potential to make billions of dollars and to fail, leaving its investors with a lower bank balance and a lot of aggravation.

Angel investors who are serious about what they do and how they do it would be wise to put their money in the technology sector. The growth and development of the Internet, apps, smartphones, and everything that comes with them have been astounding, so much so that it's hard to keep up. Investing in technology businesses isn't a guarantee, but companies that improve on social media sharing or smartphone apps that replaces manual tasks are good choices. People want more functionality out of their phones, and apps are an excellent way to expand phone capability and create efficiency.

WHAT DOES THE FUTURE HOLD?

In investing, there is a high level of risk in trying to predict the future. Still, some educated guesswork is necessary if one is to get involved in the best startups with the highest returns.

Companies that are trying to take on Facebook or push Twitter out of the way are not likely to succeed, because those social media companies have become so entrenched in daily life. People don't want to move to another site that offers the same features they already receive elsewhere. That's why Twitter did well when it first appeared; it created a need for a service Facebook did not provide. Instagram and Pinterest are succeeding for the same reason. They provide another channel for people to connect with each other and use social media.

The future is tenuous, at best, depending on the pace of technology development. It's not just apps and smartphone games; there are many other ways to use software and hardware, and those areas have to be explored. One of those areas is the medical field. Electronic health records are becoming vital to doctors and hospitals. Finding safer ways to create and share those records, help patients understand their medical data, and increase preventative measures are viable options for startups. Investors who get involved in such startups could develop medical communication that will assist in the saving and betterment of countless lives.

The technology market will become saturated. However, what you can take away from Facebook, Instagram and the other successful technology businesses today is that they addressed a need that no one thought existed. They affected the way people behaved, either by providing an easier way to connect with others or by reinventing how people enjoy creative activities. There will always be risk no matter where you invest, but keep an open mind on whether the company that comes to you for an investment will affect change. You might have a billion dollar company in your hands.

TOP 4 BIGGEST STARTUP FAILURES AND WHY THEY FAILED

The flip side of knowing how to be a successful angel investor is knowing what to watch out for. Sometimes it seems like everything is in place; the people, the product, the timing and the execution all look like they're on target. But somehow, the idea just doesn't click and the startup goes belly up.

Looking at some well-known flops of the recent past, we can see the reasons for their demise as though they were written in neon. Hindsight is 20/20; foresight is not -- so the signs were not as clear when these companies were looking for capital in the full flush of startup mode. Maybe these cautionary tales will help you avoid the next big round of infamous failures.

1. FAB.COM

Fab.com is an e-commerce website, currently owned by PCH International, and purchased for likely less than $20 million. At one point Fab.com had more than 12 million registered customers and recorded more than $100 million in sales and a valuation in excess of $1 billion. Of course, at the same time the company was losing more than $10 million in a single month. Despite attracting more than $300 million in VC money, something needed to change or this would be a short-lived party.

Fab.com had a bit of a checkered past. Founders Bradford Shelhammer and Jason Goldberg had conceived of the site as a social media meeting spot for gays. When that didn't work, they quickly decided to become an e-commerce site, selling an assortment of quirky merchandise, most based on Shelhammer's admittedly cool aesthetic taste, but some items were just plain quirky.

Initial distribution issues that had led to 16-day delivery times appeared to be resolved when Fab built its own distribution center. Visitors to the site increased more than 300 percent between 2011 and 2012 despite the fading "invitation only" and daily deals e-commerce model it relied on. Some merchandise sold out in a matter of hours, making frequent visits to Fab.com a necessary part of its fans' day. Goldberg was quick to credit the site's success to Shelhammer's sense of taste and style, and his relationships with hip designers. Things were looking good, despite Fab's underlying issues.

In November 2013, Shelhammer left the company and the downward spiral began. The company had relied so heavily on Shelhammer's style guidance that it quickly lost its way without him at the helm. But the signs were there long before his departure, as the company became a revolving door for employees.

In March of 2015, PCH International bought Fab.com for an estimated $15 million. So what had gone wrong? Practically everything.

PEOPLE:

Goldberg and Shelhammer had creative differences, as they say in showbiz. Shelhammer's interests lay in the field of design, while Goldberg was solely interested in running a business – any business, it seems. His abrasive and abrupt management style seemed to contribute to employee turnover. Heavy reliance on Shelhammer to curate the product mix meant that the company had no bench strength in the style area after his departure.

PRODUCT:

Neither founder seemed to have a strong commitment to a product or even a business model. Going from social media to exclusive products to daily deals to a bazaar that carried more than 10,000 items speaks to a business looking for a problem to solve.

TIMING:

Fab.com was always late to the party. Late to social media, it switched to invitation-only shopping just as consumers tired of that model. Daily deals had been played out before Fab opted in, and Amazon and Etsy had the "anything you want" and "artsy cool" niches wrapped up. Fab.com was chasing trends instead of chasing a true vision.

EXECUTION:

Goldberg and Shelhammer excelled at raising money, and they were able to get each idea off the ground, even if they were lacking in the innovation area. But poor management skills and inability to build a team were ultimately what did them in -- along with extravagant spending. Remember that $10 million loss in just one month?

INSIGHT:

Fab.com is an example of charismatic founders without a clear vision. They could talk a good enough game to get even seasoned investors to kick in, but there was no passion for any particular aspect of the business model. The only thing the founders had in common was admiration for Shelhammer's aesthetic sense, and that was ultimately not enough to keep them together.

2. WESABE

Wesabe was a personal financial management site, similar to Mint.com. In addition to helping users manage their finance, it included a user forum for user-to-user help and advice. Mint.com easily took over Wesabe's lead in the financial management space. Wesabe continued to run the online community for some time, but the URL has subsequently been taken down and listed for sale. The Wesabe WordPress blog hasn't been updated in years.

Wesabe seemed to have it all: A founder passionate about his idea. An innovative concept hitting the market at just the right time to capitalize on two big trends: online communities and cloud applications. Wesabe closed its first round of funding to the tune of $4.7 million in June of 2007. By June 2010, it had shut down the financial side of the site, and the community followed thereafter, despite assurances that it would continue. So what went wrong? Once again, pretty much everything.

PEOPLE:

Founder Marc Hedlund was certainly passionate about his idea. He and co-founder Jason Knight were leading the charge to online financial management for consumers. Jason Knight's departure to care for his ailing son was an admirable decision, but he had been the voice of reason to Hedlund's wrong-headed insistence on product direction.

PRODUCT:

Wesabe wasn't the only personal financial manager to hit the Internet. It wasn't even the first. However, it was one of the best at building community. Wesabe simply ran afoul of consumers' fears about disclosing bank account passwords online. In addition, Hedlund insisted on creating his own technology platform, and as a result, Wesabe was late to the party with some features and much harder to use than its biggest competitor, Mint. Apparently, the company was never clear on whether its product should have been the platform or the application, so it ran second best on both.

TIMING:

The timing was right for a Wesabe-like product, although most were struggling. Intuit swooped in and acquired Mint, choosing it over Wesabe because of its technology, ease of use and larger customer base. That was the death knell for Wesabe, which had been operating on a shoestring and struggling mightily to keep up with competitors who focused on functionality and ease of use over technology.

EXECUTION:

In interviews, Hedlund has admitted that he was stubborn about creating a platform for Wesabe rather than relying on a commercially available base such as Yodlee. This decision may not have been the only reason Wesabe failed, but it was a contributing factor. Lack of funding and Knight's untimely departure sent Wesabe over the edge.

INSIGHT:

Even with a great product idea and founders who are passionate about the product, the path to success is fraught with peril. Hedlund's failure to listen to advice about the platform was a major contributor to Wesabe's death. Having the coolest proprietary platform meant nothing to consumers who wanted ease of use, and the company failed to come up with a great story explaining why its platform was superior.

It's important to be sure that a company is clear on its objective before you invest, and in this case, Wesabe was not. In addition, the founders failed to listen to advisors, and they failed to build a team that could counterbalance or overturn the founder's obsession with technology over business success. There's a fine line between passion for quality and blind obsession–and pigheadedness.

3. PAY BY TOUCH

What a difference a few years makes! Now that Apple Pay is at your fingertips and coming soon to a cash register near you, one wonders why Pay By Touch couldn't succeed back in 2002. Biometric sensing? Check. Futuristic coolness factor? Check. Bank buy-in? Also check. What crucial factor was Pay By Touch missing?

Pay By Touch raised over $340 million in capital and had some very high profile investors. The founder, John P. Rogers, retained ownership of a super-voting class of stock that let him overrule everybody, including the board of directors. What's worse, investors were not told about his other business failures, criminal past, drug use and his general tendency to play fast and loose with other people's property. Rogers burned through his investor's money at a rate of $8 million a month and spent over $150 million buying out rival firms with similar ideas.

Pay By Touch went through four CFOs in four years and a number of board members. The turnover should have been a red flag for later investors, but money continued to pour in from investors and out because of Rogers' wild spending. The company was forced into Chapter 11 bankruptcy in November 2007.

PEOPLE:

Early investors admitted that they had done only minimal background checks on Rogers, which only serves to underline the importance we place on knowing the people behind the startups you invest in. Rogers had a string of business failures in Minneapolis and a history of drug use, including arrests for cocaine. He was accused of abuse by former girlfriends and arrested for destruction of personal property. His background was unsavory, despite his knack for charming cash from investors.

This story shows the importance of the people involved in the startup. Detailed background checks are more important than charm when it comes to knowing who you're doing business with. Along with knowing who is running your startup, you will want to be sure that your interests are protected by the company's ownership structure. There must be more than a single individual at the helm, so look for a strong and stable board as well as a team of professionals who can balance the founder if need be.

PRODUCT:

Pay By Touch had a great idea that resonated with the public. There were several other companies working on similar ideas at the same time. However, the acquisition strategy that Pay By Touch embarked on made no sense for the company, since it included companies such as S&H Greenpoints. A great product idea is not the same as a great product strategy, and Pay By Touch had no strategy.

TIMING:

Biometrics was in its infancy in 2002. While the coolness factor can't be denied, the hardware was bulky and awkward and the software unreliable. Although other companies were working toward the same idea, Pay By Touch might have been doomed to failure even without its founder simply by virtue of being ahead of its time.

EXECUTION:

The founder's story tells the tale here. There was little real interest in making the company a success and a lot of real interest in living a fast lifestyle. The C-suite turnover and the revolving door in the boardroom should have told the story here, but such was the power of Rogers' charm that even seasoned investors fell into the trap of throwing good money after bad.

INSIGHT:

We all like to think that investment firms know what they're doing, but don't rely on the list of previous investors to make your decisions. Do your own due diligence. Investigate the track record and background of the individuals at the top and make sure your ownership agreement protects your interests. While Pay by Touch could arguably have paved the way for Apple Pay, the reality is that good people lost good money because they didn't follow well due diligence practices and so fell for a good conman. This is one instance where "all good" turned out to be all bad.

4. ARGYLE SOCIAL

Social media is hot, and social media analytics hotter still. If that's true, why did Argyle Social unravel so quickly? Adam Covati had the product inspiration, and friend Eric Boggs wanted to run a business, so the time seemed right. Boggs and Covati founded Raleigh-based Argyle Social in 2010, and it seemed to quickly hit its stride. The idea behind it was to help people measure the results of their social media efforts during a time when social media marketing was just beginning to emerge as a powerful marketing channel. The team of Covati and Boggs quickly raised $1.5 million in startup capital, but even that was tough with the firm's North Carolina location. Being so far from Silicon Valley made it harder to attract talent and funding.

However, things took a turn for the worse after the firm's founding. Despite initial success in landing some early customers such as Gander Mountain and wins in technology bakeoffs, the firm struggled to become known and to compete with better funded competitors with large sales forces and professional marketing muscle. Then Boggs left in 2012 to start another company, leaving Covati to take on the role of CEO in addition to that of CTO. Despite attempts to find a buyer for the company, by the spring of 2014, Argyle posted a notice to customers that it was shutting down.

PEOPLE:

Covati had the idea and the passion, but Boggs' early departure indicates he either saw the writing on the wall early or he just wanted to run a company-any company. The commitment wasn't there. Although the firm grew to have around 100 employees, Covati focused more on the technology than on the market. Covati showed an admirable concern for his customers that bodes well for his next venture.

PRODUCT:

The product was the right idea at the right time, but with too little funding and no marketing, the company lost momentum to competitors like HootSuite and Radian6.

TIMING:

The time was right for this idea, but the team at Argyle never got the word out. By the time they shut the doors, the market had passed them by and they couldn't even find a deep-pocketed buyer for the IP.

EXECUTION:

Great technology, great functionality and great customer support. Too bad nobody outside of Atlanta got to hear about it. Had the team put even a little more effort into marketing and promotion, this might have been a very different story.

INSIGHT:

While they say that most entrepreneurs start several companies before they hit the big time, you don't want to be the one funding the education. Make sure the founders are committed to the idea and that they have broad enough backgrounds and expertise to cover all the necessary parts of making a business a success. Shoestring budgets coupled with a too narrow focus from one founder and a lack of commitment from the other seem to be what did Argyle in.

Every startup that fails has a unique story to tell, and you can learn a lot from post-mortem examinations. Put every investment you're considering through the people, product, timing and execution test and you'll save yourself some heartache along with your cash.

* * *

ROI | TOP PRIVATE ACQUISITIONS

It's always interesting to speculate on the reasons why one company acquires another. What was the strategy behind the agreement, and do the companies involved ever get what they wanted from the deal? One thing's for sure – it's not just about the ROI. Sure, it's always about the money and earning a respectable return, but sometimes it's also about egos or friendships or doughnuts. It could be about access to data or it could be about having something to prove. It's not always apparent whether an acquisition could be deemed a success in the participants' eyes, and we rarely know all the details in private equity deals. Nonetheless, here are ten of the most interesting recent private acquisitions.

1. FACEBOOK BUYS INSTAGRAM

In April of 2012, Facebook announced it was acquiring photo site Instagram for a cool billion dollars. Cash-rich Facebook needed a few of Instagram's assets, but not the physical kind. It needed to get back some of its lost "cool factor" and it needed anyone with more expertise than it had in mobile apps. Facebook was fearful that someone else might buy Instagram, causing further erosion of its former lock on the Internet picture game. It never hurts to take out a potential competitor, and one way or another Instagram was turning into a competitor.

Teens and hipsters alike were beginning to feel that Facebook was becoming increasingly stodgy and irrelevant given newer, flashier social media. Instagram, for its part, had made posting pictures on the Internet fun again, and Facebook wanted to claim a little of that fun for its own users. No matter which way you look at it, it seems Facebook bought Instagram to stay relevant in technology and to keep its fading user base engaged. The additional user data it gains from monitoring Instagram helps hone its advertising, and we all know that targeted advertising is worth big bucks.

2. GOOGLE BUYS NEST LABS

Consumers are into energy efficiency big time, and the Nest thermostat represents a way to save energy and be cool at the same time. Nest was the first IoT (Internet of Things) device to break through to consumers and open their eyes to the possibilities of controlling their homes through the Internet. Google ostensibly wanted Nest to help it in its quest to convince consumers and utilities that tracking energy usage is cool, which may even be true – or at least partly true. Nest apparently wanted the $3.2 billion Google paid for the acquisition and access to Google's endlessly deep pockets. Because of this acquisition, thousands of consumers have given the egregiously nosy Google another piece of their personal data. The prying eyes at Google not only know what you look at online; what you buy both on and off the Internet; who your friends are; your credit limits and more – they now even know the temperature of your home. Is there any area of privacy left that Google hasn't invaded? If you find one, guard it well, because Google has plenty of cash for acquiring other companies with more data to feed its ad machine.

3. BURGER KING BUYS TIM HORTONS

In January 2014, 3G Capital, a Brazilian private equity firm, bought Tim Hortons Inc., the Canadian doughnut chain, in a move designed to increase the total number of outlets. In January 2015, 3G Capital announced a name change to Restaurant Brands International amid public outcries against tax evasion through an alleged inversion acquisition. The total deal value of $11 billion didn't set people talking as much as the rumors that Burger King was moving its headquarters to Canada to avoid paying U.S. taxes. With almost half the combined company's revenue coming from Tim Hortons' 80,000 outlets, this may not be a case of tax evasion at all. Both Tim Hortons and Burger King pay about the same tax rate, so the inversion explanation appears to be less credible than the company's explanation of wanting more expertise in serving breakfast. Sometimes a doughnut is just a doughnut.

4. YAHOO BUYS TUMBLR

The most interesting aspect of the Yahoo/Tumblr nuptials was not the $1.1 billion cash acquisition price but the "wedding" vows. Yahoo CEO Marissa Mayer publicly promised not to "screw it up." Tumblr CEO David Karp was left in charge to run Tumblr independently, much as he had as its CEO before the acquisition. Yahoo benefited from Tumblr's fast-growing audience and its billions of blog posts, while Tumblr gained access to Yahoo's technology, particularly its personalization. Two years later, Tumblr is still cool, so it seems Yahoo is standing by the terms of the deal. Could Tumblr be the one thing Yahoo doesn't screw up?

5. BC PARTNERS BUYS PETSMART

In December 2014, BC Partners La Caisse de dépôt et placement du Québec, StepStone and Longview Asset Management announced they were buying out pet supply retailer PetSmart for $8.7 billion. Shareholders on record in the publicly traded PetSmart were paid $83 a share on March 11, 2015, and PetSmart shares are no longer traded on any exchange. The company has a new CEO in Michael Massey, formerly of Collective Brands, put in place to replace long-time CEO David Lenhardt. The strategy here is not readily apparent, which makes this acquisition more interesting. Longview Partners, which had owned or managed about 9 percent of PetSmart shares, stated that the change positioned PetSmart for growth. The pet supplies market is hot right now, with small specialty retailers making inroads in gourmet pet foods, designer duds and carefully curated collections of unique merchandise. The pet supplies market was about $54 billion in 2014, according to the American Pet Products Association, so PetSmart and its new owners have plenty of runway for growth if they can keep merchandise interesting enough to compete with the online boutiques.

6. EBAY BUYS BRAINTREE

EBay, owner of PayPal, purchased Braintree, a payments processing firm, in September 2013 for $800 million in cash. Braintree had raised about $69 million to fund its startup activities in 2007, and by the time of the acquisition it was processing $12 billion in payments, $4 billion of that in mobile. Internet darlings AirBnB, Uber and GitHub were among Braintree's customers. EBay wanted Braintree to help PayPal's global expansion and to up its cool factor by helping with its mobile strategy. Since the Braintree acquisition, eBay has decided to spin off PayPal all together. The market is watching to see how this may affect Braintree, which has continued to thrive under eBay ownership. EBay expects to complete the PayPal spin-off in mid-2015, and most analysts expect that Braintree will continue as an integral part of the PayPal portfolio. Braintree may even see its strategic importance grow as Apple Pay continues to make inroads in the payment landscape. Braintree has an advantage over Apple Pay in that it is device-agnostic, while Apple Pay is limited to the pool of Apple device owners.

7. BLACKSTONE BUYS GATES GLOBAL

Blackstone Group LP bought gates Global from Onex Corp and Canada Pension Plan Investment Board for $5.4 billion in April 2014. This represents a 9.9 times multiple, which is about average for a deal of this size. The sellers received about a 2.2 times return on their initial investment after the $3.5 billion payout. Gates, a maker of automotive components, was running at a revenue rate of about $2.9 billion yearly. The Gates deal was Blackstone's biggest private equity deal since the 2007 acquisition of Hilton Worldwide Holdings, Inc. Gates had been pursuing a dual exit strategy and had filed for an IPO at the same time it was looking for a buyer. Auto parts and components aren't the most glamorous or exciting products, but they generally do well in the long run. As the automotive industry has grown its global footprint, demand for components has smoothed from earlier boom or bust cycles into a steady, reliable business.

8. CARLYLE BUYS ACOSTA

The July 2014 Acosta deal with Blackstone was about $4.8 billion. Carlyle left the existing management team in place at the sales and marketing firm. Acosta works with distributors and retailers to manage the complex and confusing rules of store layout, promotions, rebates and product launches. Acosta had 110 locations housing 37,000 associates at the time of the sale. Thomas H. Lee Partners, LP owned the majority stake in Acosta before Carlyle completed the deal. Carlyle also completed several other high-profile deals in 2014, including Tyco's security business and a blood test product from Johnson & Johnson, making for an interesting portfolio.

9. ONEX BUYS SIG COMBIBLOC

In March 2015, Onex Corporation bought Sig CombiBloc, a global manufacturer of innovative aseptic packaging for the food and beverage industry. Sig CombiBloc was part of Reynolds Group Holdings, with about 40 sites around the world. The company employs 5,100 people, and Onex doesn't expect to make changes in total headcount. Onex does expect to keep the entire management team, all of whom participated in the buyout along with Onex. Onex and the management team together now own 100 percent of the company. The Sig CombiBloc deal was valued at $3.9 billion, including a contingent earn-out component. Onex may also be on the hook for up to another €175 million based on financial performance in 2015 and 2016. Interestingly, approximately 35 percent of the cash in this acquisition was paid in euros and the rest in dollars.

10. IMS HEALTH BUYS APPATURE

Founded in 2007, Appature had raised $9.6 million in two rounds of startup funding to bankroll its software that analyzes proprietary prescription data from multiple big data streams for pharmaceutical companies looking to fine-tune their marketing efforts. Seattle-based Appature customers included about half the top ten healthcare companies in the world at the time of its acquisition. IMS Health, headquartered in Connecticut, is a $244 billion global company with more than 9,000 employees and a big bucket of cash. The acquisition closed in March of 2013. The terms of the deal were not made public at the time. While insiders whispered that the Appature deal was in the neighborhood of $100 million, that doesn't seem likely at this point. In 2014, Appature's new parent, IMS Healthcare, filed for a $100 million IPO of its own and showed it had paid a total of $105 million for seven acquisitions in 2013. Whatever the price, combining big data analytics and healthcare–two of the hottest markets around–can't possibly be a bad thing.

11. STARR PARTNERS BUYS MULTIPLAN

In February 2014, Starr Partners bought MultiPlan, a company that manages insurance claims, for $4.4 billion. The previous owners were two private equity firms that had bought MultiPlan in 2010 for $3.4 billion with the intention of making a two- to three-year investment. Starr Partners holds its investments for longer periods, in the range of five to seven years. Starr is reported to have approached MultiPlan's owners with a buyout proposal in late 2013, and they worked out the details from there. At the time of the acquisition, MultiPlan worked with 900,000 healthcare providers and processed about 40 million claims each year. The relationships in this deal go way back. Reportedly, Hank Greenberg, CEO of Starr Partners, and Mark Tabak, CEO of MultiPlan, have been friends for years. Could that friendship be the reason Starr approached MultiPlan's prior owners?

It's easy to see the strategy behind some of these acquisitions, while others seem baffling. Nonetheless, even if we're not privy to the details, the companies went into each acquisition with high hopes and at least a semblance of a plan. With the staggering sums that changed hands in these transactions, let's hope that all parties to the deals get what they want from the acquisitions. That's the only way the acquired companies will have the opportunity to keep on doing whatever it was they were doing that made them attractive targets in the first place.

TOP STARTUP CASH FLOW DISASTERS

One of the hardest tasks a management team can face is managing cash flow so that the business runs smoothly and that priorities such as R&D are adequately funded. Even seasoned managers in large, well-established companies sometimes get into cash flow trouble, so imagine how much harder it is for startups. With little or no infrastructure in place, the demands for funds seem limitless while the VC money seems vast. It's no surprise that so many startups succumb to cash flow disaster. Here are a few of the most spectacular flameouts.

1. PETS.COM

   Slightly ahead of its time, Pets.com sold pet supplies online. Several other startups with similar business models have gone on to at least modest success since pets.com folded, so what went wrong with this one?

   Spending was out of control. The company spent millions on marketing and advertising, including a pricey Super Bowl ad and a branded balloon in the Macy's Thanksgiving Day Parade. While advertising seemed to be important to help Pets.com stand out from the crowd of companies with similar business models, the Super Bowl ad alone ate up $3 million dollars. The company was running with negative margins, meaning that it incurred a loss for every item it sold.

It seems the management team didn't realize that the old saying about making up for losses with volume is a joke, not a sound business strategy.

The company suffered massive losses in every quarter it was in operation. It lost $21.7 million in the third quarter of 2000 alone. Despite moving its base of operations to lower cost digs, the company never recovered from the wasteful ways of its early days. As late as August 2000 it was still buying competitors such as Petstore.com with cash from its successful IPO. Pets.com shut its doors in November 2000, after laying off the bulk of its workforce and a mere six months after its IPO raised $82.5 million.

2. BOO.COM

Boo.com was one of the earliest fashion e-tailers. The founders envisioned a globally appealing brand targeted to the next younger generation. The founders were among the earliest dotcom millionaires, having launched and sold an earlier business successfully. Boo.com was considered a sure bet and managed to attract $130 million with its fresh approach and cutting edge technology.

Boo.com had a virtual personal shopper to guide users through the site, and users could drag and drop items on models that could spin and rotate in 3-D to give a complete view of how the clothing would look in real life. Since the 1990s, such features seem commonplace, but at the time, Boo.com was pushing the envelope and developing the technology itself. In addition, management felt that the best way to gain traction would be to launch globally at the same time, so they poured additional money into country-specific, local language versions of the site.

Internet speeds were slow at the time, and performance of the site was painfully slow. Additional millions went into improving performance. The detailed photography necessary to support the 3-D models ran close to $200 per item, which meant a $500,000 a month bill simply to photograph goods for the site. The company launched a fashion magazine to supplement its website and attract traffic, adding to the monthly nut. Expensive marketing campaigns in every region drained cash. One investment that did pay off was the company's distribution system, which allowed them to ship approximately 100 percent of orders on time. Even today, many e-tailers would envy that record, but it doesn't happen without putting money into the processes and facilities.

Sales never materialized to the level necessary to support the infrastructure. Despite the wow factor of the shopping experience, users wouldn't wait for pages to load and the planned for conversions and orders never materialized. The founders tried to raise cash to keep the site running, but failed. As of May 2000, Boo.com was no more.

3. SPIRALFROG

SpiralFrog was an early entrant into ad-supported downloadable audio. While SpiralFrog was not alone in attempting to supplant iTunes as the music source of choice for the 18 to 34 year old target audience, they sorely misjudged their audience. First, they didn't support the iPod or even Microsoft's ill-fated Zune. So, what was left that it did run on? Second, the DRM rights were restrictive since users could only download to one PC and two devices. PC, iPod, iPhone, and iPad. Even though the iPhone wasn't released until 2007 and the iPad in 2010, users already had more than 3 devices at the time of SpiralFrog's demise. Downloads were slow, even given the standards of the time and the music selection was poor. Songs expired after 60 days unless the user remembered to log in. SpiralFrog failed to obtain rights to some key music libraries. Advertising and spending to attract users increased, but SpiralFrog was unable to attract advertising dollars to offset its own spend. Nonetheless, SpiralFrog continued spending on advertising in a futile attempt to attract and retain users. They ran through the $12 million in VC money and pulled the plug more than $10 million in debt.

4. DEN.COM

Digital Entertainment Network created videos for teenagers and blew through $100 million in its quest to land an audience. While much of that went to producing content and creating marketing promotions designed to land viewers, much of it also went to fund the founders' unsavory life styles. An attempt to go public failed to raise the necessary cash, and the company went bankrupt amidst allegations of drugs, guns and child pornography. It was the not the first startup headed by Marc Collins-Rector, nor was it the first to fail. Investors who had used our "People, Product, Timing, Execution" model might not have been taken in. The fallout from this disaster lingered as former employees won a $4.5 million dollar judgment against Collins-Rector and the other founders in 2001, and additional allegations of misconduct continued to surface as late as 2014. This disaster could have been avoided with a simple background check that would have uncovered Collins-Rector's criminal record and history of bad business dealings and immoral conduct.

5. FLOOZ

Flooz had an interesting idea – currency not backed by any government and only available for use on line. The company signed up several sites to accept the new form of payment and launched an expensive marketing campaign featuring Whoopie Goldberg. Oddly enough, consumers stayed away in droves, preferring to continue using credit cards. Rumors at the time insinuated that Flooz had sold $300,000 worth of Flooz to Russian credit card thieves. Customers began noticing fraudulent credit card charges, and processors put a hold on Flooz's accounts, reportedly holding back over $1 million. Between the lavish spending and the ill-advised Russian deal, Flooz hit the wall and collapsed. After running through $35 million, Flooz declared bankruptcy in 2001 after less than two years in business and a fruitless search for an acquirer to rescue them.

6. WEBVAN

WebVan, an online grocery site, had a great idea and a billion dollar infrastructure to support it. They targeted the mass market but their selection and quality was more upscale, putting the product beyond the reach of many consumers. Instead of starting small and working out the kinks in one or two cities, WebVan rolled out in 26 cities right away. Setting up each city cost $50 million, with no guarantee of success. WebVan had managed to raise $1.2 billion in VC money, and they spent it all with minimal revenue to show for it. WebVan declared bankruptcy in 2001.

7. GOVWORKS.COM

The founders conceived Govworks as a place where everyday citizens could interact with the government and pay parking tickets. While it sounds noble, the company didn't have a real plan to monetize the idea. The founding partners spend vast sums on custom technology and computer systems. The firm was also the subject of a documentary movie called "Startup", which painted the failure in a very unflattering light. Govworks.com was sold for $7.5 million in debt and cash.

Lifelong friends, the partners have gone on to start another venture, but they left $59 million of wreckage in their wake. Due to its massive failure, Govworks was even featured in a 2001 documentary called Startup.com.

8. ETOYS.COM

This was another great idea with poor execution. eToys managed to garner $166 million from its IPO in 1999, but by 2001 the once highflying shares were selling for just a few pennies. The firms' big mistake, as with so many of the era, was spending lavish sums on marketing and advertising to attract an audience. As eToys expanded its product line from the original concept of educational toys to more mass-market toys, orders increased but distribution couldn't keep up. During the 1999 Christmas season, the flood of orders broke the company's fragile systems, and children missed having their coveted toy under the tree, EToys had made children cry and parents angry. Worse yet, they gave Santa Claus a bad name. Late deliveries, wrong items, lost orders, back orders – the litany of delivery errors covered every possible bad outcome. The heavy spending on marketing had attracted a customer base that the company couldn't support. EToys never recovered and eventually KayBee Toys bought its remaining assets for pennies on the dollar.

With our Angel Kings formula, investors would have been saved!

PEOPLE:

As a rule of thumb, while startups are almost by definition run by inexperienced people, make sure there's also a team around the founders with some expertise to help out. And go one step further and do actual background checks. If a founder is willing to submit to a background and credit check, you'll be able to better assess his or her future success.

PRODUCT:

Evaluate the product. Is there a market for the product or service, and does the company have a strategy to target the market? Would you buy it or use it?

TIMING:

Is the time right for the product, or do other factors have to come into play before the market will be ready to adopt the idea?

EXECUTION:

Is the technology available to support the plan or is the company banking on creating their own? Are they executing tactically against the plan? How are they balancing spending against revenue, and is the product rollout plan sustainable? A few simple questions could save you from the investing in the next Harvard case study on startup disasters.

3 Lessons Learned:

1. Spend wisely. Cash is king. Don't waste it.
2. Don't have unnecessary inventory. Inventory depletes your business more than you could ever depreciate.
3. Of course, build something innovative and different, but make sure the demand exists first before you launch.

5 WAYS TO FIND THE NEXT BIG STARTUPS

It may be the dream of every investor to discover the next big thing and that you end up rich beyond your wildest fantasies while the world praises you for your astonishing insight and vision. This is an excellent and rewarding fantasy, but it is probably not going to happen. However, you can make a lot of money and have fun investing in startups if you follow these proven strategies, used by such successful VCs as Marc Andreessen, Fred Wilson and even the greatest investor of all-time, Warren Buffett. The concepts are simple and you can apply them to startups in any industry.

1. DOES THE PRODUCT OR SERVICE SOLVE AN ACTUAL PROBLEM?

Startups are often new ideas that nobody has ever thought of before, or they may be about a better way to address a problem. You don't want to invest in a startup like Flooz, the online-only currency. Flooz was a solution looking for a problem, and it ate up $35 million of somebody's cash before it crashed and burned. The problem for Flooz was that a solution to the problem of secure online shopping already existed. The solution was credit cards – small, lightweight, useable anywhere and offering protection against fraud. Not only was there a pre-existing solution, the existing solution was better than what Flooz had to offer.

Don't think that a problem doesn't exist simply because nobody is talking about it. Consumers weren't bemoaning the lack of a table in their lives before April 2010 when Apple introduced the first iPad, but consumers sat up and took notice. Sales of the iPad were astonishing. Despite recent slowdowns, the iPad is inarguably one of the most successful products of all time. When they saw it, consumers realized that the iPad was, in fact, the solution they had been looking for. Lightweight, portable, useful and sturdy, the iPad was a better mobile device for Internet use than smartphones with their tiny screens. Apple had the vision to develop a product that solved a problem. Just because consumers had not yet articulated the problem didn't mean they weren't looking for a solution.

Sometimes the energy and enthusiasm of the founders can make you see a solution where none exists, as in the case of Flooz. Sometimes it's a solution that solves a real problem that is just starting to emerge. You need to evaluate products carefully to ensure that the problem is real and that the solution actually solves it. It helps if you know and understand the industry.

Most successful investors suggest sticking to what you know or staying in industries where you understand the business. Not only will that help you understand the market for the product but also you can more evaluate whether it is a real solution to a real problem.

Warren Buffett looks for recurring revenue, as in the razor followed by the perpetual razor blade sales. In technology, the cloud represents a source of recurring revenue that can sustain a company more comfortably than selling one off licenses. Just ask Marc Benioff of Saleforce.com about the benefits of a SaaS model and recurring revenue.

2. WHO IS ON YOUR TEAM?

The founders and the startup team are important, but they may not have startup experience or business experience. You should spend time getting to know the team and observe how they handle themselves in various business situations. Notice what the office looks like, and ask about their plans to move or renovate as they grow.

Just before the dotcom bubble burst in the early 2000s, Aeron chairs were expensive, superfluous office items prevalent in the startup world. However, when the cash flow ran out, the dotcoms couldn't pay the people who sat in those chairs. What a waste of VC cash. Marc Andreessen says he pays careful attention to a company's burn rate. Too high and he'll pass.

Good advice. Money should be spent on real priorities, not window dressing that only serves to feed the ego of the management team. Money should be spent on adding necessary features to the product, not recreating the wheel out of a bad case of the sad and misguided "not invented here" syndrome.

So dig into the budgets and the tactical plans. Make sure the team has their eyes on the prize and that suddenly having millions of dollars won't send them off on a wild spending spree.

In addition to the founders themselves, you should evaluate the team around the founders. The best you can hope for would be if they've brought in experienced people to help run the business. If all you see in meetings are frat boys, this may not be a prudent place to park your cash. Marc Andreessen says he looks for "the magic team." As you're evaluating the team, remember the wisdom of Peter Thiel: "Scientists never make any money. They're always deluded into thinking that they live in a just universe that'll reward them for their work." That's another reason why you need a balanced team with varied skills and expertise.

It wouldn't hurt to do background checks on the founders, by the way. You never know until you check and learn about a founder's financial and personal history.

Also consider who else is backing this endeavor. If you're the first angel in the first round, you don't have much insight, but if the startup can point to Andreessen Horowitz, Sand Hill Partners, Warren Buffett or another well-respected investment group, you are in good company. That doesn't excuse you from doing your own due diligence. It just means you're in good company.

3. IS THERE A PLAN?

The latest thing in startups is bragging about the "pivot" where the company changes direction because they found a new idea they like better. This is called ADHD in small children and we treat it with medicine. In startups, we often treat it with cash, which makes no sense at all.

If the original plan was good enough to ask for money to fund it, then why is it no longer good enough to run with? The only exception is if you are funding a company that is still in the market research phase and you are funding that research.

There are certain parts of the plan you should pay special attention to. One is the monetization strategy. There should be one, and it should be well thought out, supported by research and viable. If the plan calls for millions of marketing dollars to find hundreds of thousands of revenue dollars, it is not a good plan. The startup should be able to point to other companies that have used the same strategy successfully. That doesn't mean they have to be in the same industry. It simply means pointing to a successful business that uses the same model.

Fred Wilson has said that people should consider investing in startups that achieve a strong customer base before generating revenue, as was the case with Facebook. It may be the right strategy for a particular startup, but there should still be a monetization strategy at the end of the customer and user acquisition period.

Look for scalability. Many a company starts with a product that doesn't scale and they all suffer an unhappy fate. Think of WebVan with its $50 million per city infrastructure costs. Think of Boo.com with its half million a month in photography fees. Think of the total market. How many people will want this product or service? If the market is too small you will saturate it before you've earned back your investment. Peter Thiel has been quoted as saying that it's always a mistake to go after a big market on day one. Dotcom history has proven the wisdom of that sentiment.

You should also ask about the exit strategy and timing, and the founders must understand and actively support your need to earn a return on your investment. Unless your plan is to treat this cozy little company like a retirement hobby, the founders must actively support a mutually agreeable exit plan and timing. Otherwise, you can grow old before you see your money again.

Look for momentum in the company, the market and the product. You should see the company adding people to the team as they approach market readiness. You want to see signs and stirrings that the market is seeking the solution you are about to unveil. You want to see new beta versions that perform better or have more features.

4. WHAT ABOUT THE FINANCIALS?

If the company has been in operation, you should be able to see its financial statements to evaluate the team's spending habits and use of funds. Both of those may change once the founders have millions of dollars in hand rather than just a Visa card, but you may get an inkling of the future.

Along with the existing financial statements there should be some projections as part of the business plan. Make sure the written business plan jibes with what you hear the founders saying. If they're talking a nationwide rollout but the plan shows barely enough spend to cover the neighborhood, you're dealing with a naïve or unrealistic team.

While you're looking over the financials with your advisors, check out the legal documents too. Look for consistency among all the paperwork and the financial plans. Make sure you are comfortable with the ownership structure and that there are safeguards to protect your interests.

5. CAN YOU AFFORD THE LOSS?

Even with the right product, a brilliant plan and a stellar team with conscientious spending habits, things happen. There is always risk in investing, especially with startups. Before you hand over your hard earned cash, make sure you can afford the loss if you never got your money back.

As you've been reading this, you may have noticed that the well-known angel investors recommend various evaluation approaches, but they all focus to varying degrees on People, Product, Timing and Execution, just as we do. Add to that the caveat to understand your limits. Just as you would in poker, decide how much you can put onto the table for investing, and never stray from your investment strategy.

BIOPHARMACEUTICAL FUNDING TAKES OFF

Biopharma is a hot sector for VC investment. There are always new ideas and if you have the patience to wait for the extended approval process, the rewards are great. On fact, Forbes recently reported that the weighted average return hovered in the neighborhood of 9 X for pharma and biotech. The recent months have brought record setting deal sizes and more VC funding than at any time in recent memory. According to Thompson Reuters, investors funded 202 life science deals with $2.75 billion during the last quarter of 2014 alone. While that wasn't a record setting amount, it was darn close. Like most areas of investment, some areas within the sector are hot while others are not. Here's a look at some of the hottest sectors and most interesting deals.

Last year two biopharma deals in particular were notable for their jaw-dropping returns. Roche Genetech bought Seragon for $725 million upfront with $1 billion additional in earnouts. Seragon makes treatments for hormone driven cancers, including breast and uterine or endometrial cancers.

In the second big deal, Johnson and Johnson bought Alios, maker of antivirals to treat respiratory diseases including the common cold, for $1.75 billion. Estimates are that both deal earned investors 20 X payouts.

Recent high dollar investments include two notable deals:

Moderna Therapeutics has been through five rounds and raised a total of $674.6 million. Investors include Wellington management, Viking Global Investors, RA Capital management, Alexion Pharmaceuticals and Flagship Ventures. Moderna Therapeutics develops messenger RNA molecules to provoke creation of antibodies.

Intarcia Therapeutics has been through nine rounds and raised a total of $534.3 million. Investors include GGV Capital, New Enterprise Associates, Venrock, New Leaf Venture Partners, Marker, Fred Alger Management Farallon Capital Management, Foresite Capital, RA Capital Management, Quilvest Ventures, Alta Partners and Omega Funds. The latest round of over $450 million occurred in January 2015. Intarcia Therapeutics develops therapies for long term chronic disease treatment.

BIOTECHNOLOGY

Biotechnology was the hottest area for venture funding during 2014. VCs put more than $4.8 billion into the sub-sector. Early stage funding was at an all-time high in the fourth quarter with $1.3 billion, representing a 41 percent increase over Q4 2013's $956 million. Year over year, early stage funding increased 35 percent to $3.7 billion. Late stage funding increased by 55 percent to $660 million in the quarter and 21 percent for the year to $2.3 billion. The average early stage deal size was $18.2 million, another increase over prior years. Late stage deals averaged $17.4 million.

Within biotech, certain sub-sectors were hotter than others. The four hottest subsegments included biosensors, biotech equipment, pharmaceuticals and biotech research. While still hot by any standards, industrial and animal biotechs were slightly less heated. Key areas of research include genomics, Alzheimer's and personalized, targeted cancer treatments.

The areas receiving the most funding in the recent past include startups focused on targeted genetic treatments for certain cancers or chronic diseases. Revving up the human immune system to ward off viruses and creating 'customized" antibodies for cancer treatments that avoid the side effects of traditional chemotherapy are doing well. Nanotechnology to fight chronic disease is becoming an area of increased interest as well. Several recent startups have been working on fast and reliable substitutes for in vitro and animal testing by replacing these controversial methods with inanimate "organs on a chip."

Over the last several years, there have been more than 85 exits that generated record numbers in this sector, which puts it among the most desirable sectors for investing.

FOURTH QUARTER 2014 VC FUNDING BY SUB-SECTOR

- Biotech human ran to $1,706 million for a 46 percent increase.
- Pharmaceutical hit $155 million and a 60 percent increase.
- Biotech equipment funding reached $100 million for a 148 percent increase.
- Biotech research investment was $39 million for a 1 percent increase.
- Biosensors received $28 million, an increase of 259 percent in Q4 2014 over the same quarter in 2013.
- Biotech - industrial was down 74 percent with $7 million.
- Biotech - animal was down 64 percent with only $10 million.

TOP TWELVE COMPANIES TO WATCH

1. **Unum Therapeutics** for universal cellular therapy. The concept is to mobilize T-cells to create antibodies directed to a tumor, sparing surrounding tissue. Unum is based in Cambridge Massachusetts. They received $12 million in Series A funding in October 2014 from three investors, including Sanofi-Genzyme BioVentures, Atlas Venture and Fidelity Biosciences.

2. **Navitor Pharmaceuticals** is working on nutrient sensing to regulate cell growth and functioning. Also based in Cambridge, Massachusetts, they raised $23.5 million in Series A funding in June 2014. Investors include SR One, Johnson & Johnson Development Corporation, Atlas Venture and Polaris Partners.

3. **Intellia Therapeutics** is using gene editing technology to treat genetic diseases. Located in the biopharma heartland of Cambridge, Massachusetts, Intellia raised $15 million in Series A fund in November 20014. The three investors included Caribou Biosciences, Atlas Ventures and Novartis.

4. **Synlogic** is attempting to create therapeutic microbes to find and treat diseases. Once again Cambridge Massachusetts based, Synlogic raised $34.4 million in two rounds of funding. The most recent occurred in October 2014. Investors include the Bill and Melinda Gates Foundation, New Enterprise Associates and Atlas Venture.

5. **Quartet Medicine** aims to use neural pathways to regulate pain and inflammation. Also in Cambridge, Massachusetts, Quartet has been through one round of financing in October 29014. They raised

$17 million from Pfizer Venture Investments, Novartis Venture Fund and Atlas Venture.

6. **Voyager Therapeutics** is working on CNS-focused gene therapies for central nervous system diseases. Cambridge again. Voyager went through its first round of funding in February 2014, raising $45 million from Third Rock Ventures.

7. **Editas** is using genome editing to create precise corrective molecular modifications that could be used treat a variety of diseases. In its Series A round during November 2014, Cambridge, Massachusetts based Editas raised $43 million from partners Innovation Fund, Third Rock Ventures, Flagship Ventures and Polaris Partners.

8. **Caribou Biosciences** is working on cellular engineering for use in industry, agriculture and therapeutics. Based in Berkeley California, Caribou has been through two rounds of funding, raising $2.9 million from a single investor, Novartis. It is notable that Caribou invested in Intellia.

9. **Scholar Rock** is using a new class of biologic niche modulators to selectively target disease by regulating dysfunctional cell growth. This Cambridge, Massachusetts firm had four investors for its first round of funding in September 2014. The $20 million came from EcoR1 Capital, Kraft Group, Polaris Partners and ARCH Venture partners.

10. **Emulate** is creating organ functionality on a chip to enable simplified and faster clinical trials. First round funding from Cedars Sinai Medical Center and NanoDimension raised $12 million for this Cambridge Massachusetts company in July 2014.

11. **Nortis** has a similar concept, creating tissue-engineered microenvironments for an alternative to in vitro and animal testing. Based in Seattle Washington, Nortis received $12 million in July 2014 from undisclosed venture investors. That followed from a march 2014 infusion of $1.2 million also from an undisclosed venture investor.

12. **Lysogene** is using gene therapy to target rare and severe central nervous system pathologies in children. Based in Paris, the company nonetheless recently entered a partnership agreement for continued research and collaboration with University of Massachusetts Medical School and Auburn University in Alabama. Lysogene received $22 million in Series A funding in May 2014. Sofinnova Ventures was the sole investor.

GEOGRAPHIC CONSIDERATIONS

During the fourth quarter of 2014, Boston and Chicago received the most sector funding. Boston received $959 million in 32 deals. Two out of the three largest biopharma deals since 1995 went to Boston area firms in 2014. Those deals included Intarcia Therapeutics for $200 million in April 2014 and $446 million in January 2015 to Moderna Therapeutics.

Other regions with a strong presence include the San Francisco Bay area with $580 million in biotechnology in Q4 2014. The New York metro area and Research Triangle area round out the hottest areas, although their totals, while sizable, were miniscule in comparison to the investments in Boston and San Francisco.

Biopharma will continue to be a hot area, as shown by the mega deal Moderna Therapeutics landed. When looking for investments in this sector, most targets will be found in Boston and the San Francisco area. Genetic therapies for targeted disease treatments will continue to be the go-to sector for biopharma investments.

DOES THE LEAN STARTUP WORK?

"In my first startup, I had an initial advertising budget of $5 per day total."
– Eric Ries

New entrepreneurs often buy in to the corporate mantra that cash is king, but many companies over the years have made it on determination, intelligence, strong designs, and a bit of luck. For angel investors, these companies can be a great investment, because buy-in is very small in the beginning. Founders who are willing to bootstrap have a different idea of budget, and they can often get more done with less funding. If the startup succeeds, then investors might even see a generous return on a relatively small cost.

In our article on the hottest software startups, we talk about Apttus, a successful software company that bootstrapped its way through seven years before seeking traditional investor funding. In such a case, investors have an even greater advantage: the startup is generally further along with its research, plans, and products. It might even have products on the market, providing investors with solid data on which to make a decision. Even then, investment asks may be lower than with non-bootstrapped companies.

ERIC RIES AND THE LEAN STARTUP

Bootstrapping isn't a new concept; entrepreneurs have been using their last dimes to launch companies for centuries. Funding a small endeavor on little more than your own sweat and what cash you can scrape together is a risky strategy, though, and most angel investors are likely familiar with statistics about how many of these small businesses fail each year.

Planning and methodology brings a bit more stability to the bootstrapping risk, and one of the more successful methods today is Lean Startup, which was pioneered by Eric Ries. Ries, like many founders featured in our book, began in the technology field. After graduating, he worked for a California company that would fail within a few years. In 2004, Ries cofounded IMVU, a social network company, through which he met investor and mentor Steve Blank.

Blank invested in IMVU, but he required that Ries and his cofounder audit a class he taught on entrepreneurship. Through that relationship and class, Ries would learn about Blank's beliefs on customer development–a strategy he used to quickly deploy IMVU products and later to create the foundation of his lean startup method. Reis's efficient approach to the startup meant that the product launched within six months. By 2011, the company was generating revenue of $40 million with an equal number of users. At that time, Ries had moved on to other things, however, remaining simply a board observer with the company. Ries's early successes and failures put him in a position to advise other startups, which he did independently and as part of the team at a venture capital firm. He also used his experience, and what he learned from working with other startups, to create his philosophy of Lean Startup.

SUMMARY OF THE LEAN STARTUP METHOD

Lean Startup methods for any product follow a few common steps and guiding principles.

ELIMINATING UNCERTAINTY

Lean Startup brings a method to startup endeavors. Founders don't have to over manage, over analyze, or over work their ideas, products, and execution, but they do need a plan and a way to test. As with Lean Process Management–a methodology pioneered by Toyota and used across the manufacturing world today–Lean Startup requires constant questioning and testing. Startups should always be moving forward; at the same time, they should constantly be asking if that next step is the right step.

WORKING SMARTER

Entrepreneurs often ask the wrong question. You shouldn't wonder whether you *can* do something, but whether you *should* do it. Is there a viable need and does your product meet that need for businesses and consumers?

In Lean methodologies, the startup is an experiment, and the conclusion of that experiment is a product. By working through the experiment quickly to test a hypothesis–and not concentrating on making a perfect product first time out–startups can get to market faster.

DEVELOPING AN MVP

The core of the "work smarter, not harder" principle relates to developing a minimum viable product, or MVP. Once a startup identifies a problem that needs a solution, it should develop the minimum viable product that offers that solution. The MVP is the minimal product that can be brought to consumers without being a complete flop–it does not, however, have to be perfect. Often, an MVP is distributed as a beta product to a smaller subset of users. Those users provide feedback on the product, and the startup enters a cycle known as build-measure-learn, which we'll cover in a moment.

Developing a minimum viable product lets startups determine rapidly whether the market will demand a product, which is good for both startup and investor. You find out if a gamble is likely to pay off with a reduced amount of time, resource, and work. It's the equivalent of getting an early peak at some of your opponent's cards in poker-or, perhaps more accurately, being given a cheat sheet on your opponent's tells early in the game.

VALIDATED LEARNING

Lean startups measure progress by what Ries calls validated learning. While a beta launch may be valuable, lean startups don't wait for all the data to come in-or even for the beta to launch. Any data or information that can be obtained, especially from customers, is integrated quickly. The product can be improved in small increments, letting the startup make faster strides toward something that will generate successful and consistent revenues.

THE 5 PRINCIPLES OF LEAN STARTUP

1. Entrepreneurs are everywhere.
2. Entrepreneurship is management.
3. Validated learning.
4. Innovation accounting.
5. Build-Measure-Learn.

Let's examine the concept behind each step and how it applies to the lean startup.

1. ENTREPRENEURS ARE EVERYWHERE

The stereotypical view of an entrepreneur veers between the brilliant college student and the driven scientist, but in reality, entrepreneurs are everywhere and come from all walks of life. By definition, an entrepreneur is a person who organizes and operates a business, sometimes – but not always -- taking on high levels of risk to do so. Entrepreneurs are not restricted to technology startups or cutting-edge biotech.

The importance of this point cannot be overlooked, even though it sounds simple. Opportunities for startups abound in every industry and in every region. When you are looking to fund a startup, you don't have to be confined to a narrow range of opportunities. Find a sector that intrigues you and focus your attention on startups in that sector.

2. ENTREPRENEURSHIP IS MANAGEMENT

Going back to the definition of entrepreneur, we see that a core concept is operating a business. The definition does not include brilliant ideas or wild spending habits or even a degree of coolness. It's about management, which means harnessing available resources to meet goals or at least to provide the best possible outcome under given circumstances.

Management is about discipline and creating processes that help the organization reach its goals.

To make a startup successful, the entrepreneur needs to impose processes and disciplines on the organization. Management is about making good decisions faster even when based on limited information; it's about getting the best from a team. Sometimes a manager is a coach and sometimes a manager is a dictator or a friend – or a naysayer. A manager manages, and gets things done.

This is a fundamentally different view of entrepreneurs, who often exhibit diva-like tendencies and go off on expensive ego trips leaving reality behind. Investing in a lean startup means your cash won't be wasted on some of the excesses and errors committed by entrepreneurs such as leaders at Pets.com, WebVan, Den.com, Boo.com or Flooz. These companies all failed.

3. VALIDATED LEARNING

Using lean startup principles, companies continually test their vision with the only people who can validate it – potential customers. Most startups take the "Nike" approach. They just do it, working diligently to bring a product or idea to fruition and then springing it as a completed product with no time, resources or room for changes or improvements. Many entrepreneurs are disappointed by this approach when the expected sound of trumpets heralding their vision fails to materialize and instead, all they hear is a resounding thud as the doomed product hits the trash.

The MVP, "Minimally Viable Product," idea strives to find the product that has the fewest features and requires the least effort to create that will still have appeal to a broad enough market to sustain the company's goals. The minimally viable product feature set does not spring directly from the entrepreneur's mind, nor will it ever happen in a vacuum unless it's a fluke of the universe.

Enlisting early adopters is fundamental to this process. The startup needs the feedback from users to measure the product's viability. By the time the product is ready for full-scale distribution, it has a built-in user base and a history of solving real customer needs.

4. INNOVATION ACCOUNTING

Startups have sometimes felt that they were immune to the realities of business that exist in established industries, but startups need to be even more conscious of the mundane metrics. The entrepreneur's role is to define the process and provide the roadmap including specific milestones and priorities. This is more than project management and far more than standard accounting. It is a new kind of accounting that measures startups on their business imperatives. It's a fascinating topic that Ries explores in detail in his book, "The Lean Startup."

5. BUILD-MEASURE-LEARN

Creating an innovation process is key to the MVP concept and the entire lean startup idea. It involves the product learning cycle: Build-Measure-Learn. The process starts with early prototypes that are shown and tested with multiple customers. Customers provide their feedback on what they like, didn't like, or what they need to have added before they would be willing to buy the product. The startup measures the product's current features for acceptability to its target market. The development team takes this learning, adds features that fulfill the identified need and repeats the process until they have come up with a design that meets the need without adding unnecessary cost, extended development cycles or unwanted features.

With Lean Startup, you will eliminate or at least reduce uncertainty in the startup process. Your team will be able to work smarter, not harder as you answer the fundamental question: Should this product be built? Most entrepreneurs ask "What can I build?" or How can I build it?" The lean startup works on the premise that you shouldn't build a product unless there is a sustainable business to be built. Like the original idea for lean manufacturing, it eliminates waste:

- Wasted time.
- Wasted effort.
- Wasted resources.

The Lean Startup is one of many possible ways to build a billion dollar company. It's not perfect. In fact, continuing to iterate one MVP after another can squander precious time. If you haven't found a customer after your fourth or fifth iteration, there's probably a bigger issue with the founding team, product, execution or timing. But if you're a startup with little funding and you've got an engineer who can build something fast, give it a shot. As my father once said, all diets work. Whether you're on a low carb, low sugar, low sodium or low fat diet, each make you more disciplined and thus make you lose weight. Likewise, a Lean Startup approach can work to get you to market quicker, even if others like Peter Thiel argue there are other approaches that work better.

THE MOST SUCCESSFUL LEAN STARTUPS

1. AARDVARK

Google acquired Aardvark because the product was highly successful at querying users for subjective information and graphing the results.

They used the MVP process to test each iteration of the product, and by the sixth iteration they had their MVP.

2. DROPBOX

When the CEO of Dropbox started using principles from The Lean Startup, the company increased its user count by a factor of 4x in just a little over a year. Dropbox attributes this to product improvements identified during customer tests.

3. IMVU

IMVU is a 3-D chat and gaming community with more than 50 million registered users and an annualized run rate of $40 million. They use experimentation and innovation processes to develop features that keep their customers coming back.

4. VOTIZEN

Votizen aims to mobilize voters by becoming the first social media network for voters. Votizen users managed to drive the first social media promoted bill into the Senate.

5. WEALTHFRONT

Wealthfront aims to enable ordinary investors to have access to the most successful investment managers and hedge funds. Despite operating in an SEC-regulated environment, Wealthfront practices the principle of continuous deployment and now manages more than $200 million and $2 million a day in transactions.

6. CARBONMADE

Carbonmade is a portfolio app that lets creative professionals show their stuff online. The product began as an in-house tool for the startup, which spent its time concentrating on a different product while the portfolio app grew quietly among an audience of friends, friends of friends, and friends of those friends.

The startup was founded by Dave Gorum, Jason Nelson, and Spencer Fry. From the beginning, the three knew they wouldn't seek investors right away due to their experience with previous startups. During the course of founding the company, Gorum developed a product for displaying his own creative work–he and others liked the app so much, they shared it with friends, which is where the growth story began.

In 2007, the three used the app to launch Carbonmade, offering a $12 per month plan for users. The team intended to create a suite of apps aimed at the creative audience, but within a year they realized several things:

- They had a viable product consumers were demanding.
- They *liked* working on the product.
- The community surrounding Carbonmade was passionate about the brand.

The trio made a decision to drop the other product in development and concentrate on making Carbonmade–the thing customers wanted–better. As of 2015, the company offers three portfolio packages ranging from $6 to $24 per month, and consumers pay for over 880,000 portfolios.

Carbonmade illustrates the validated learning premise from Lean Startup. By reevaluating its goals and interests–as well as listening to what the customers were saying–Carbonmade turned its attention to a proven product. The result? Millions in revenue every month.

7. PLENTY OF FISH

After working for a number of tech startups, Markus Frind decided to launch his own company in 2003. Frind settled on the online dating market and bootstrapped his company from his apartment, where he received the company's first Google AdSense paycheck–for a whopping $1,100.

By 2007, the company was reportedly worth close to $1 billion, and at that point, Frind started hiring people to help him. For the first four years, however, he did most of the work himself and generated a great deal of revenue through a freemium website that was funded by advertisers.

Frind didn't stop there. Over the years, Plenty of Fish followed the build–measure–learn model we discussed above. It eventually gave up funding by an ad–based, freemium model. By offering paid subscriptions, the startup hoped to better engage users.

Frind also made a timely decision after studying consumer use and the market. He integrated his product onto mobile platforms, which he claims is responsible for a large increase in both user and revenue growth. Between 2013 and early 2015, Plenty of Fish experienced doubled revenues. By early 2015, it had 100 million users and expected annual revenue of $100 million.

Frind once stated that he didn't know anything about SEO, community, venture capital, or advertising when he began his startup experiment. What he did know is how to learn: he stated that, "I spent every waking minute when I wasn't at my day job reading, studying, and learning."

8. GITHUB

GitHub is another company that started as a private solution. Coders Tom Preston, PJ Hyett, and Chris Wanstrath were all using Github, which is an open source version control software. When they found they had trouble sharing their code with others after creating it, however, they decided to make a solution. The solution–GitHub–began as a simple weekend project for a group of coders. They funded the minimal resource needs–hosting and a domain–and shared the tool with friends.

It wasn't long before GitHub went the way of Carbonmade, with word of mouth spreading the product outside of the founders' social circles. At that point, the trio decided to launch GitHub as a business. Together, they were able to cover initial formation costs, but they didn't have enough cash to support themselves as fulltime employees. Instead of seeking immediate investment and spending cash resources on themselves, they worked other jobs and did consulting work to pay the personal bills while they grew the business.

By 2009, the company boasted 100,000 users and an award as the best bootstrapped startup. By 2012, GitHub was stable and impressive enough to score $100 million in investor funding from SV Angel and Andreessen Horowitz.

9. TECHCRUNCH

TechCrunch is the story of a bootstrapped startup that went from launch to a $30 million acquisition in five years. Founded in 2005 by Keith Teare and Mike Arrington, TechCrunch is a blog and news site that covers the technical industry, which didn't require much in the way of capital. Monetizing through advertisers, the startup experienced a rapid rise among followers and readers. Today, it's one of the most-read websites about the tech industry across the globe.

After about five years, Arrington reportedly owned 85 percent of the company, which had done little to seek funding from investors. Still, AOL found the site to be valuable and bought it for $30 million in 2010.

10. SPARKFUN

Nathan Seidle and his startup, SparkFun, are great examples of part of the Lean Startup model. Seidle bootstrapped his startup for a number of years, pumping profits back into the company whenever possible. He also immediately created a learning environment for himself as a business owner when he launched SparkFun.

The company sells electronic parts and is currently a major player in the open source technology market. When Seidle launched the company in 2003, however, he did so because he himself ran into a problem. He burned out some electronic components when working on a project, but couldn't find what he needed for replacement parts easily online. With SparkFun, he wanted to bring necessary parts to individuals and small businesses, but he also wanted to provide education and encourage people to get involved with electronics.

To fund the launch of his fledgling company, Seidle used $2,500 in personal debt to purchase products. Since he wasn't sure which products would hit home with consumers, he started with a random assortment of parts–setting up the experiment environment Ries talked about with Lean Startups. As small trickles of orders began to come through, Seidle tracked the success of each product and learned which items to reinvest in.

In Chapter 3, we talk about how companies don't have to be first to market with a solution, and they don't have to be the first to provide a certain type of product. They *do* have to provide an innovative twist on the solution, or in some way make the solution more convenient for the consumer. SparkFun delivers this innovation by including datasheets and tutorials for all of its products as open source hardware.

In less than a decade, SparkFun grew from a bootstrapped startup–whose founder couldn't afford a new coat because he funneled everything back to the company–to an enterprise worth $10 million. Seidle has over one hundred employees and his company supplies a global Maker community.

11. INDEED.COM

In Chapter 2, we discuss the importance of investing in established, experienced people, which describes the cofounders behind the site, Indeed. Paul Forster and Rony Kahn already founded, ran, and sold a company before they began to bootstrap Indeed. It's not surprising that they didn't bootstrap for an extensive amount. After a beta release of the popular job listing site, the company raised $5 million in funding, which a Union Square Ventures (USV) representative said investors had to convince the cofounders to take.

According to that same USV associate, by the time the investment came, Kahn and Forster had launched the Indeed service and were on the way to success. Forster said a major principle of Indeed was to run efficiently and to remain laser focused on building the product over time. By 2012, that focus had paid off. Indeed generated around $150 million a year and had 550 employees. It was also poised for either a successful IPO or an acquisition. In the end, the company–which was valued at over $750 million–sold for an undisclosed amount. Guesses at the time were that the acquisition price ranged between $750 million and $1 billion.

12. APPSUMO

As with all great startup stories, AppSumo begins with someone addressing a need. This time, it was Noah Kagan, who was working with a Facebook games company. Through interaction with partners of that company, Kagan discovered that many businesses and users were having a hard time discovering innovative applications and web products.

Kagan realized someone could offer a product that connected those innovative products and services with the market. Using open-source code, Kagan built part of his product and hired an outsourced coder for a total of $60 to do the rest. The same month, he launched AppSumo, which was to offer deals on products Kagan found online. The first deal he offered was a pro account at Imgur for 50 percent off. Advertised on Reddit, which is a clever target audience crossover decision, the deal sold to 200 buyers.

David Cramer then joined Kagan as a cofounder. The two rebooted AppSumo with updated code and a new offer. They sold 500 of the new offer. The pair continued in a rinse and repeat pattern, learning as they went. Within a few years, the startup boasted 200,000 subscribers and a growing network of customers, startups, and advertisers.

13. GAWKER

Gawker founder Nick Denton is another example of someone who founded and sold another company before turning to bootstrapping for his next endeavor. Denton launched Gawker, a media and blogging company, in 2002. For many years, he did most of the work himself, bringing on other bloggers as needed in contract or work-at-home positions to keep costs down. Denton slowly expanded Gawker operations outside of his home by renting an inexpensive storefront to house his growing team of bloggers. Six years after he launched, he invested in a more traditional office for the company. Within about ten years, Denton's bootstrapped media company weighed in with valuation estimates around $150 million.

ANGEL INVESTOR CONSIDERATIONS

Bootstrapped startups often have something of the Cinderella story. You might want to cheer them on; you might even want to get involved in helping them succeed. For angel investors, separating the cheering section from the business section is critical. Bootstrapping shows initiative, but just because a founder chooses to work lean, doesn't mean he has a sustainable idea or a great execution plan. For every successful bootstrapped startup we might list, there are dozens, if not hundreds, of garage and dining room startups that never make it past the front door.

When dealing with bootstrapped startups that have moved into seeking investments, angel investors should ask:

- Why is the startup choosing to seek investors now?
- Has the model, product, or service seen some success, or is the company running out of resources and attempting to salvage itself with funding?
- How does the company fair using our checklists for people, product, timing, and execution?
- Is there still enough room for an investor to profit? In some cases, the company may have bootstrapped itself past the startup stage, in which case an angel investor might not be the best match when it comes to funding.

Angel investors that decide to pair up with bootstrapped startups tend to benefit from a few things. First, anyone who has bootstrapped a startup to the point that attracts investors has a strong work ethic and adaptability, which promises company growth to an investor. Second, many successful bootstrappers are familiar with the startup process. They've either successfully launched or exited their own startups, or they have been part of a failed startup either as a founder or an employee. As it did with Eric Ries, that experience colors a founder's outlook and adds to his or her skill, leading to better execution plans and an ability to adapt and change tactics as new information is gleaned.

* * *

ALL-TIME BEST ANGEL INVESTORS

Venture capitalists don't usually become widely known celebrities, although a few do achieve the status of celebrity. Others start out as celebrities and become known for their astute investing in various sectors. Ashton Kutcher comes to mind. Still others, such as Warren Buffett, are the stuff of legend for investment prowess and down home wisdom. Angel investors and venture capitalists come from all over and have fascinating and varied backgrounds. Here is a look at some of the all-time top investors.

1. MARC ANDREESSEN

Marc Andreessen has one of the highest profiles among angel investors. Andreessen was one of the founders of Netscape Communications, which introduce the browser that made the Internet accessible to regular people who were not technologists. Netscape Navigator, the browser originally called Mosaic, eventually lost its dominant market position to Microsoft's Internet Explorer, which Microsoft bundled free with Windows. As Navigator's market share dwindled, the company sold it to AOL. Andreessen went on to found a software company, Opsware, which he later sold to Hewlett-Packard. He also founded LoudCloud, a Web hosting service and a company widely credited with starting the current trend toward cloud computing. Andreessen serves on the board of several companies. He is a founding partner in Andreessen Horowitz, one of the most prolific and widely respected Silicon Valley investment firms. Andreessen Horowitz counts Actifio, Airbnb, Asana, Box, Bump, Coho Data, Digital Ocean, Facebook, Fusion IO, Groupon, Jawbone, Oculus, Pindrop, Pinterest, Platfora, Rockmelt, Shapeways, Skype and a host of other prominent technology firms.

Andreessen was born in Iowa in 1971, but he spent his childhood in Wisconsin. He attended the University of Illinois at Urbana-Champaign, where he received a B.S. in Computer Science.

As far as investing philosophy, Andreessen focuses on the people with whom he invests. He has been quoted as saying he looks for the "magic team" – a group with the drive and business sense to make a go of an endeavor. He also concentrates on a firm's burn rate, and he has been known to slam "spendthrift" entrepreneurs who spend wildly on non-essentials. He predicts that these startups will "vaporize" quickly.

2. PETER THIEL

Peter Thiel is the cofounder of PayPal and an early investor in Facebook, so he knows his way around technology. Born in 1967 in Frankfurt, Germany, he was raised in California. Thiel attended Stanford University and Stanford Law School. His current net worth is over $2.2 billion. He is president of Clarium Capital and a managing partner in Founders Fund. He founded Thiel Capital Management in 1996, before starting PayPal. In 2012, he opened Mithril Capital Management.

He has received numerous awards and accolades, including a TechCrunch Crunchie Award as venture Capitalist of the Year in 2013.

Thiel has special interests in technology, including machine intelligence, anti-aging research and seasteading.

His investment philosophy is to invest in smart people who solve difficult problems. His portfolio has included Airbnb, Facebook, Palantir, Spacex, Spotify, Stencenrx, Stripe and ZocDoc.

Recently Thiel's interests have turned strongly to biotechnology and he joined Y Combinator, a startup incubator. He has invested in Cambrian, Emerald Therapeutics and Stem CentRX through Founders Fund.

His investment philosophy is that it's better to have a dominant share in a small market than a small share of a large market. He also enjoys investing in contrarian concepts and hard tech startups. He does not currently invest in social media, websites or IT. He invests based on the people involved, and he believes in the creation of actual value as a basis for investing.

Perhaps the most telling anecdote about Thiel is that he handed unknown and unproven Mark Zuckerberg $500,000 to fund Facebook because he believed in Zuckerberg. He also runs a "20 under 20" project to encourage promising young people to start a company.

3. FRED WILSON

Fred Wilson is a managing partner at Union Square Ventures. The fund has holdings in Disqus, Canvas, HeyZap, Zynga and Twitter, among others, and he is on the board of Etsy.

Wilson was born in New York City in 1961. He was educated at MIT and the Wharton School. He got his investing start by founding

Flatiron Partners, which specialized in follow on investments. In 2004, he started Union Square Investors. While he's not against investing in technology or social media, his criteria include both a large network and engaged users. He also checks out a company's social media presence before committing.

4. NAVAL RAVIKANT

Naval Ravikant is the founder of AngelList, a social media site whose mission is to connect startups with investors and investors with each other. The site makes money by taking a carry on all profits from the syndicate. He is the managing partner at Hit Forge and a well-known investor. He is interested in crypto currencies such as Bitcoin and he heads his personal website with a quote from author Neal Stephenson's book, "Snow Crash." Stephenson is the author of numerous books on cryptography and finance, including "The Cryptonomicon."

Ravikant is the coauthor of "Venture Hacks" and a founder of Genoa Corp, Epinions.com and Vast.com. He advises many startups, including Bix.com, iPivot and XFire. His investments include Twitter, FourSquare, Docverse, Mixer labs, Jambbol, SnapLogic, PlanCast, Stack Overflow, Heyzap and Disqus.

Ravikant spent a great deal of time lobbying legislators to pass the JOBS Act, which enables ordinary people to invest in startups. He organized an e-petition to show support, and has been vocal about helping to open up the tight clique of angel investing and allowing entry to new blood.

Born in India, his family moved to America when he was nine. He lived in New York City. He later attended Dartmouth. He moved to

Silicon Valley during the first wave of dotcom fever, and worked at @HomeNetwork, Intrinsic and eventually he founded Epinions.

5. CHRIS SACCA

Chris Sacca is the founding and managing director of Lowercase Capital. His top angel investments range from Heroku, Facebook, Twitter, Kickstarter, Optimizely, Twilio and Uber. He also has a phenomenal reputation as being an advisor and mentor for many startups across the country.

Chris graduated from Georgetown University Law Center, and worked at Speedera Networks and Google, before getting into major angel investments.

Any list that includes top VC and angel investors has to include Chris.

6. TIM FERRISS

Tim Ferriss was born in 1977 in East Hampton, New York. He graduated from Princeton University with a degree in East Asian Studies and is the author of several books, including "The Four Hour Workweek", "The Four Hour Body", The "Four Hour Chef", and "Escape 9-5, Live Anywhere and Join the New Rich" which was on the New York Times Bestseller list.

His first company was BrainQuicken, which he founded in 2001 to sell nutritional supplements online. He sold it in 2010. He starred in two television series, *Trial By Fire* and *The Tim Ferriss Experiment*. In 2013, he began an audiobook publishing venture, Tim Ferriss Publishing.

Ferriss has been an advisor to Facebook, Twitter, StumbleUpon, Evernote and Uber. He has been an angel investor to such firms as Posterous, DailyBurn, Shopify, Reputation Defender, StumbleUpon, Trippy, Badongo, Foodzie, RescueTime, TaskRabbit, Uber and SimpleGeo. He worked with Shyp on AngelList. His current investments include Soma, Exo Protein Bars, SkyKick, grove labs, WealthFront, Expa, FOBO, Shyp, Zendrive, Sano, Blackjet, Cozy, Artillery, Duolingo, Milk, Unsubscribe.com, Vittana, SimpleGeo and DailyBurn.

Ferriss' influence is widely felt. A blog post can send a book to the top of a bestseller list and his AngelList work with Shyp raised $250,000 in under an hour. As much a media star as he is angel investor, Tim Ferriss was named the seventh most powerful online personality. Inc. Magazine named his blog one of the, "19 Blogs You Should Bookmark Right Now." New Yorker magazine called him "this generation's self-help guru" and compared him to Norman Vincent Peale and Napoleon Hill.

7. ASHTON KUTCHER

Ashton Kutcher is a television star and an astute angel investor. He has invested in such success stories as Skype, Foursquare, Airbnb, and Path. Association with Kutcher gives a boost to companies because of his huge fan base from his acting career. He is also technically knowledgeable and works as a product engineer for Lenovo.

Born in 1978 in Cedar Rapids, Iowa, Kutcher got into modeling and acting at an early age. He starred in That '70s Show and Two and a Half Men on television and in movies such as "Dude, Where's my Car?" He was married to actress Demi Moore and is currently in a relationship with Mila Kunis, his 70s Show costar.

Kutcher is an avid social media user. He was the first person ever to garner more than 1 million followers on Twitter. His blog, A+ (a plus), has 50 million readers and recently raised $3.5 million. He also just started a new venture capital firm, Sound Ventures. Kutcher favors consumer technology and social media investments.

8. MARC BENIOFF

Marc Benioff was born in 1964 in San Francisco California. Benioff graduated from University of Southern California with a B.S. in Business Administration. He is currently believed to be worth in the neighborhood of $3.5 billion as a result of his ownership position in Salesforce.com and other investments. Benioff founded Salesforce.com in 1999.

He worked at Oracle Corporation in sales and marketing for thirteen years before leaving to found Salesforce. He was named one of the fifty smartest people in technology by Fortune magazine in 2010 and one of the Top 50 People in Business. In addition to his business interests, Benioff is a philanthropist who pioneered the 1/1/1 business model in which companies give back to the community. He has also donated hundreds of millions of dollars to UCSF Children's Hospital. He was one of Barron's Top 25 Most Effective Philanthropists in 2010. In February 2014, he started SF Gives to fight poverty in the San Francisco Bay area, kicking it off with a $4 million dollar deposit and raising more than $10 million from other companies. He won the "Best CEO" award at the Crunchies in February, 2015. His company, Salesforce, was named "World's Most Admired Company" for two years in a row. It is ranked as number seven on the list of the World's Best Places to Work.

Along with Mark Andreessen, he is an investor in Leap, the hip San Francisco bus service. He is on the board of CloudWorks, Brigade and Cisco. His investments include Highfive for $32 million of Series B, MileIQ for $12.1 million Series A, Hampton Creek for $90 million Series C, Connect for $10.3 million Series A, Helium for $16 million Series A, MetaMind $8 million in the venture round, 12 labs $765,000 in the seed round and Breezeworks, $5 million in Series A. His special interests include mobile, social and cloud in technology along with health.

Benioff's strategy includes five simple steps.

1. Give back.
2. Do what makes you happy.
3. Put your priorities over your ego.
4. Get out of the stream of business.
5. Pace yourself and look at the long term.

9. JEFF CLAVIER

Jeff Clavier is the managing partner and founder at SoftTech VC. Softtech has closed more than 150 investments since its founding in 2004. Jeff has invested in such success stories as Mint, Kongrgate, Brightroll, Milo, Wilfire, Bleacher Report, Fitbit, EventBrite, Sendgrid, Poshmark, Hired, Postmates and Vungle. His exits have included acquisitions by Intuit, GameStop, eBay, Google, Groupon, Twitter, Facebook, Yahoo and AOL.

Clavier was born in France. After completing his education there, he joined a financial services startup, which was later acquired by Reuters. He moved to Silicon Valley in 2000.

Jeff is in demand as a speaker at conferences and events, as well as a frequent blogger.

10. WARREN BUFFETT – THE ORIGINAL ANGEL

While not considered primarily an angel investor he is considered the, "best living investor." Buffett has investments in virtually every sector. He invests in startups as well as established companies. He prefers to invest in businesses with strong brands and simple business models. He is sometimes called the "Oracle of Omaha" because of his uncanny ability to predict the market. His personal net worth is more than $70 billion, making him the third richest person in the world.

Buffett lives in Omaha Nebraska and was born there in 1930. He was educated at Columbia Business School and the University of Nebraska--Lincoln.

Warren Buffett prefers to invest in existing businesses that meet his criteria. He likes businesses with sustainable business models, and he likes the "razor and the razor blade" business model because of its potential for recurring revenue. Although he invests primarily in existing companies, Buffett's best advice for evaluating investments in startups follows:

1. Invest in a great team.
2. Invest in what you know.
3. Invest in companies with recurring revenue.

These investors have known amazing successes as well as a few failures. Each has a specific philosophy for deciding where to invest their money. Many of them speak about investing in the people, knowing that the right team will find a way to reach their goals. Nearly all express disdain for sloppy management and freewheeling spending. They look for the team at the startups they invest in to be able to execute against a plan, and all have expressed believe in having the right product for the market is important.

The most defining characteristic of the top angel investors is that they know how to:

1. Assess people and a founder's potential for success.
2. Take calculated, early risk after doing their research.
3. Believe in companies with a greater mission.

*   *   *

ALL-STAR, HONORABLE MENTIONS

David Cohen (TechStars)

Scott and Cyan Banister

Jeremie Berrebi (Kima Ventures)

Paul Buchheit (Y Combinator)

David Lee (SV Angel)

Dave McClure (500 Startups)

Joshua Schachter (Former CEO Tasty Labs)

Garry Tan (Y Combinator)

David Tisch (BoxGroup)

Christine Tsai (500 Startups)

TOTAL ADDRESSABLE MARKET ("TAM")

DETERMINING MARKET SIZE FOR A STARTUP AND WHY IT MATTERS

How much is the magic market share number? It depends on how much the investment ask is: you don't need a $20 billion market share to make a profit; niche companies often succeed with much small shares–they just succeed on a smaller scale.

In this section, we'll cover some basic ways you, as the angel investor, can estimate the addressable market share. We'll also talk about how to drill down in a startup's pitch deck, what to look for when the startup talks market share, and how to protect yourself against poor investments with regard to market.

BACK-OF-THE-NAPKIN CONSIDERATIONS

You can do some back-of-the-napkin math to estimate a startup's future share of the market. The more you know about the industry or product type in question, the more accurate your math is likely to be, which is one reason many angel investors choose to operate in fields with which they have experience.

For a solid estimate of TAM, you'll need five pieces of information.

1. ## THE TOTAL POPULATION OF POTENTIAL USERS

   This may be a geographical consideration: There are 100,000 people in the city where a restaurant wants to launch. More likely, this is a more abstract number, since the majority of angel investors are opting for opportunities in Internet, software, e-commerce and other virtual spaces. A total possible population for a mobile app launching in the United States, for example, might be up to 182 million people in 2015, according to Statista's numbers on smartphone users in the nation. The site also forecasts smartphone user population to grow to 220 million in 2018.

2. ## DEFINITION OF THE MARKET SEGMENT AND ESTIMATED PERCENT OF TARGET CUSTOMERS.

   Your product limits the percent of your market segment. Angel investors should ask: Who is this product for? Who is likely to want, need, and purchase this product? Are people already buying similar products, and if so, who are those people?

   Consider an app that acts as a virtual storybook for babies. The obvious market for such an app would be new parents with smartphones. There are a total of 318 million people in the US; if 182 million have smartphones, then approximately 57 percent of the population has a smartphone. There are around 4 million babies born each year—applying some dirty math, we can assume that 57 percent, or around 2.28 million, of those babies have at least one parent with a smartphone. That's the target audience for our app.

This back-of-the-napkin math is rough: the population numbers used to arrive at the above percentages counted young children and older individuals, which are less likely to own smartphones. Child-bearing parents are more likely to own the devices, which means the target audience could be as high as 3 million. For ease of estimation, let's assume 2.5 million. Out of 182 million smartphone users, that's approximately 1.4 percent.

3. **HOW MANY OF THE PRODUCTS WILL BE PURCHASED AT A TIME?**

   If a company is selling software through licenses, businesses can purchase multiple instances of the product. Someone with a hot new cupcake recipe is going to sell in multiples as well; our baby app, however, is most likely to sell once to each user.

4. **HOW OFTEN WILL THE PRODUCT BE PURCHASED?**

   Does the product lend itself to repeat purchase? Is it a commodity or necessity that will be used up, so consumers must refill or restock? At first glance, a software product is going to be purchased once for each user, but what about new versions and upgrades? Are those free, or monetized?

5. **WHAT IS THE INTENDED SELLING PRICE OF THE PRODUCT?**

   We'll look at two possibilities with our baby app example. First, the startup may charge for its app. Given app store prices, and depending on how much functionality the startup is going to provide in its app, price might range from 99 cents to $7.99. For the example, assume the startup charges $2.99.

The other possibility is that that startup offers the app free to users, but plans to monetize it through ads, in-app purchases, or professional relationships. In this case, the angel investor needs to see the startup's projections on how much per user the app might generate. For our example, let's assume the startup estimates $5 in revenue per user, per year.

POSSIBLE MARKET SHARE FORMULA

The basic market share formula multiplies all of the data points above. So, for our baby app, basing market share solely on the purchase price of $2.99, maximum market share would be:

*182 million smartphone users * 1.4 percent target audience * 1 purchase at a time * 1 purchase (no repeats) * $2.99*

The *maximum* potential market share would be approximately $7,618,520 per year.

DRILLING DOWN: THE STARTUP'S PITCH DECK

That $7.6 million market share number for our imaginary baby app is unrealistic-but some startups are optimistic enough to publish such numbers in their pitch deck. No matter how great the product and timing is, you aren't going to get 100 percent to buy-in from your potential market-and remember, the math we did to get to $7.6 million was all estimates and quick Internet statistics searches. You have to assume the numbers are off a bit.

Startups tend to make sweeping statements about market targets in their pitch deck. They might state, "We're targeting 1 percent of a $20 billion market by 2022." As the angel investor, you have to do your own math, as shown above, to vet the total market claim, and then you have to evaluate whether you think the startup is on point with their target. How likely is the 1 percent goal? At Angel Kings, we like to see startups that provide more specific market definitions, even if that reduces opportunities to $500 million instead of $20 billion.

IS THE STARTUP'S PLAN BACKED BY DATA?

Startups with specific market definitions have some data to back up claims; as the angel investor, you should vet that data against your own research or knowledge of the market. The statistics we used to create our assumptions for the baby app market share are an example of data that anyone can vet. Startups should source such information, but a quick online search turns up information too. You should also download the app yourself, try it out, and see if people would care enough to pay for it.

It's harder to tack down the percent of potential market a startup hopes to obtain. Ask how the startup came up with that percent. Did they conduct market surveys? Are they basing the data on comparable products? The startup launching our imaginary baby app might have polled 500 new mothers and mothers-to-be to find out if they would be interested in purchasing an app, and then applied that data to the overall market to determine that 20 percent of possible consumers would make a purchase.

Despite how much data the startup presents, you as the angel investor have to make a judgment call. Do you buy in to the market assumptions the startup makes? Do you think they are probably too optimistic? Even if the startup's assumptions are too optimistic, does the market share potential *you* see make the investment worthy?

TOMORROW'S MARKET, NOT TODAY'S

As an investor, you are worried more about tomorrow's market than today's market. Understanding today's market lets you make evaluations of future market potential. In some industries, you can also use benchmarks, expert guidance on industry trends, and forecasts to estimate future market behavior. With our baby app example, an investor might use the estimated smartphone user growth from several statistical sites to gauge how much the potential market will grow.

PRIMARY DEMAND VERSUS SECONDARY DEMAND

Numbers and data are important, but investors must also understand the difference between primary and secondary demands. Primary demand references the market size for a specific product or product category–baby apps, cupcakes, virtual hard drives, and point-of-sale software, for example.

Secondary demand refers to the size of the market for a brand.

When dealing with early-stage startups in most industries, angel investors are concerned with primary demand because fledgling startups often tout a single product idea. While concentrating on primary demand, keep secondary demand in mind as it plays a role in growth potential. What are the brand goals and plans for the startup? Will the startup pull its audience through branding more so than product, and does the startup plan to branch out with products that could capture greater shares of the market in the future?

In a few niche industries, secondary demand is the primary evaluation point. This might be true when evaluating biotech or social startups, for example, where audience buy-in to an idea is much more important than the product itself.

SETTING LIMITATIONS AS AN ANGEL INVESTOR

You know the saying about going to the grocery store hungry or without a list? Chances are, you walk out spending more than you wanted and with items you don't need. As an angel investor, enter evaluation phases with limitations in mind to avoid getting caught up with the people and idea and failing to see the potential market pitfalls.

Some angel investors won't consider a startup that doesn't have a potential minimum market share of $500 million or more. Others won't invest in a company where growth projections can't be reasonably estimated at 10 percent a year or more. You shouldn't set targets and ranges like this.

Even more important than arbitrary limitations is your own awareness of earning potential. No investment is 100 percent safe, but by calculating market share, the angel investor has a better understanding of the type of returns that can be expected if the startup is successful.

THE TOP 5 SOFTWARE STARTUPS

In 2014, The Economist noted that software startups were exploding across the world; venture capitalist Marc Andreessen went so far as to say, "Software is eating the world."

Though timing as of 2015 is somewhat favorable for any software startup founder with a strong product and plan, not every fledgling software company makes it. Many don't even make it to the seed stage of investing, partly because the ample competition in the niche makes it more difficult to attract investors. In this section, we'll cover some recent hot software startups in a variety of stages and discuss some reasons they stand out from the global crowd.

1. APTTUS - INTEGRATING WITH SALESFORCE.COM

Product is definitely the deciding factor that's landing this hot software startup millions every time it steps up to the pitching mound. In early 2015, Apttus scored $41 million in funds as part of a Series B investment round, with much of the funding coming from Salesforce Ventures, an investing arm of Salesforce.com.

Apttus provides a number of solutions targeted primarily at e-commerce companies. Its first, and powerhouse, product is Quote-to-Cash, a platform that makes it easier for companies to move efficiently through revenue cycle and drive sustainable cash growth. Interestingly, Quote-to-Cash's entire product line, as well as other solutions from this startup, is that the entire Apttus product line is based on Salesforce.com. In effect, Apttus piggybacks the extremely successful ERP solution with a number of integrations that improve experience for businesses using Salesforce.com.

Aligning its products with Saleforce.com gives Apttus at least two major benefits as a startup. One thing we like to see with a startup is that its product idea isn't first to market–a product that builds successfully on something else is much more likely to succeed. It's also more likely to see success faster than a ground–up venture, and faster success means faster time to value for an investor. By basing its product on the existing Salesforce platform, Apttus doesn't have to grow an audience from scratch. And, if you're going to tie yourself to another software company, why not pick one of the most successful? Salesforce itself grew 33 percent from 2013 to 2014, and was the fasted growing software company at the time.

The second reason the Salesforce.com connection makes Apttus a strong software startup is that it provides for an excellent chance at a future acquisition. At Angel Kings, we never invest in any startup that doesn't have an exit strategy, and linking arms with a company that is growing massively each year *and* has a history of generous acquisition purchases is about as good as any strategy we've seen.

Previous companies acquired by Salesforce.com include Buddy Media for $745 million in 2012, Radian6 for $326 million in 2011, and Exact Target for $2.5 billion in June 2013. As of early 2015, however, Salesforce.com appeared happy to invest in a growing Apttus rather than acquire it outright; in fact, according to Apptus, Safesforce.com's contribution to the startup's Series B funding is the highest investment amount from Salesforce.com that wasn't part of an acquisition.

Apptus also began as a traditional bootstrap, which is rare for software startups these days. Lean management during the first seven years meant slow growth, but once the company did come to investors, it had a strong project and a plan with many kinks worked out. Current CEO Kirk Krappe says that primary goals are to continue building a great company, but he acknowledges what many investors seem to be banking on: Apptus is positioned well for an IPO or sale in the future.

2. CIPHERCLOUD - COMPETING WITH LEGACY SOLUTIONS

As of 2015, CipherCloud has around five years and $80 million in investments under its belt, and even the internal team couldn't provide a specific reason for attracting $50 million in Series B funding in an investment round in 2014. We're not surprised this startup has been successful so far-it punches most of the buttons on the Angel Kings investment checklist, including strong people, product, and timing.

The founder behind CipherCloud is Pravin Kothar. Kothar has plenty of experience in the technology and security space, and he's also got a history of launching successful startups. He was the founding Vice President of Engineering for ArcSight, which launched in 2000 and was acquired by Hewlett-Packard in 2010. Kothar was also involved with startup Agiliance, which garnered $24 million in investments from 2005 to 2015 and boasted an impressive growth rate of 4,909 percent from 2007 to 2010.

An experienced and established founder is one that investors can get behind, but he also needs a marketable product. CipherCloud entered the market at a time when cloud-computing itself was becoming a mainstream service, but users were still anxious about security concerns. With security an ever growing concern-and cloud computing an ever growing requirement among global organizations looking for cost-savings and efficiencies–CipherCloud's service is positioned to meet demands and psychological needs for an enormous market. No company wants to feel vulnerable to hackers, particularly those in sensitive niches. In fact, CipherCloud's first four years netted them 3 million users–including top banks, healthcare organizations, and government agencies.

CipherCloud doesn't offer a new solution; many companies in the second decade of the 21st century are bringing cloud security solutions to market. What CipherCloud does offer is out-of-the-box solutions that integrate with some of the biggest cloud software solutions on the market. The company offers security for Salesforce.com, Office 365, and Box, among others. Like Apttus, this smart startup used the tailcoats of larger organizations to get up to speed. Now that it's caught the eye of investors, CipherCloud intends to develop additional products and move into new markets.

3. **SLIDEMAIL – EMAIL STARTUP PITTED AGAINST GMAIL GOLIATH**

SlideMail is an exciting startup that's newer than the two previously mentioned. The fledgling company managed to land $120,000 in seed investments through Y Combinator in mid-2014. What makes SlideMail hot is the way it takes a space that's been mined by giants such as Yahoo, Gmail, and Hotmail and makes it new again with a little bit of intelligence and one feature that may make SlideMail technology one of the big tech acquisitions of the future.

SlideMail is an app that helps you handle email interactions. The app does what a lot of the browser-based email applications attempt to do, but SlideMail's intuitive programming does it better. Much of the technology is based on natural language programming, which lets SlideMail interpret simple phrases within email as a human does. If an email contains phrasing about dinner tomorrow night, SlideMail makes a note within the app. As times approach, the mail program brings appointment- or time-based emails to the surface, ensuring users don't miss time-based messages in the hustle of daily communications.

SlideMail uses similar logic programming to adapt to user behavior. If you archive email from a certain person to the same folder repeatedly, SlideMail might prompt you to set up automatic archiving. It also suggests email actions in an intelligent fashion, which lets users move through over-burdened inboxes more efficiently.

These functions may sound familiar to users of existing email programs. Outlook and Gmail both have some functionality that can recognize times and dates, for example, and users can set up rule sets in both programs to automatically handle email. With SlideMail, however, the app suggests these things based on actual behavior so users don't have to come up with a list of behaviors on their own. Products that meet existing needs in a more efficient or convenient manner are often successful, which is why SlideMail would score well on Angel Kings' product checklist.

Even more than convenience, SlideMail's privacy option gives it an edge. With increasing news stories about the eternal nature of online data-and a growing number of scandals involving hacked or leaked emails-users are growing more wary of email use. According to SlideMail, however, all data is stored within your instance of the application rather than on third-party servers. By deleting the app, you delete all information related to your email account. It's not perfect privacy, but it is more than most mobile email users get.

SlideMail hasn't hit its stride with marketing. Users and tech gurus have pointed out a number of branding and marketing options for the startup, however. The convenience and time-management features will resonate with college-aged audiences, particularly those who are always willing to step away from mainstream applications such as Gmail. Another market might be older users, who still rely on Yahoo or other sites for email and would like a robust mobile email program–SlideMail works with existing accounts through POP access.

4. MIXPANEL – EQUIPPING OTHER STARTUPS

Mixpanel topped CNN's annual list of startups to bet on in 2015, and investors have agreed with that evaluation for about five years. The startup has received a total of $77 million in investments over the course of four rounds and five years. The latest round of investing was a Series B round in December 2014, which landed the startup $65 million of its total–all from a single investor. At the time, Mixpanel cofounder Suhail Doshi stated the startup was valued at $865 million–a huge step up from its Y Combinator roots in 2009.

So, what launched Mixpanel to the top of the hot software list in half a decade? The product, which is a serious analytics program, had a lot to do with the company's success. In fact, the program meets consumer needs so well that all the startups seem to be using it. According to a report in 2012, Andreessen Horowitz found that Mixpanel was a favorite among growing companies, which is why it invested in one of the first rounds. The firm just happened to be the investor that returned two years later for the impressive Series B funding mentioned above.

Doshi credits some of Mixpanel's success with an intelligent early move by the company. While Mixpanel analytics do work on websites, the startup originally concentrated on mobile. Doshi said it was a big bet, but with numerous bigger analytic players slow to respond to growing needs for mobile data, Mixpanel's decision positioned it to become what Doshi calls the "king of mobile analytics." According to numerous industry reporters, it's not posturing or marketing language on Doshi's part-despite being a young company with little more than 100 employees, Mixpanel is the name that comes up most when discussing mobile analytics.

Timing, then, was on Mixpanel's side. The startup also worked from the bottom up within the industry. The majority of the company's clients were startups, too, which made for a lot of turnover, but allowed Mixpanel to build quickly on previous successes and scale to larger clients over time.

5. SLACK - THE MESSAGING APP THAT COULD

With a CEO whose credentials include cofounding popular photo-site Flickr, which sold to Yahoo for $25 million in 2005, it's not surprising that Slack has seen some success. What's surprising is *how much* success the messaging and chatroom app has seen: In nine months, the startup moved from launch phase to a $1 billion valuation.

Even before launching in 2014, the startup was laying down a road to success. Since its first seed round in 2009, the startup has raised $180 million in investments, and by 2015, it became one of the fastest growing business-to-business applications in history with a half million active users and counting.

The application offers coworkers a quick way to communicate about projects, but it's more than a chat room or forum. Slack lets users create and manage channels to segregate content, upload documents into libraries, search posted content for answers, and participate in private chats or direct messaging. The app houses all the functions required for daily business communication, making it a favorite among small teams, freelancers, and workforces in disparate locations.

PEOPLE, PRODUCTS, EXECUTION, AND TIMING

Most of the startups are strong in all four areas, but all of them hit it out of the ballpark with products and timing. While software in general is timely now, these few startups illustrate the point that winning angel investments involve companies that have strong founders with a great idea, a well-thought out plan, and an understanding of when to hit the market.

FIVE WAYS TO VALUE A STARTUP

We'll cover five different methods for valuing startups, concentrating on valuing early startups and those that are in pre-revenue stages.

1. THE BERKUS METHOD

This method, which is used and defined by active angel investor David Berkus, involves a lot of estimation. The reason Berkus came up with the method is that he personally found that lengthy revenue forecasts rarely turned out to be accurate. According to Berkus, only 1 in 20 startups hit revenue forecasts, so he opted for an "eyeball" approach using a few key elements. The method applies best to technology companies, but can be applied to other products.

First, Berkus says that investors should believe the company has a potential to hit $20 million or more in revenues by the 5th year of operation. Then, he applies a scale to five components of a startup, rating each at up to $500,000. The components are:

- The startup has a sound idea–a product that provides a basic value with acceptable product risk
- There is a prototype, which reduces technology risks
- The startup has or plans for a quality management team to reduce risks in execution
- Strategic relationships are already in place, reducing risks for competition and market

- Product rollout and sales plans exist (not applicable to all pre-revenue startups)

Using the method, the highest valuation would be $2.5 million; a pre-revenue startup could only score $2 million. This is a very back-of-the-envelope method, but it can be a useful tool for angel investors evaluating startups in the earliest of stages.

Some disadvantages do exist with the Berkus Method, however, illustrating the point that no type of data should be considered in a vacuum. For example, this method doesn't consider market or competitive environment, which may be of importance in many situations.

2. COMPARABLE TRANSACTIONS ("MARKET COMPS") METHOD

A comparable transaction is a common method used to value companies that are for sale, but it can also be used when considering startups. The basic principle is similar to the idea of valuing real estate based on what a comparable home on the street sold for recently, except investors have to take into account multiples of some kind because the new social media startup isn't going to have revenues and values equal to a company such as Facebook.

One comparable method calculation involves the EV/Sales ratio. The ratio is defined as the enterprise value of a company divided by its annual sales, or:

$$\frac{\textit{Market capitalization} + \textit{Debt} + \textit{Preferred shares} - \textit{Cash and cash equivalents}}{\textit{Annual Sales}}$$

You have to make sure you select one or more appropriate comparables – select companies from the same niche or industry that are as similar in market and solution to the startup as possible. When available, use startups from similar geography.

For example, you might have a startup with current annual revenues of $2 million. You could review a second company, which just sold for $50 million with annual revenues of $15 million, which is an EV/Sales ratio of about 3.3. Applying that ratio to your similar startup gives it a value of $2 million x 3.3, or $6.6. For a better chance at accuracy, you'd want to consider multiple comparables and value the startup at an average or median number.

The benefits of using a comparable approach is that you can pull information about existing companies from easily accessible data, and the calculations are simple and easy to communicate. Comparables also provide investors with benchmarks for valuations. Because actual data is used, however, the valuation could be influenced by temporary market factors that are not relevant to the startup being reviewed. It can also be difficult to find enough relevant comparable companies to get a good baseline for more accurate valuations. Investors can complete comparables valuations on their own, but some complex valuations may require the assistance of accounting professionals.

3. RISK FACTOR SUMMATION METHOD

Like the Berkus Method, the Risk Factor Summation Method is a bit back-of-the-napkin. It does take more factors into account, however, and applies to a broader selection of startups. The method considers 12 categories and applies a simple scale to each. The scale is:

- ++ (excellent performance)

- \+ (good performance)
- 0 (neutral performance)
- \- (poor performance)
- -- (excessively poor performance)

The investor adds or subtracts monetary value based on the rating for each category as follows:

- ++ (add $500,000)
- \+ (add $250,000)
- 0 (no change)
- \- (subtract $250,000)
- -- (subtract $500,000)

The 12 categories graded are:

1. Management
2. Stage of the business
3. Legislation/political risk
4. Manufacturing risk
5. Sales and marketing risk
6. Funding/capital raising risk
7. Competition risk
8. Technology risk
9. Litigation risk
10. International risk
11. Reputation risk
12. Potential lucrative exit

Let's look at how an investor might have used this method to value one of the hot software startups from a previous section: Apttus.

Remember, this valuation has nothing to do with the company's current value, but might have been what an investor used before Apttus generated revenue.

1. **Management.** In very early stages, investors might need to rate management based on the founder and plan. A case could be made for rating Apttus 0, +, or ++ at that stage, so let's use the middle rating and add $250k.
2. **Stage of the business**. As we're discussing a very early startup, 0.
3. **Legislation/political risk**. Apttus offers a service with little to know political risk, so ++ and $500k.
4. **Manufacturing risk**. Apttus products are software, which means no manufacturing risk, so ++ and $500k.
5. **Sales and marketing risk.** By linking up with Salesforce.com, Apttus minimizes its sales and marketing risks. Likely ratings might be + or ++; for this example, we'll use ++ and $500k.
6. **Funding/capital raising risk**. Investors might look at Salesforce.com's history of funding and give Apttus a + rating solely on the likelihood of the larger software company chiming in with funds at some point, so $250k.
7. **Competition risk.** The e-commerce sector is rife with competition, so an investor might get conservative here and rate Apttus --, for minus $500k.
8. **Technology risk.** Since Apttus planned to base its product on another platform, technology risks get at least -, or minus $250k.
9. **Litigation risk.** This is tricky, as everything comes with litigation risks. Simply because the software deals with money matters, we might give it -, so subtract $250k.
10. **International risk.** Probably minimal to none, so + for $250k.
11. **Reputation risk.** While Apttus itself doesn't seem to have a large reputation risk, aligning itself with another company so closely does reduce its control, so a rating might be 0.

12. **Potential lucrative exit.** We covered in the hot startup section that Apttus has a potential for sale to Salesforce.com, so ++ for $500k.

From these metrics, we come up with a valuation of $1.75 million for the fledging Apttus startup. Note that the example provided above used basic information to rate each element–the more information you have about a startup, the better you can rate and value it using this method. Like the Berkus Method, this is a tool for investors to use in evaluating a startup, and not likely to be a tool used to value a company during a purchase transaction.

4. DISCOUNTED CASH FLOW ("DCF") METHOD

Discounted Cash Flow valuations are the most complex of the five methods we're covering in this section and involve a series of formulas that take into account cash flow during a certain period and a discount rate applied based on the risks of the cash flow. The benefit of DCF is that it can be extremely accurate. The disadvantage of DCF is that a slight miscue on projections can throw the valuation off by millions.

DCF is particularly difficult to apply to early startups, which have little to no historic cash flow data to rely on. Established companies at least have past trends that can be built on to project future cash flow, but startups base that information on a lot of conjecture and guesswork. Some founders are better at others in that guesswork, and many can present data to back up projections, but it's safe to assume that a founder is going to err on the side of optimism when presenting his or her financials to investors.

Even with established companies and plenty of data, DCF valuations can go wrong. Pim Keulen of Seeking Alpha took a look at a DCF valuation of Nike in early 2015. Keulen cites an article by another Seeking Alpha author, Andrew Labutka. Labutka uses the DCF method to calculate a value for Nike of $107 per share, which was over the share price of $95.03 at the time. Keulen contended that Labutka made a few mistakes in his DCF analysis, including using incorrect number of shares outstanding and FCF numbers. By Keulen's calculations, Nike valuation would be between $60.06 and $63.22 per share—much lower than the company's stock price at the time.

The Nike example is a good one, because it illustrates that, even with a well-known, well-published company and DCF math, valuations can range widely. It also shows that even financial professionals using DCF can make small mistakes that skew final numbers by a great deal. DCF works much better with public companies vs. private companies.

5. ASSET-BASED VALUATION METHOD

Asset-based valuation is also known as book value valuation. Out of all the methods described in this section, asset-based valuation may provide the easiest way for investors to get a hard look at what a startup is currently worth in real value, but the number garnered through this approach isn't always helpful for angel investors evaluating a new opportunity.

In asset valuation, the original cost of all assets is adjusted by impairment costs and depreciation. The total physical asset values are added to any balance sheet values–cash on hand, accounts receivables, and other positive balance sheet items. Liabilities–outstanding debts or

---

· Keulen, Pim. *Don't Get Fooled By This DCF Valuation: Nike is Overvalued, not Undervalued.* http://seekingalpha.com/article/2799025-dont-get-fooled-by-this-dcf-valuation-nike-is-overvalued-not-undervalued. Jan 5 2015; 2027 ET.

expenses–are subtracted from the total to get the asset-based valuation.

The problem with this method in valuing startups should be obvious: investors aren't betting on the current state of the startup, but on the future state. Asset-based valuation fails to take into account the intrinsic value of ideas or the future success of the product. Investors *can* apply asset-based valuations to projected assets, liabilities, and cash flow, but you run into the same possible issues as with DCF models.

OVERVALUED STARTUPS: IS SNAPCHAT OVERVALUED?

Angel investors evaluating opportunities should never rely on a single valuation method. Employing one or more of the five methods above–or other industry methods–gives you a broader idea of whether a startup is going to return value. And remember, even when numerous industry experts are involved, consensus on valuation isn't likely.

In December 2014, Snapchat – one of our top Mobile to Consumer apps – was valued between $10 billion and $20 billion. Many experts chimed in on this valuation, saying that Snapchat was overvalued because it generated almost no revenue. Others compared the app to Twitter, stating that Twitter had about 2.7 times the users Snapchat did and was valued at $23 billion; using quick and dirty comparative math, the users said Snapchat was not too overvalued at the $10 billion mark.

Whatever the online community has to say, Snapchat was successfully raking in investors at the time. Someone, somewhere, was using a valuation and evaluation method that made the startup attractive.

HOW WE VALUE STARTUPS AT ANGEL KINGS

We base our entire valuation on the four parts of our formula—people, product, execution, timing—and we supplement this with our financial analysis. The best method would be to pick one of the above methods and then use the Angel Kings' scoring formula as described on our website, http://AngelKings.com in order to determine startup valuations.

***

THE TOP 3 SECTORS TO INVEST IN BY 2020

Many angel investors have favorite sectors, and some sectors lend themselves to angel investing. Software or Internet services require less capital than manufacturing startups, for example, which means large venture capitalists aren't always required for seed and series rounds. Single founders or co-founders are also more likely to approach angel investors, and many of those individuals are currently working in tech-based fields. Given those observations–and the current global market—it's not surprising that two of our three hottest sectors are tech based: cybersecurity and big data. The third sector that's poised for prime growth through 2020 is biotechnology.

CYBERSECURITY (VISIT ANGELKINGS.COM)

Cybersecurity refers to the software, hardware, and services that protect networks, computers, and data. Protection may be any destruction, access, or change that is unauthorized by the user or is unintentional. The bulk of what we refer to as cybersecurity concentrates on protecting against cyber threats–hackers, malware, and criminals that would vandalize or appropriate data or networks for illicit use. Other cybersecurity products might protect against outages or disaster scenarios.

WHAT MAKES CYBERSECURITY ATTRACTIVE TO INVESTORS?

As of early 2015, Angel.co lists 127 cybersecurity startups with an average valuation of $4.7 million. Such startups are attractive to investors for a variety of reasons, not the least of which is a general high potential for IPO and acquisition events for any small company in the industry. A startup with a good idea draws attention from bigger companies, and experts believe the cybersecurity market will continue to be dominated by big players such as Dell. That doesn't alter the value of smaller companies–Aaref Hilaly, a partner at investment firm Sequoia Capital, says that larger organizations rely on startups for major innovation across the technical space.

Another reason cybersecurity startups make good investments is that the best companies tend to scale up quickly. Tech firms in general are experts at building on existing technology; they rarely start from scratch, letting then bring viable products to market in short time spans. Because those products tend to meet an urgent psychological and actual need for users, an apt marketing campaign or integration is often all it takes for good products to find sales success.

Investors in cybersecurity can also be assured of a continued and growing need for these types of products. Startups that show an understanding of the market are likely to be able to navigate future needs to tweak or develop products for continued viability. Cybersecurity startups tend to be launched by individuals with high-level technology degrees, backgrounds with large tech companies or security agencies, and, often, some background in startup management. As these companies hit IPO and acquisition stages early on, it leaves founders available to launch new products–and provides angel investors with experienced people to invest in.

WHAT ARE SOME COMPANIES POISED TO THRIVE IN THIS SECTOR?

Dozens of startups are positioned for strong growth in cybersecurity over the next few years, and new companies hit investment rounds every month. One company poised to thrive is CipherCloud, which we covered in our section on the hottest software startups. Another startup poised for success in the cloud security arena is SkyHigh Networks.

Founder Rajiv Gupta says that part of SkyHigh Networks' success is that it collaborates with larger security companies rather than competing with them. In launching SkyHigh Networks, Gupta and his cofounders looked for the hole in cloud security they could plug. Rather than developing another solution simply to protect cloud networks or data, Gupta and his team addressed the psychological needs of companies directly. Specifically, SkyHigh Networks offers technology that lets companies analyze cloud-based security risks, monitor and manage employee cloud behaviors, and encrypt data stored on the cloud. The company secured $66.5 million in investments over three rounds since 2012.

Other companies to watch in this sector include Shape Security, Palo Alto Networks, Recorded Future, LaunchKey, and 405 Labs.

WHAT CATALYSTS MAKE THIS SECTOR LIKELY TO TAKE OFF?

Cybersecurity has already taken off, and rapidly evolving technology keeps the floor swept for new startups and success. Growing sophistication among hackers and cyber criminals mean legit operations have to work even harder to keep up, and there's always a new threat or security need to be addressed. Since companies can't cut networks and

Internet from their processes, cybersecurity products will continue to be a major need.

Every five years or so, the industry sees a major architectural shift in how businesses and people use computers and technology. Recent shifts have been to cloud and mobile, and experts are expecting future shifts to include genetics, biotech integrations with computers, and increasing virtual environments. Each shift drives a new wave of startup and investing opportunities.

The globalization of economies and businesses also drives cybersecurity. Users are more connected than ever before, but laws, cultures, and infrastructures are not. Businesses that can't rely on global governments to protect virtual assets are willing to pay for services and products that will.

WHAT ARE THE RISKS FOR STARTUPS AND INVESTORS IN THIS SECTOR?

As strong as the industry is, cybersecurity investments are not without risks. The sheer number of founders running in the industry's direction makes saturation and competition a risk, though a number of the illustrations used throughout our book demonstrate that excellent ideas and execution can triumph in the face of robust competition. Another risk for cybersecurity startups is the possibility of quick obsolescence as technology evolves so rapidly. For angel investors, evaluating the people behind the product can help determine whether founders will be able to adapt to the market when necessary.

BIOTECH AND RESEARCH

"Biotech", or biotechnology, includes the field of all startups that are biology-based technology companies. Some types of companies in the field include pharmaceutical companies, R&D firms with a biological focus, and equipment and tech firms servicing research labs and scientists. The combined purpose of most of these companies is to develop knowledge, technology, and products that fight diseases or provide solutions for other global issues such as hunger or resource scarcity.

WHAT MAKES BIOTECH AND RESEARCH ATTRACTIVE TO INVESTORS?

With 2,560 companies and an average valuation of $5 million on Angel.co's biotechnology startup list, there are plenty of opportunities for investors in this space. As with cybersecurity, biotech startups offer a good chance at IPO action. In 2013, the industry saw more IPOs overall than it had for the past 13 years. While the industry is more volatile overall than other options, no one will argue that biotech will continue to be relevant through 2020, and many biotech firms offer long-term investment opportunities that can balance out the portfolios of angel investors with a lot of hot-burning software investments.

WHAT ARE SOME COMPANIES POISED TO THRIVE IN THIS SECTOR?

A number of hot startups in biotech are covered in chapter 6, including Counsyl, Science Exchange, Transcriptic, Benchling, and Cambrian Genomics. Companies to watch that are crossing pharmaceutical and biotech spaces include Portola Pharmaceuticals, Tear Glucose Research, Dual Therapeutics, and Prosena Holdings.

One interesting startup poised for ongoing success in biotech is 23andMe. Founded in 2006, the startup is one that has managed to thrive sans IPO for almost a decade. Since 2009, the startup has garnered over $111 million in funding, including a 2014 National Institute of Health grant.

23andMe differentiates itself from other biotech startups in a number of ways, one being that its launch and current flagship product would probably not be considered a necessity for many people. The company offers a mail order DNA kit that lets any consumer swab the inside of their mouth and return the saliva sample for analysis. The consumer can then access a detailed report about their DNA, including ancestry breakdowns. Users can opt in to databases to find long-lost relatives across the world and build family trees using DNA connections.

The product is compelling on many levels for consumers, who are living in a technologically connected world. As family structures evolve, many individuals are wondering where they come from–and 23andMe gives them that knowledge at an affordable rate and through a process that is convenient. However, 23andMe has faced serious regulatory hurdles with the FDA, who stated that by providing reports that detail a consumer's vulnerability to certain diseases, 23andMe is considered a medical device and must comply with FDA regulations.[*]

What makes 23andMe a likely long-term investment opportunity and player in biotech isn't just the consumer-friendly product, though. The company has execution plans that go beyond basic family-tree research. First, it leverages all the DNA it gathers to fuel genetic studies. Consumers can opt into research programs, and each sample offers additional information in more than 230 studies. Second, 23andMe has plans to enter

---

[*] FDA. In Vitro Diagnostics and Radioactive Health. *23andMe, Inc. 11/22/13.Inspections, Compliance, Enforcement and Criminal Investigations.* Alberto Gutierrez, 22 Nov. 2013. Web. 29 Apr. 2015.

health-related markets. It already provides DNA-based health reports to consumers in Canada and is awaiting FDA approval in the United States to do the same.

WHAT CATALYSTS MAKE THIS SECTOR LIKELY TO TAKE OFF?

Health concerns, resource needs, reemerging and new diseases, and growing regulation in biological and healthcare fields are all fueling biotech growth and are likely to do so through 2020. New technologies are also driving research and development in fields such as disease treatment, vaccines, and genetics. Thanks to technologies such as nanospectroscopy, researchers can view the world of viruses, proteins, and genes like never before, and those technologies are only improving. A desire to fix global issues—as well as a certain level of consumer fear about such issues—will make biotech a big business for decades.

WHAT ARE THE RISKS FOR STARTUPS AND INVESTORS IN THIS SECTOR?

Biotech hit hard in 2013, but the industry demonstrated an overall poor performance in 2014, so it's not without risks for investors. In fact, the volatility of the industry is a primary risk. Investors adverse to moderate or greater risk may not find biotech is right for them.

Another risk common to biotech startups is a lengthy time to value. Many biotech startups are founded on a research discovery or idea—unlike 23andMe, they don't yet offer a specific product or monetization option. Angel investors working with idea or research-based startups should always tread lightly in early stages.

BIG DATA

The data industry covers a wide range of startups, from those that provide data analysis software to cloud storage providers. Any company developing products and services that make it easier to move, store, secure, analyze, or access data would fall into this category.

WHAT MAKES DATA STARTUPS ATTRACTIVE TO INVESTORS?

Angel.co lists 2,435 big data startups, 1,187 big data analytics startups, and 290 data mining startups; in each listing, average startup valuation was over $4 million. With hundreds of successful data startups, investors can pick from diverse solutions that are meeting needs across every single industry on the market. So much data exists that companies can't keep up with analytical needs. According to Forrester Research, businesses estimate using only around 12 percent of data that's available to them-tools that let companies capture more of the data pie without expending extra resources are sure to find favor among business consumers, which is a strong point for investors.

WHAT ARE SOME COMPANIES POISED TO THRIVE IN THIS SECTOR?

In our section on the hottest software startups, we covered Mixpanel, a data startup that everyone seems to agree is poised for big things. Other data startups poised to thrive in upcoming years include MuSigma, Domo, Cloudera, Kaggle, Precog, and CrowdFlower.

Data is an interesting sector for investors because you don't have to stay within the business and software scope. A number of startups are bringing mobile-to-consumer applications into the data space, and with so many consumers seeking to organize and order their lives, these companies are seeing success. One interesting startup, which has garnered $8 million in funding since 2010, is Yummly. The startup piggybacks preference-based delivery ideas offered by products such as Netflix and Pandora, but applies those ideas to food.

Yummly uses data-both intrinsic and personal-about food and food preferences to deliver recipes and food recommendations via its website and app. The startup has even teamed up with another of our favorite companies-Instacart. Users can generate grocery lists based on Yummly data and recipes, and then order those items through Instacart's one-hour grocery delivery service.

While it's not in the business sector, Yummly does illustrate a characteristic angel investors should look for when investing in data companies. Data alone doesn't do much, so startups need a plan for integrating their product with other companies, software, or industries.

WHAT CATALYSTS MAKE THIS SECTOR LIKELY TO TAKE OFF?

According to Rob Bearden of Hortonworks, data volumes at the enterprise level are trending to grow 50 times year-over-year through 2020. With 85 percent of that data coming from sources such as mobile, machine-generation, and social networks, analytic challenges are expected to plague companies over the next few decades. Those challenges fuel the market for unique products that offer data solutions. With IT professionals in all industries struggling to keep up with hardware and

---

* "A SIEM Is Not Enough: Moving to a Complete Cyber Security Solution." *Big Data Cyber Analytics*. N.p., 20 Apr. 2015. Web. 29 Apr. 2015. http://www.ikanow.com/a-siem-is-not-enough-moving-to-a-complete-cyber-security-solution.

software demands, data needs often get shunted to the side–also a reason organizations are more than willing to turn to new solutions.

* * *

THE HOTTEST HARDWARE STARTUPS: WHAT YOU NEED TO KNOW

A number of hot hardware startups are covered in a few other chapters in this book, and many are mentioned in chapter 6. For angel investors, hardware is a fun and adventurous space, because it covers so many niches. From gaming to home automation, you can find a hardware startup that address needs in almost any industry. Pebble, the Kickstarter darling, brings smartwear to the wrist, and Boosted lets urban dwellers get around quickly on a motorized longboard. Hardware even enters the tobacco market with companies such as Ploom, which used its ties with a Japanese tobacco firm to create sleek vape devices.

Below, we look at a few other hot hardware startups and discuss why these companies are catching investor eyes.

1. FORMLABS

Formlabs, launched in 2011, is an illustration of what happens when founder know-how meets impeccable timing. The company, which received $1.8 million in seed funding in November 2011, further drove its 3D printer product to market with help from a 2012 Kickstarter campaign. The campaign offered rewards ranging from a virtual high five and a file copy of the printer model to a package containing the actual printer plus fun printables. In its Kickstarter campaign,

Formlabs claimed it intended to disrupt the 3D printing market with an affordable, high-quality 3D printer.

The startup was able to garner additional funding in 2013, when a Series A round brought it $19 million for product development and expansion. It's not surprising investors were happy to get in on funding Formlabs. By that time, it had already made good on a number of its Kickstarter promises; by December 2013, Formlabs had fulfilled all the Kickstarter rewards and shipped more than 1,000 of its Form 1 3D printers throughout the globe; this hardware startup had a strong execution plan.

Why all the hype around Formlabs' product? First, Formlabs' Kickstarter project, came at a time when 3D print technology was becoming a household topic. News media was covering the technology, which sounded futuristic and frightening to many-op-eds asked "What if people print guns?" and entrepreneurs bubbled excitedly about manufacturing concepts. For many users, though, the technology was entertaining to consider, but far from daily reach.

Formlabs' Kickstarter campaign meshed with the audience because it made the concept relevant, less frightening, and affordable. For $2,299, a backer received the printer and some supplies. With businesses paying a thousand or more for copy machines, that price for a 3D printer opened the technology to small business users and individual inventors.

That covers product and branding, but for the angel investor, the people behind FormLabs are also an attractive investment. Natan Linder managed Samsung's R&D center in Israel and was a lead designer with a robotics company. Maxim Lobovsky's 3D printer experience dates back to FabLab and Fab@Home projects as does

David Cranor's. All three founders also came from a background at MIT Media Labs.

With so many criteria pointing to a high chance at success, we aren't surprised that FormLabs made several expansion announcements in early 2015. This startup is looking to grow rather than seek an IPO. In a single week, the company announced expansions in both Germany and China.

2. PICOOC

Picooc is a Chinese health device maker with some products that are similar to US-based Fitbit, which we covered in chapter 6. Through two investment rounds, Picooc raised a total of $25 million. By its second round of funding, which garnered $21 million of that total, Picooc was already known for its flagship product: a smart body scale that integrates with fitness apps and other devices.

Picooc's scale lets users see metrics such as body water, muscle mass, body mass index, and body fat. Users can tie that data to a fitness tracking application, which integrates the information with user-entered figures and data from wearable fitness devices. The result is comprehensive fitness tracking in a world where users globally are becoming more health conscious and more aware of how data can tell a story about fitness.

Picooc certainly isn't first to market, and its products do bear some similarities to products from Fitbit. Where Picooc wins–and investor

---

Krasserstein, Brian. "Formlabs Heads to Germany, Opens Office in Berlin, Partners with IGo3D." *3DPrintcom*. N.p., 16 Mar. 2015. Web. 29 Apr. 2015. http://3dprint.com/51309/formlabs-germany-igo3d/
Molitch-Hou, Michael. "Formlabs' SLA 3D Printing to China - 3D Printing Industry." *3D Printing Industry Formlabs Brings LowCost SLA 3D Printing to China Comments*. N.p., 10 Mar. 2015. Web. 29 Apr. 2015. http://3dprintingindustry.com/2015/03/10/formlabs-brings-low-cost-sla-3d-printing-to-china.

interest comes into play–is that it beat Fitbit to the ample Chinese market. And it did so at a lower price point. Picooc's scale retails for around $72 in China; comparable Fitbit scales, which didn't launch in China until June 2014, retailed for $198. Anytime a startup can do something as well as or better than the competition and at a lower price point, angel investors should take notice.

3. OUYA

Ouya is an interesting hardware startup to consider, because its story isn't one of immediate success. The startup was founded in 2012 and received funding over two years for a total of $23.6 billion. The product was an open-access television gaming console that would bring hundreds of free games to user televisions for a price around $99. Think Roku for the app gaming market.

The product, which launched in 2013, let game and app developers publish their products to Ouya just as they do to social media or mobile apps, but users could easily play the games on televisions. The intent was to open the console gaming market to developers and players outside of the culture of PlayStation or xBox, but the product debut was a mixed bag. The product sold out before launch, due in part to a stunning Kickstarter campaign that raised both $8.5 million and ample awareness about the product. Those with industry knowledge also anticipated the product because it was designed by Yves Behar, a recognized name with ties to UP and Jambox.

Ouya's product kickoff was problematic, however, pointing to possible problems with the startup's execution plan. Early buyers complained about late deliveries, and the product itself had consistency issues. Another issue, which might have muddied branding waters, is that the company managed to get the console into high-end retail locations before it met promised shipping dates for Kickstarter backers. Unlike Formlabs, which used its Kickstarter funders as the first rung in a loyal following, Ouya may have burned some of those bridges. The result of all these issues was that industry publications started to declare the startup dead, which might have you wondering why this hardware company is on our hot list.

We like the Ouya story because it illustrates a point about flexibility for both startups and investors. As we said in our product chapter, angel investors back people and ideas, not perfect products. And the Ouya team demonstrates the ability for startups with good ideas and people to bounce back from poor product launches or performance.

In early 2015, Ouya announced that Chinese Internet company Alibaba was investing in the startup. Both companies held investment details close to the chest, but did talk about why they were teaming up. By 2015, Ouya had developed a gaming library of over 1,000 games. The plan is to integrate those games with Alibaba's existing technology.

Ouya founder Julie Uhrman was asked why the product might see better success in China than it did in the United States. She pointed out the ample opportunity for gaming developers in the global space and stated that many concentrate on the saturated US market because it's what they know–perhaps a mistake that even Ouya itself made. By partnering with the Chinese company, Uhrman's startup not only opens global doors for itself, but for all the app developers that launch via the Ouya platform. That open-market mind set and ability to make execution changes that might be better for the startup and investors is why Ouya makes our list.

4. THALMIC LABS

With over $15 million in investments since it launched in 2013, Thalmic Labs is an exciting hardware startup in an earlier stage than the previous three we covered. The company's first product is an armband, called the Myo, which senses muscle movement in a user's arm and integrates with computers for virtual-reality style control. The armband offers more precise control than some other devices on the market, and Thalmic Labs originally showcased its prerelease product by flying a drone with it. The armband can also be used to control computing functions, including PowerPoint navigation, and some games.

With a release price of $199 each, Thalmic Labs didn't expect its products to hit wide consumer audiences at first. It was relying on early adoption crowds—techies, industry insiders, and gaming and computer developers—to buy its products on first launch in 2015. The startup did make what seems like a smart product launch choice—it launched on Amazon for added exposure and easy distribution.

While the Myo isn't going to be an international bestseller right away, the product and the company are exciting for investors because of the promise of future growth. The Myo is one of those rare products that is slightly before its time but is not first to market. There's a platform ready in the space for these types of control devices, and other hardware and computer uses are catching up, positioning Myo and Thalmic Labs to be big players in the next few years as drastic changes are made to the way users interact with computers.

5. LITTLEBITS[4]

Launched by Ayah Bdeir in 2009, littleBits won over 20 awards at the MakerFaire Bay Area in the same year. Between then and 2013, the startup garnered over $14 million in funding for its product: kits and components that bring DIY electronic and programing capability to almost anyone. The kits include a variety of small modules, such as sensors, sound and light components, and power, and let users create anything from home security components to a toy Mars Rover. Consumers can buy kits for certain projects, or purchase deluxe kits that contain basic modules needed for multiple electronics products.

Bdeir's product isn't the first in the electronic education space-soldering kits have been around for years. But littleBits are easier to use thanks to snap-together technology, and the small, colorful modules lend to education in a variety of environments. We like littleBits as a hardware startup because of the sheer diversity and market potential of the product. DIY electronics gurus can invest in dozens of kits, including an Arduino coding kit. Schools can use the electronics to teach computer, design, engineering, and basic science lessons, and littleBits even works with other hardware companies to engage consumers and boost awareness of STEM activities and education.

In early 2015, littleBits partnered with 3D printing company Shapeways to host a contest. Entrants had to modify a traditional home object, such as a toothbrush, using littleBits modules and 3D printing to make the object more useful, efficient, or smarter. Such interactive marketing tactics are bringing littleBits slowly into the

---

[4] On June 25 2015, littleBits raised $44.2 billion for its Series B round of fundraising.

public eye, which bodes well for the continued success of this hot hardware startup.

6. NINJA BLOCKS

Another startup in fairly early stages, Ninja Blocks has identified what it considers a growing problem in modern homes: everything is connected, but connections are disparate and lead to poor user experience. The company, which is cofounded by Pete Moore, has received $1.7 million in funding so far, but the open-source nature of its product has let it move forward with development and preorder processes.

Pete Moore isn't new to tech startups; he previously founded Cenqua, which was later acquired by Atlassian. He is also an angel investor and startup advisor. For the Ninja Blocks launch, Moore teams up with cofounder Daniel Friedman.

One reason investors should watch this young company is that Ninja Blocks is poised to bring a wide-ranging solution to a growing and hungry market. Right now, it is targeting home automation–a market that is flooded with high-dollar solutions, service companies, and products that require mobile device access.

Ninja Blocks is looking to provide the same solutions without the excessive expense or mobile requirements. Its open source policy also lets other product developers integrate control access, so the single Ninja Blocks device may be able to control entire homes and more in the future.

HARDWARE: PRODUCTS POWERED BY PEOPLE AND PLANS

Looking at these hot hardware startups, products play a big role in this sector. Without a strong product, hardware companies flounder. But for angel investors, people and plans are equally important–when products, such as Ouya, have less-than-optimal launches, the people and execution of a startup can make proactive changes, saving both companies and investments.

STARTUP GROWTH | USERS VS. MONEY

AND WHAT MATTERS MOST

Strong user growth for a startup is undoubtedly an attraction for angel investors. The ability for a startup to generate user growth of any type means it has a product that is at least interesting to consumers and some type of marketing plan. But at some point, user growth needs to turn into money; that means converting each user to profitability. There are examples on the market now where startups continue to concentrate on user growth to the advantage of the angel investor.

WHY INVESTORS SHOULD CARE ABOUT PER-USER PROFITABILITY

When evaluating a startup, angel investors need to look for a future plan for per-user profitability. With a physical product-centric startup, user profitability is usually obvious: individuals will buy the product at a certain price, and as long as the startup is accurate on cost projections, each user presents a profit or a potential profit.

More complex situations are presented with the growing number of tech, mobile, software, and biotech companies relying on nontraditional product models. Apps that are offered free to users–such as email programs–or biotech research don't come with an obvious per-user profit point. In this environment, startups may rely heavily on user growth for years, even developing wildly successful platforms from a market and branding point of view. The problem for angel investors is that a popular platform that doesn't generate revenue also doesn't generate a return–unless there's an acquisition involved.

STARTUPS WITH STRONG USER GROWTH AND NO REVENUE

We've talked about Snapchat in several sections and chapters of this book. Not only is Snapchat one of the hottest startups, but it also has no revenue to speak of. What the startup does have is users–lots of users in prized demographics. The app is popular among teens and twenty-somethings, which is always a market that advertisers are looking to engage with. The app launched in 2011; four years later, it has a global reach. Users sent 760 million photos and view stories over a billion times a day via the app, which is an enormous scale that certainly has possible ramifications for monetization in the future. As of late 2014, the app boasted 100 million users a month.

Another social media app with little to no revenue and ample user growth is Instagram, which was acquired by Facebook in 2012 for a whopping $1 billion. Instagram, which was only two years old at the time of the acquisition, boasted 30 million users and high download rates on both Apple and Google platforms. Just a week before the purchase, investors valued Instagram at $500 million.

The Instagram story illustrates one scenario in which high user growth and no revenue ends up beneficial for a startup and its investors. Value isn't always found in profit, and Facebook placed a value on the Instagram product itself. Specifically, Instagram brings a strong mobile presence to Facebook–a component that has been seen as a weak point for the social media giant. Other acquisitions that involved low- to no-revenue ventures included Hot Potato, GroupMe, Zite, Dodgeball, and even YouTube.

3 REASONS NO-REVENUE STARTUPS GENERATE IPO AND ACQUISITION INTEREST

In the absence of a plan for per-user profitability, startups need a strong exit plan–having both is the best bet. There are a number of reasons companies are willing to pay big bucks for startups that come with little in the way of existing revenue.

1. PRODUCT DEVELOPMENT

Markets are competitive, and even the big players need a steady stream of new products in the pipeline. For many conglomerates, it's less expensive to buy a startup that has done the research, development, and troubleshooting work already. Even if a product isn't generating revenue yet, the publicity of an acquisition and potential for a new lineup can boost overall performance for a larger company. In social and mobile spaces, "products" may equate to users and audience–in the Instagram example above, Facebook got both a product and a possible subset of new users.

2. INDUSTRY KNOWLEDGE

Larger companies in a number of spaces rely heavily on startups to fuel learning, development, and innovation. R&D is expensive and time consuming, and one of the easiest ways for corporations to gather data is to buy startups that are at the forefront of the industry. This is especially true in the biotech field, where enterprises purchase startups that have launched solely on a research discovery.

3. PEOPLE

We've said many times in this book that people are a main pillar of any investment, and that's true for large enterprises as well as angel investors. A third reason corporations purchase startups is for the team. Considering the expense of recruiting, especially at specialized and high levels, startup acquisitions may be an affordable option for enterprises, which then benefit from knowledge, research, and a ready-made team to implement solutions.

WHEN IS IT OKAY TO CONTINUE WITH USER-BASED GROWTH?

Profits are great, and enough profits let startups grow into larger companies that return continued value to investors. Some examples of startups on this trajectory include 3D printing company Formlabs and software company Apttus. But for some companies, concentrating on user growth over revenue is a success tactic because it either invites IPO action or positions the company for strong revenues later in the game.

The startup is seen as valuable, which is what matters on the market. It's a fine line to walk, and one that startups shouldn't stride for too long. The market is powerful, but it's also fickle. Interest can wane, and without revenue, a startup may be lost once investors and acquisition possibilities dry up.

It's also okay to continue seeking user growth if the plan is to brand first and profit later, as long as there is an exit strategy. Many social networks take this road, offer free models to build a large, loyal following before turning to monetization. A network or app with millions of users puts itself in a power position when negotiating with other brands and advertisers, which can boost future revenues by a large percent.

SWITCHING FROM FREEMIUM MODELS

In some cases, per-user revenue plans involve converting users from freemium to paying models. Startups can take several routes toward that conversion, and each tactic has its own risks and rewards.

A common method for driving user growth that can then be converted to profitable per-user arrangements is offering a free version of a product with options for upgrading to paid versions. Often employed in mobile app, software, and Internet service models, this is probably the safest way to approach switching from freemium models because it doesn't place an expectation or burden on the consumer. The risk is that consumers may find the free model sufficient enough and never buy in to paying products, so startups must plan carefully. Companies have to provide a free product that is attractive enough to entice users while leaving users wanting-and willing-to pay for more.

Another version of this model is popular with apps such as Candy Crush, which provides a free product but offers enhancements within the game at a cost.

A second option is monetizing a product in a way that doesn't hit user pockets. Generally, that means incorporating advertisements into the product, but some companies have become creative with this method. ZenBenefits, for example, partners with other vendors to drive revenues while offering its product free to consumers. Other platforms use consumer data-with consumer permission-to drive revenues through other marketing and integration efforts. The biggest risk with this method is that the revenue-generating activity may make user experience less than enjoyable-where ads are involved.

A third option for switching from freemium delivery is to offer users limited-time free access. After the trial period, the user must begin paying for the product or service. It's a timeless marketing method that has worked for young companies over the years, but it may be the most risky option simply because consumers who are used to getting a thing for free are often unhappy when asked to pay for it. The key to success with this method is transparency and ample communication so consumers are never surprised by a transition.

CONSIDERATIONS FOR ANGEL INVESTORS

Throughout this book, we've looked at startups that seem to be winning with both models, and the few examples in this section illustrate how investors can get returns either way. Ultimately, considerations for the investor come down–again–to our four pillars – the formula - for evaluating and scoring startups.

As an investor considering the user vs. revenue question about a specific startup, ask yourself:

- Does the startup have a strong exit strategy?
- Is the startup in a space that is likely to support IPO or acquisition without revenue?
- If the startup plans to concentration on user growth first, does it have a plan for converting to revenue?

ARTICLES EXPANDED

TOP 5 DORM ROOM FOUNDERS

Here we present the top Dorm Room Founders. Though we mentioned some earlier in the book, our Angel Kings team felt that these deserved mention.

1. REDDIT

Reddit is a website that provides a free exchange of ideas, imagery and information on a grand social scale. College students Steve Huffman and Alexis Ohanian built Reddit while attending the University of Virginia. The original concept was to create a sharing platform with a voting tool that would move good ideas to the top of the list of visibility and bury other posts that simply weren't interesting. In doing so, the site usage created its own product creation, generating the most popular material consistency every time it was used.

Reddit founders realized the power of marketing and awareness could push a product farther than the benefits of the product itself. So, to make Reddit look interesting and popular as a website, the initial company bunch faked the functionality of the website with multiple accounts until the popularity grew to a sustainable level. Then they backed off and let real users take over and keep expanding the site exponentially. This approach, which is considered a standard reason for banning an account on most social platforms, represents a thinking-out-of-the-box move, which is why Reddit got notice and worked. Tried and true paths don't usually find breakthroughs with new products.

Between the growing awareness and the fake account seeding information and posts on Reddit, the site became popular quickly. In fact, it exploded to 1.6 billion visits and views monthly. That established Reddit as the top website being visited worldwide, bar none. It also grabbed the attention of corporations who wanted to have a link and connection to an Internet presence with that much digital presence. Today, Reddit is a collection of forums and posting halls versus just one big one. Each sub-forum is specific to a topic or group of ideas, making it searchable and focused on specific conversations. That increased popularity with even more diversity being supported.

Reddit as a dorm room idea was an extreme success and still continues to be so. And for anyone who doesn't think that Huffman and Ohanian invented something useful, try explaining that idea to Conde Nast, the high end travel magazine company, who bought the website and is now the main owner of the business.

2. DELL

$1,000 may not seem like much today due to inflation, but in the mid-1980s it was exactly what Michael Dell needed to get his company going from his college room. Dell was able to take that same company started in 1984 and produce a corporation that today is worth billions of dollars with employees worldwide. While not a popular website owner per se, he proves that any kind of business can be launched from a dorm room, and even at a time when the Internet wasn't even a critical component of the business model (the Net didn't start to take off until the 1990s).

At age 19 he leveraged a simple amount of money into a product that people wanted. Dell tuned into what was considered advantageous with physical computers. At the time, IBM was still the big player of computers. There was the MAC of course, but this was a bulky box with a tiny screen in black and white. The IBM system, on the other hand, was a steel cast PCU, a big monitor and a standard size keyboard to boot – all that just to play around in DOS or WordPerfect or Lotus spreadsheets. There was plenty of room for something more, a sleeker product that did more with computing and didn't feel like driving a Sherman tank down the interstate slow lane.

Dell also had timing working to his advantage in addition to producing a product people wanted. This is a key factor for dorm launches. Sizing the opportunity when it has the most potential to run positively is critical for a dorm company to launch. Then, secondly, the next timing point is to keep it growing exponentially. Dell hit both windows perfectly. His computer product fed into people's growing need for a better desktop unit. Additionally, personal computing was booming, and making his product consumer-friendly fit the growing market just as it was budding and well beyond IBM's projections. No surprise, by a decade later Dell's company had multiple manufacturing facilities nationwide, plenty of investors behind as a public corporation, and a growing sales opportunity going forward.

Dell also jumped onto e-commerce early in 1996 when the Internet 1.0 was just getting warm. With an online ordering presence, he expanded his company again exponentially by going global with sales. While many computer producers stuck to retail stores, Dell marketed heavily a better product that could be custom-made to a buyer's preferences, including the software packages as well. The idea stuck and today Dell sees a good portion of its regular sales from online orders.

Again, Dell's venture started with just the right amount of seed money for the time, his will to make it happen, and good timing. It's a classic story of being in the right place at the right time, and Dell also proves anything can become a dorm room success; companies don't have to be just Internet websites trading information.

3. YAHOO!

Before Google's dominance in the search engine field there was Yahoo!, which still competes today for the same market and users. Yahoo! is among a number of launches that started at Stanford University. As the Internet began to grow in the mid-1990s and become user friendly as a place to find information, David Filo and Jerry Yang realized that getting into the information sorting business was a viable venture. They created "Jerry and David's Guide to the World Wide Web," and awkward-sounding but useful resource that captured and sorted website pages to make them easier to find. Realizing the popularity of the tool, Filo and Yang reconfigured their information product, and renamed it Yahoo instead. By January 1995 they had set in place the main cornerstone of the company by securing the Yahoo.com domain as well.

Because the Internet and website in general were very much like the Wild West at the time, two sorts of users existed. The bulk of computer-naïve folks were going through conduits like AOL, which created a bulky user-interface for most services as well as clunky browser software for actual Internet searching. This option forced people to search through AOL's databases first for information before going to the web itself. The second group of users was those who went direct to browser and just starting moving around from known site to known site, linking more as they went. They became the bread and butter of Yahoo, users who wanted a searchable system where term could be punched in and all related sites would pop up on a link list.

Because Filo and Yang figured out how to create the software that generated search engine results and connected it to a website, their business skyrocketed and soon made AOL-type platforms of Internet use obsolete. They refined their product, and the pair also made the use of the search engine essential for anyone else who wanted to build a new thing, "traffic," to their website to produce more attention or sales. The formula of a search engine being a useful middle man traffic cop for Internet activity became obvious in its simplicity.

Ironically, they had to make some basic but critical decisions early on. The company name Yahoo alone had already been taken. So Filo and Yang did a quick fix and added an exclamation point to the end to stay legal and retain their brand name, ergo Yahoo! It's often the little things that can break an empire before it gets going.

The Stanford University project boomed during the dot-com era of the late 1990s and became the hit San Francisco corporation. More importantly, however, it had enough staying power to survive the dot-com crash and keep going because the product was still essential for Internet use. The company has since gone through numerous versions and renovations, as well as multiple CEOS good and bad. But the thing that made Yahoo! a hit in its early college days is still in play and extremely strong – people still need a filter for the Internet to find what they are looking for.

While Yahoo! today is nowhere near the presence of Internet importance it once had, Filo and Yang's product had the same success as other dorm room ventures that made it big – they had a product that everybody wanted to use and the timing matched the need perfectly. A well-positioned idea executed into a simple but useful product continued to be the key formula for a dorm room launch to corporate status. And the science and technical basis of Yahoo! paved the road for its competitor and successor, Google, as well as that of others like Ask!, Alta Vista, and other search engines that popped up on the Internet by the 2000s.

Dorm room CEOs and their companies may product also sorts of services or products but the dynamic of what makes the next Dell or Yahoo! follows a couple of specific patterns that become big predictors of success. First, the obvious one is that the product or service invented needs to be both original as well as simply and basic to use. The inherent ease with which to use the new product is what makes it so easy to spread and grow in popularity fast. Complexity slows down product adoption that is critical early on as a company gets started.

Secondly, these dorm room launches have incredibly good timing with the market's need. It's not enough to have a product everyone needs, but the product has to also be made available when that need is so obvious everyone beats a path to the company door to get it.

Third, the door room launches produce a service or product that has staying power and remains essential. They do not boom and then fizzle like a fad or fashion. In most cases, the product is a tool that has ongoing benefits. Communication-type services or data exchange can continue to be beneficial as long as the network it is connected to stay viable. However, other products like physical computers can continue to be useful for years and years, as long as they are revised and modified to stay technologically relevant.

Finally, but nowhere the least, the people involved with the dorm project matter immensely. These characters are driven to see the project reach fruition. In most cases, they have a knack for seeing things outside the box, and they aren't hesitant to bend a few conventional rules to see that happen. They are risk takers and 100 percent invested in their idea, almost to the point of being hazardous to their health. Without this kind of zeal and commitment, most college company ideas won't get off the ground. It's one thing to have funding, but the person making the company become a reality is the catalyst for the growth.

From a venture investment perspective the above factors are the aspects to look for. There are thousands of college projects now that it has become apparent a dorm room CEO is a real possibility. This actually makes it more difficult to find good ideas since one has to wade through far more chatter. However, there are plenty of ideas yet to see the light of day, and colleges continue to be incubators of some amazing inventions and concepts from those starting out in life. So with a bit of savvy hunting and good filtering, as well as a lot of patience for listening, venture investors can still find plenty of opportunities for the next big thing.

*** * * *

FIVE WAYS TO VALUE A STARTUP

THE STARTUP'S PERSPECTIVE

"Any idea, plan, or purpose may be placed in the mind through repetition of thought."
– Napoleon Hill

Investors need more than just a gut feeling, or someone approaching them with an idea, in order to put their money on the line. Fortunately, there are more formulaic ways for VC firms and angel investors to choose which startups they want to fund. Not every investor is going to focus on the same things, of course, but there are many indicators of a potentially successful startup that are common to the majority of investors.

Anyone who plans to start up a company must consider those indicators, because getting funding is a vital part of success for a startup. For the investor who is looking for his or her next big investment, the startup that meets the right criteria is going to be moved to the top of the list. While founders of startups shouldn't create their companies based solely on what they think investors want to see, they may want to consider the kinds of startups that are commonly funded.

That way, they can tailor their idea to investors while still offering the product or service they originally intended to provide. To that end, there are five main things that most of the top investors look for in startups. Focusing on as many of these things as possible can mean a better chance of funding for startups, and a lower risk and higher return for investors who take a chance on those startups in an effort to help them succeed.

1. A PERSON (OR TEAM) INSTEAD OF AN IDEA

When considering what kind of startup an investor will fund, it's vital to look at the person (or team) behind the startup, not just the idea that has been created for the business. An idea that revolutionizes an industry is a wonderful thing, but it won't get off the ground unless the right people are behind it. Some people have "it," and others don't. The people who *do* are the people investors want to work with. They operate different from others, and they have characteristics and traits that just aren't seen in the overall population.

The top investors in the world, along with many smaller-time investors, know that the quality of the people behind a startup can make all the difference when it comes to how successful that startup will be. Those who are uncertain about their ideas or where to go next can make investors nervous, because they lack the confidence to push their ideas and see them through. That has to be considered by any investor who is serious about financial goals, and who is thinking about taking a risk on a startup company.

Vetting the founder(s) of a startup is common for investors. Who the person is, where that person came from, and anything else that can be discovered will be found out. Anyone can come up with a great idea, but only certain people can carry that idea through to the end. The goal of an investor is to find someone with a winning idea, who also embodies the traits needed to carry that idea through and turn it into something wonderful. Vetting a startup founder is necessary and important. Investors have to know that the people and companies they invest in are actually going in the right direction.

When an investor considers a company and is able to vet the founder(s) of that company, that information provides the investor with a platform from which to work, and knowledge from which to build when it comes to making an important and significant financial decision. Investors can't always know everything about a prospective startup and its founders, but those investors can find out much more than the founders may have expected. Thorough research is the only safe way to gain enough knowledge when making an investment decision in a startup company.

While the idea may be an amazing one, if the people behind it don't have the traits the investor is looking for, it's likely that the investment money will be used elsewhere. There will always be other people coming up with big ideas, and eventually one of them will hit on the right combination of people and plans that will cause an investor to sit up and take notice. Until that happens, though, an investor would be wise to hang onto their money, and wait for the best combination of opportunities, delivered at the right time by people who have been vetted and found to be what the investor is looking for.

2. A PRODUCT THAT WILL STAND UP TO THE TEST OF TIME

Despite the importance of people in the creation and development of a startup idea, the product also has to be a good one. It's unrealistic to think that an investor will put money into a startup with a good product idea but poor leadership. It's also unrealistic to assume that investor will provide funding for a startup run by great people, but who have a product that is not going to hold up to scrutiny. Startup products (or services) have to be the best. They need to be new, innovative, and also timeless in a way.

Flash in the pan options may make some quick money when they're first launched, but they aren't going to stand up to the test of time. These types of products are bad for investors, because they don't provide the long-term growth and development that's necessary for making back their investment plus a good return. Even if the product starts selling wildly when it's first created, if those sales die down to nothing after six months, the investors are left wanting. That's a poor investment for anyone.

While it can't always be avoided and mistakes do happen, even to the best investors, there are some ways to get around the problem and make the best choices when it comes to products that will stick around. Looking for a product that stands the test of time means asking some tough questions, and doing some thorough research about other products that are on the market and that might be similar in some ways. How does the new product differ, and how is it the same? What does it do to build on the current products in some way? Is there room for another product in that particular market area?

Those are all important questions, since the products that stand the test of time are usually similar enough to other products to get people comfortable with them, but still different enough to draw in consumer interest over something that they just can't get in another product. That's the way to get people interested in something new and keep them coming back. It's why products like smartphones do so well when new ones come out. It's also why software and app developers do well as startups. People are already familiar with the type of product they're selling, but their version of it does something new and different.

Even if people aren't sure if they need what the product does, if they find it interesting or think it might be useful, they'll buy it and give it a try. That's what investors should be looking for – a product that people will buy and try for a long time to come. As time advances the product may have to change and evolve, but the overall plan and design for it should be one that holds up to the test of time. It can't be so unique that it won't be viable in 5 or 10 years, but yet it has to be different enough that people won't pass it over because it looks like the same thing they can get everywhere else.

There must be a reason behind the product and a value to it that isn't found everywhere else. Investors who take the time to look for those things, and to vague the value of the products over time, are generally going to have more success than investors who avoid doing those things, or who aren't clear on how to do them correctly. By the time someone gets involved in a VC firm, or becomes an angel investor, the experience to avoid these kinds of problems has generally already been developed. Still, there's success, and then there's *success* – the kind of mind-blowing returns that may only come around once or twice in a lifetime.

To be an investor that achieves that level of success hinges on several things. Timing and luck can be part of the equation, but the right product or service is almost always behind those extreme returns that have sometimes been seen. Companies like Facebook and Google were able to provide those kinds of returns for some of their early investors, and those who got involved with the company later didn't make as much. That's important to note, as investors who are considering getting involved with a startup product or service don't want to wait too long.

If they spend too much time trying to decide whether to invest, they can miss out on the early-stage investing that can allow them to buy in to the company in large amounts without spending a lot. When the company grows and develops, and the product takes off, it's those early-stage investors who see the best returns and make a lot of money from the products that are able to stand the test of time and turn into something that people want and need in their daily lives. These "household name" products and services can bring amazing returns, because they entrench themselves so strongly into society.

3. A FOUNDER WITH INTEGRITY AND TRUSTWORTHINESS

Building on the idea of people instead of ideas, an investor will also be looking for a couple of important qualities in the founders of startups: integrity and trustworthiness. Both of those traits need to be there, and in large amounts, for an investor to feel comfortable putting money into a company. Startup founders who have integrity can be relied upon to mean what they say, and to say what they mean. They know that they have something important going on, but they also know that they need help and investment dollars to make it happen. They aren't going to lie to investors to try to get money, and they aren't going to waste an investor's time.

They also won't waste their own time or talents with others who are not serious about what they are doing. These kinds of founders are serious about the development of their product or service, and they seek to work with those who feel the same way. They want to succeed, and they know they *can* succeed, if they get the funding and the guidance they need. They're willing to take direction, and willing to listen, but they won't give up the vision they have for their work. Meeting their goals is important to them, and they aren't the kinds of people who make empty promises. If they say they'll do something, they do it.

That's vital to the success of a startup. Companies that are trying to get off the ground require a different kind of leadership, and often a different level of it, than companies that have already gotten going and are better established in their industries. With that in mind, investors are going to be more drawn to a startup where the founders are people of integrity, and people who have a proven track record of doing what they say they're going to do. They need to be people the investor can trust, or there's little point in investing in their company. The risk is simply too high with people who can't be trusted.

Investors put a lot of their own money on the line, and they do that because they want to make good returns, but also because they believe in the company or companies in which they're investing. They see the people behind them as good quality people, and they feel their ideas are solid and will hold up to scrutiny. However, if they don't feel they can easily trust everything the founders say, or they don't feel the founders are living a life of integrity when it comes to their business dealings, it's often best to walk away. Mitigating risk is one thing an investor needs to learn quickly, or there won't be any more money to invest with.

It's not always possible to avoid risk, as there's some in every business transaction. Additionally, what seems to be vetted, excellent choice for an investor can turn bad quickly if something that was previously undiscovered comes to light. Taking a careful look at the company and the people running it can help to lower those kinds of risks, but it won't remove them entirely. That's why it's so important for an investor to be able to trust a startup founder, and rely on the founder's level of integrity to be what's needed for a successful business relationship.

When startup founders lack the integrity they need to successfully build their business, or when they've been proven to be people who can't be trusted, they lose a lot of opportunities for funding that they would otherwise have. That's unfortunate for the startups that were hoping to see money from those investors, but it's a good thing for the investors themselves, who likely dodged a metaphorical bullet in avoiding the funding of these kinds of startups.

People who are serious about investing in startups know that there's much that goes into the process of finding the right ones, and that it's a poor choice to work with people – and give money to people – who can't be trusted to keep their work. Investors wouldn't give their money to untrustworthy people in their personal life, so there's no reason they should do it in their business life, either. The more vetted and trustworthy a startup founder is, the more likely that founder will be to see money from solid investors with whom a strong relationship can be built.

4. A LEVEL OF RISK THAT EVERYONE UNDERSTANDS

The level of risk that comes with investing can vary greatly. It depends on the type of business being created, the actual product or service that the company is developing, how much funding is needed, what that funding will be used for, the abilities of the founders, and other factors. These are all issues that have to be considered, and there is no true level of risk that is acceptable or unacceptable – it's all what the investor decides he or she wants to take on, and it can be anything from almost no risk to a high risk.

It's an individual decision, and not one that can be made across the board for every occurrence. Another thing the level of risk needs to be is understood by everyone. Investors who don't understand risk levels well, or who can't gage how much risk they may be setting themselves up for will often struggle, and can make bad investments simply because they judge their level of risk to be lower than it is. On the other side of the coin, though, are those investors who think everything is too much of a risk, and who won't take chances. They can end up losing out, since they didn't invest in that next big thing.

While other investors are getting rich off of companies with reasonable levels of risk, shy or conservative investors are sitting around with small returns, wishing they would have put more money into the company, but there was (in their opinion) just too much risk. Investors have to decide the level of risk that's right for them, but they also have to decide if they're being realistic with that level of risk. To do that, they need to have a good understanding of the risk level in which they're being asked to engage.

Others who need to understand the risk levels include the founders of the startup. They may see a level of risk that's much lower than what the investor sees. If that's the case, it's important to explore why they feel that way. Is it because they believe in their company? Are they blinded by the idea of getting rich from their product or service? Do they have inside information that hasn't been given to investors? Are they simply better at judging risk? There could be a number of reasons why a startup founder feels something is less risky than an investor does, but everyone involved in the transaction needs to work toward getting on the same page.

If the startup founders and the investors don't understand risk on the same level, it's possible they'll not be able to come to an agreement regarding whether investment in the company is a good idea. It's also possible the founders will be looking for a much higher funding level than the investor will be comfortable with, because of the perceived risks involved. Sitting down and talking openly about the level of perceived risk can be helpful for startup founders and investors, so they can determine why they have such different views on the subject. That can help them reconcile their thoughts on risk, and agree on something that could move the company forward.

It's also possible that they just aren't a good fit, and that another investor should be sought out to help fund the company. Since everyone sees risk differently, what isn't acceptable to one investor might be perfectly fine for another. The key is to find an investor and a startup founder who see risk the same way, and who both understand the level of risk they're undertaking. When they're on the same page and have the same type of thinking about the risk levels, they're much more likely to work together successfully.

That will get things moving in the right direction, and can help the founder build up a successful company that will provide good return to the investors. Ultimately, that's what both are looking for, despite any risks that are being taken. The founder wants to see the company succeed, and the investors want to make money on their investment. With an acceptable level of risk that's understood by both parties, it's completely possible for everyone to walk away happy – but that only comes with an understanding of the true level of risk faced.

5. A COMPLETED, COMPREHENSIVE BUSINESS PLAN

Business plans still exist. They aren't some archaic idea that got scrapped as soon as people went digital and started doing everything through their smartphones and crowdfunding sites. Startup companies that want to succeed need good business plans. They have to be able to show investors what they're about and where they're headed. That doesn't mean some rough ideas sketched out on paper, either. It means a comprehensive plan to get the business off the ground, keep it sustainable, and grow it into something more than it will be when it starts up. The original Sun Microsystems business plan achieved this in two pages.

Many business plans are for five years, although some can be for 10. It's hard to design a business plan that goes beyond that, because so much can change in that length of time. While businesses want to have a good plan based on where they're going, that plan has to be flexible enough to allow them to adapt and change as conditions warrant. The plan also has to be realistic. It's one thing to spell out where a startup plans to be in five years, but how's it going to get there? What are the specific steps it will take to make sure it arrives at its desired location?

If the founders of the startup don't know the answers to those questions, they aren't ready to look for investors yet. They need to go back to the drawing board and focus on what they're doing, so they can find a way to build their business realistically. It's not easy, but if it were easy, everyone would be doing it. Startups come with a lot of work and a lot of risk – but they can also come with amazing rewards if they're handled correctly. Taking time to create a comprehensive and detailed business plan might not seem "cool," but it's a requirement for startups that want to be taken seriously, and that want to attract significant investment dollars.

Founders who aren't sure how to create a business plan can find someone who can help them. Whether they have to pay that person, can pay them with a percentage of the new company, or can get a volunteer will depend on a large number of factors. Either way, though, the development of a business plan is not something that should be overlooked, or slapped together in a hurry in the hope of getting it in front of investors. Those who invest in startup companies know what to look for in a comprehensive business plan, and they aren't going to settle for less.

If the startup doesn't know where it's headed and how it's going to get there, it's hard for investors to take it seriously. That can mean a low level of investment dollars, or none at all, which can end a startup before it gets off the ground. To avoid that, investors will need to see something that indicates that the startup founders are serious about their plans, and that they've thought those plans through carefully. Speculation is important and necessary, but the entire premise of the company can't be based on thinking and hoping that something may go a particular way.

There need to be solid, concrete ideas, and back-up ideas if the company is forced by market circumstances or other reasons to take a different direction. No matter what kind of product or service a startup is going to provide, it's a business and has to be run like one. Investors aren't going to spend much time listening to an idea that doesn't have anything behind it. The next gadget or gizmo that *should* be invented to make people lives easier sounds great, but getting from that concept to something that can be bought on the shelves of the local retailer is a big process.

Startups can't just "wing it," and good investors know this. The business plan can be key to answering investor questions, and helping them determine if the startup is somewhere they want to put their money. For startups that aren't sure where they're headed, a business plan can also help develop clarity. That will help the company and any potential investors make better decisions.

* * *

FINAL THOUGHTS

My father once said, stop being the person who always talks about others; be the person about whom people speak. Ironically, I spent an entire book talking about the billion dollar successes that other people have had by either building their own companies or investing in companies themselves. No more. Now, it's your turn too to be the investing king.

Remember: investing is easy, but making big returns is hard. Whether you want to beat the market, earn greater returns, be part of that big deal, or just advise startups, you have the tools and the knowledge, now you must execute.

Before you invest in the next "billion dollar" startup, just remember to ask these five critical questions:

1. Who are the people behind the idea (Hackers, Hustlers and Mavens)?
2. Would the product be something you would use now, 10, 20 years from now?
3. Do the founders have a plan to make money by building a company or is it just a hobby?
4. Will someone care enough to hand over their credit card and give the startup money?
5. Do the financials support the startup's growth?

And use our formula. We built this for you too. After all, there's plenty of money to go around the world and back. If you have questions, or need help, let me know. There's no reason to miss out on the next big deal. You have everything you need and now just need the courage to make it happen.

To less luck, and more skill,

Ross D. Blankenship
CEO | Angel Kings Investments
AngelKings.com

*To learn about Angel Kings and venture capital investing, get started by going to:

www.AngelKings.com

*BONUS:

HOW TO GET STARTED WITH VENTURE CAPITAL AND STARTUP INVESTING

#1 Know the laws:

Before investing, there are three primary regulations you need to know:

Regulation D, 506 (b) – Private Fundraising

Companies can raised unlimited amounts of money from accredited investors and a maximum of 35 unaccredited investors.

Under Rule 506 (b), startups are only allowed to advertise fundraising to accredited investors.

Examples: AngelKings equity funds, WeFunder, FundersClub

Regulation D, 506 (c) – Private Fundraising

Companies can publicly raise an unlimited amount of capital, but must verify investors are actually accredited.

Examples: AngelList, and AngelKings equity funds

Regulation A (Section 401 of JOBS Act)

Companies can advertise and raise funds from *non-accredited* investors. This is akin to the Wild West; Regulation A opens a brand new frontier for startup investing. In fact, Regulation A is kind of like a small-IPO, and for the first time startups will be able to circulate an offering to investors of all sorts – from billionaires to retail investors.

Overall, we support the free markets that are driving new investments in startups; none of these regulations are perfect. The only right thing to do, whether you are accredited or not, is to use the formula and diligence we discussed in this book before making investments in startups.

*At Angel Kings we have a hybrid of funds devoted to both early-stage venture capital, and later stage investing. We prefer accredited investors and have strict membership criteria.

#2 Do your due diligence:

The Angel Kings formula contains everything you need to get started in venture capital investing. From the people, product, execution, timing and then financials to support, you must use each ingredient wisely.

Trust your gut less. Make more calculations with less public information. Build rapport with the founding team and ask yourself whether this is a "startup" or a long-term company that will give you a massive return on your investment.

And always read the terms sheet. Never invest without getting your money back. For a more analytical guide to terms sheets, we recommend reading *Venture Deals* by Brad Feld and Jason Mendelson.

#3 Meet everyone you can:

We host events at Angel Kings. Our conferences allow you to meet many of the top angel investors in the world. Through Angel Kings, you can meet, greet, and ask questions from the best. Whether you're a beginner angel investor, or have invested in many startups, you're welcome to continue learning from the best venture capitalists in America.

INDEX

12 labs, 294
23andMe, 327, 328
405 Labs, 324
A+ (a plus), 293
AAA, 205
Aardvark, 277
Aaref Hilaly, 323
Acosta, 244
Actifio, 288
Adam Covati, 237
Agiliance, 307
Airbnb, 22, 288, 289, 292
Airware, 126
Alexion Pharmaceuticals, 264
Alexis Ohanian, 347
Alibaba, 206, 336
Alios, 263
Allegis Capital, 140
Alta Partners, 264
Amazon, 97, 105, 106, 107, 129, 206, 231, 337
Anaplan, 182
Andreesen Horowitz, 310
Andreessen Horowitz, 215, 259, 282, 287
Andrew McCollum, 187
Angel Kings, 4, 5, 19, 20, 21, 23, 25, 27, 34, 35, 36, 38, 44, 45, 46, 56, 61, 67, 68, 76, 79, 80, 85, 86, 88, 95, 98, 117, 118, 120, 122, 123, 132, 141, 146, 149, 152, 155, 158, 166, 167, 174, 302, 306, 307, 309
Angel.co, 323, 326, 329
AngelList, 125, 290, 292
ANNOVAR, 142
Anolinx, 141
Appature, 245
Apple, 20, 25, 68, 70, 72, 74, 76, 77, 79, 80, 88, 94, 97, 98, 160, 234, 237, 244, 257, 342
AppSumo, 284, 285
Apttus, 270, 305, 306, 308, 316, 317, 318, 344
ArcSight, 307
Argyle Social, 237
Artillery, 292
Asana, 131, 182, 288
Ash Rust, 158
Ashton Kutcher, 287, 292
asset-based valuation, 319, 320
Atlas Venture, 266, 267
Atlas Ventures, 266
Authy, 123, 124, 132
Ayah Bdeir, 338
Badongo, 292

BC Partners, 243
Benchling, 142, 326
Berkus Method, 313, 314, 315, 318
Betable, 169, 170
Bill & Melinda Gates Foundation, 191
Bill and Melinda Gates Foundation, 266
Bill Gates, 34, 46, 190, 201
Bill Kirtley, 171
BillGuard, 150
biotech, 27, 141, 263, 264, 274, 303, 325, 326, 327, 328, 341, 343
biotechnology, 119, 146, 213, 214, 268, 289, 326
Bix.com, 290
Biz Stone, 127
Blackjet, 292
Blackstone, 244
Bleacher Report, 294
Blockscore, 132
Boo.com, 249, 250, 260, 275
Boosted Boards, 123
Box, 288, 308
Brad Rosen, 171
Bradford Shelhammer, 230
BrainQuicken, 291
Braintree, 243
Brandon Ballinger, 133
Breakeven, 102, 108
Breezeworks, 294
Brigade, 294
Brightroll, 294
Buddy Media, 306
Buffer, 113, 114, 115, 116, 120, 121, 122
BufferApp, 120, 121, 122, 123
BugCrowd, 134
Bump, 288
Burger King, 242
Cake Health, 147
Caltech, 199
Cambrian, 145, 289, 326
Cambrian Genomics, 145, 326
Candy Crush, 170, 209, 210, 345
Canvas, 289
Carbonmade, 279, 280, 281
Caribou Biosciences, 266, 267
Carlyle, 244
Cashbet, 170
Chris Hughes, 187
Chris Sacca, 291
Chris Wanstrath, 281
CipherCloud, 215, 307, 308, 324

Cisco, 294
Clarium Capital, 288
Clinical Methods, 141
Cloudera, 329
Cloudflare, 183, 184, 185
CloudWorks, 294
Coca-Cola, 71
Codementor, 175, 176
Codementor.io, 175
Coho Data, 288
comparable transaction, 314
Connect, 294
CoreOS, 181
Cornell, 4, 12, 198
Couchbase, 180
Counsyl, 143, 144, 326
Coupons, 205
Coupons.com, 205
Cozy, 292
Crave, 166
CrowdFlower, 329
CryptoSeal, 183
cybersecurity, 27, 136, 322, 323, 324, 325, 326
DailyBurn, 292
Daniel Friedman, 339
Daniel Palacio, 124
Dartmouth, 290
Dave Gorum, 279
David Berkus, 313
David Cramer, 285
David Cranor, 334
David Filo, 350
David Karp, 242
David Lenhardt, 243
DCF, 318, 319, 320
Dell, 181, 323, 348, 349, 350, 352
Digital Entertainment Network, 251
Digital Ocean, 288
DigitalOcean, 180
Disconnect.me, 135
Disqus, 289, 290
Divya Narendra, 155
DNAnexus, 144
Docker, 180
Docverse, 290
Dodgeball, 343
Domo, 329
DraftKings, 166
Drew Houston, 87, 88, 93, 95, 98, 99
Drizly, 172
Dropbox, 22, 86, 87, 88, 89, 90, 91, 92, 93, 94, 95, 97, 98, 99, 120, 174, 278
Dropcam, 159
Drync, 171
Dual Therapeutics, 326
Duolingo, 292
Dustin Moskovitz, 187

EBay, 243
EcoR1 Capital, 267
Editas, 267
Eduardo Saverin, 188
Elijah Murray, 152
Elon Musk, 34, 36, 37, 38, 42
Emerald Therapeutics, 289
Emulate, 267
enterprise, 119, 139, 179, 181, 182, 283, 314, 330
Epinions.com, 290
Eric Boggs, 237
Eric Ries, 67, 270, 271, 286
eToys, 253
Etsy, 109, 110, 111, 112, 231, 289
Ev Williams, 127
EV/Sales ratio, 314, 315
Evan Blair, 136
Evan Doll, 160
EventBrite, 294
Evernote, 292
Exact Target, 306
Exo Protein Bars, 292
Expa, 292
Experiment.com, 145, 146
Fab, 104, 105, 106, 107, 108, 111, 229, 230, 231, 232, 333
Facebook, 19, 20, 22, 25, 27, 42, 43, 69, 77, 135, 162, 187, 188, 197, 203, 224, 225, 226, 227, 240, 260, 284, 288, 289, 292, 294, 314, 342, 343, 358
FedEx, 191
Fidelity Biosciences, 266
fintech, 119, 151, 154
Firebase, 125
FitBit, 148, 294, 334
Flagship Ventures, 264, 267
Flatiron Partners, 290
Flaviar, 172
Flickr, 311
Flipboard, 160, 164
Flooz, 251, 256, 257, 275
FOBO, 292
Foodzie, 292
Ford, 91, 92
Foresite Capital, 264
Formlabs, 333
Formlabs,, 332, 336
Forrester Research, 329
FourSquare, 290, 292
Fred Alger Management Farallon Capital Management, 264
Fred Smith, 191
Fred Wilson, 256, 260, 289
Freshbooks, 151
Fusion IO, 288
gates Global, 244
Gawker, 285

Genoa Corp, 290
GGV Capital, 264
Github, 123, 243, 281
Gmail, 92, 308
Google, 25, 26, 47, 69, 92, 94, 97, 125, 133, 135, 140, 189, 190, 196, 226, 241, 277, 280, 294, 342, 350, 352, 358
GoPro, 22, 52, 53, 54, 55, 56, 58, 59, 60, 61, 63, 207, 208
Govworks.com, 252
GroupMe, 343
Groupon, 288, 294
grove labs, 292
GrubHub, 208
Hampton Creek, 294
HandyBook, 131
Harvard, 42, 46, 188, 190, 191, 197
Helium, 294
Hello Inc., 126
Heroku, 291
Hewlett-Packard, 287, 307
HeyZap, 289, 290
Highfive, 294
Hired, 294
Hit Forge, 290
HootSuite, 121, 238
Hortonworks, 330
Hot Potato, 343
Hotmail, 75, 79, 308
Huddle, 179
Hullabalu, 129
Hulu, 94
Illumio, 182
Imgur, 161, 284
IMS, 245
IMVU, 271, 278
Indeed, 283, 284
inDinero, 149
Instacart, 130, 161, 330
Instagram, 224, 225, 227, 240, 342, 343
Intarcia Therapeutics, 264, 268
Intellia Therapeutics, 266
Iodine, 147
iPivot, 290
Ipsy, 150
Jack Ma, 206
Jambbol, 290
James C. Foster, 136
James Proud, 126
Jason Goldberg, 105, 230
Jason Knight, 232
Jason Nelson, 279
Jason Tan, 133
Jason van den Brand, 152
Jawbone, 288
Jay Kaplan, 139
Jeff Bezos, 126

Jeff Clavier, 294
Jerry Yang, 350
Joel Gascoigne, 120
John P. Rogers, 234
Johnson & Johnson Development Corporation, 266
Johnson and Johnson, 263
Julie Uhrman, 336
Junglee Games, 170
Kaggle, 143, 329
Kai Wang, 141
Khosla Ventures, 216
Kickstarter, 126, 145, 154, 332, 333, 335, 336
King Digital Entertainment, 209, 210
KINGS over ACES, 21, 22
Kirk Krappe, 307
Kleiner Perkins, 214, 226
Klout, 121, 158
Kongrgate, 294
Kraft Group, 267
Larry Page, 47, 189, 201
LaunchKey, 138, 324
Leafly, 169
Lean Startup, 67, 68, 270, 271, 272, 276, 277, 278, 280, 282
Lee Holloway, 183
Lenda, 152, 153
Lending Club, 153, 209
Lenovo, 292
Life360, 159
LinkedIn, 69, 155, 156
littleBits, 338
Living Social, 152
Lookout, 132
LoudCloud, 287
Lowercase Capital, 291
Lysogene, 268
Marc Andreessen, 224, 225, 256, 258, 287, 305
Marc Benioff, 257, 293
Marc Collins-Rector, 251
Marc Gobe, 76
Marc Hedlund, 232
Marissa Mayer, 242
Mark Cuban, 39
Mark Kuhr, 139
Mark Zuckerberg, 21, 42, 46, 187, 197, 201, 289
Marker, 264
Markus Frind, 280
Massroots, 167
Mathew Prince, 183
Matt Mullenweg, 192
Maxim Lobovsky, 333
Medium, 127
MetaMind, 294
Michael Massey, 243
Michel Valdrigh, 192
Michelle Zatlyn, 183

Microsoft, 25, 97, 190, 191, 250, 287
Mike Little, 192
Mike McCue, 160
MileIQ, 294
Milk, 292
Milo, 294
Minimally Viable Product, 275
Mint, 232, 233, 294
Mint.com, 232
MIT, 197, 289, 334
Mithril Capital Management, 288
Mixer labs, 290
Mixpanel, 179, 310, 311, 329
mobile to consumer, 119
Moderna Therapeutics, 264, 268
Mosaic, 287
MultiPlan, 246
MuSigma, 329
NarrativeScience, 157
Natan Linder, 333
Nathan Seidle, 282
Naval Ravikant, 290
Navitor Pharmaceuticals, 266
NEA, 213, 214
Netflix, 94, 150, 330
Netscape Communications, 287
Netscape Navigator, 287
New Enterprise Associates, 213, 264, 266
New Leaf Venture Partners, 264
Nick Denton, 285
Ninja Blocks, 339
Noah Kagan, 284
Nortis, 268
Novartis, 266, 267
Novel Startup, 67, 68
Nutanix, 181
Nutanix Virtual Computing Platform, 181
Oculus, 288
Office 365, 308
Omega Funds, 264
OnDeck Capital, 207, 209
Onex, 244, 245
Opsware, 287
Optimizely, 174, 215
Oracle Corporation, 293
Ouya, 335, 336, 340
Overstock.com, 205
Palantir, 289
Palo Alto Networks, 324
Pandora, 162, 330
Paper by FiftyThree, 161
Path, 292
Paul Allen, 190
Paul Forster, 283
Pay By Touch, 234, 235, 236, 237
PayPal, 36, 37, 38, 68, 154, 193, 243, 288
Peachtree, 151

Pebble, 126, 332
Pebble Technology, 126
Percolate, 129
Pete Moore, 339
Peter Thiel, 19, 68, 193, 222, 224, 225, 226, 258, 260, 288
Pets.com, 248, 249, 275
PetSmart, 243
Pfizer Venture Investments, 267
Picooc, 334
PillPack, 147
Pindrop, 288
Pinterest, 22, 67, 68, 69, 70, 73, 74, 76, 77, 79, 80, 227, 288
PJ Hyett, 281
PlanCast, 290
Platfora, 288
Plenty of Fish, 280
Ploom, 167, 332
Pocket, 164
Polaris Partners, 266, 267
Portola Pharmaceuticals, 326
Poshmark, 294
Posterous, 292
Postmates, 130, 294
Pravin Kothar, 307
Precog, 329
Pre-revenue, 102
profitability, 22, 106, 107, 109, 113, 115, 222, 341, 343
Profitable, 29, 102
Prosena Holdings, 326
Quartet Medicine, 266
Quickbooks, 151
Quilvest Ventures, 264
Quote–to–Cash, 305
RA Capital management, 264
Radian6, 238, 306
Rajiv Gupta, 324
Ravikant. *See* Naval Ravikant
Rdio, 162
Recorded Future, 324
Recurly, 150
Reddit, 172, 284, 347, 348
Regalii, 156
Reid Robinson, 141
RescueTime, 292
Richard Branson, 210
Risk Factor Summation Method, 315
Rob Bearden, 330
Rob Francis, 136
Robert Herjavec, 25
Roche Genetech, 263
Rockmelt, 288
Roku, 93, 94, 335
Rony Kahn, 283
SaaS, 114, 115, 174, 257

Salesforce, 293, 305, 306, 308, 317, 318
Salesforce.com, 293, 305, 306
Sand Hill Partners, 259
Sano, 292
Sanofi-Genzyme BioVentures, 266
Scholar Rock, 267
Science Exchange, 143, 326
Sendgrid, 294
SendHub, 158, 159
Sendwithus, 175
SEO, 281
Sequoia Capital, 323
Seragon, 263
Sergey Brin, 47, 189
Shape Security, 140, 324
Shapeways, 288, 338
Shopify, 128, 292
Shyp, 129, 292
SiftScience, 133, 134
Sig CombiBloc, 245
Signifyd, 138
SimpleGeo, 292
SkyHigh Networks, 324
SkyKick, 292
Skype, 288, 292
Slack, 177, 178, 311, 312
Slack App, 177
SlideMail, 308, 309, 310
Snapchat, 89, 90, 162, 196, 320, 342
SnapLogic, 290
SocialPicks, 175
Sofinnova Ventures, 268
SoftTech VC, 294
Software as a Service, 174
Soma, 292
Sound Ventures, 293
SpaceX, 36, 37, 42
SparkFun, 282, 283
Spencer Fry, 279
SpiralFrog, 250
Spotflux, 135
Spotify, 162, 289
SR One, 266
Stack Overflow, 290
Standard Treasury, 154
Stanford, 47, 175, 189, 193, 196, 197, 288, 350, 351
Starr Partners, 246
Stem CentRX, 289
Stencenrx, 289
Steve Huffman, 347
Steve Jobs, 20, 21, 34, 38, 66, 76, 88, 93
StopTheHacker, 183
Stripe, 126, 153, 289
StumbleUpon, 292
Suhail Doshi, 310
SumZero, 155, 156

SV Angel, 216, 217, 282
Synack, 139, 140
Synlogic, 266
TaskRabbit, 292
Tear Glucose Research, 326
TechCrunch, 282, 288
Tellme, 160
Tesla, 36, 37, 43
Thalmic Labs, 337
Theranos, 142
Thiel Capital Management, 288
Third Rock Ventures, 267
Tim Ferriss, 291, 292
Tim Hortons, 242
Tom Preston, 281
Transcriptic, 146, 326
Travis Kalanick, 49, 52, 63
Treehouse Island, 130
Trippy, 292
True Link Financial, 134
Truecar, 204, 205
TrueVault, 145
Trulioo, 135
Trustev, 138
Tumblr, 242
TuteGenomics, 141
Twitter, 69, 77, 127, 164, 168, 172, 178, 203, 227, 289, 290, 292, 293, 294, 320
Uber, 22, 27, 49, 50, 52, 53, 54, 55, 57, 60, 63, 75, 129, 130, 131, 162, 172, 243, 292
UC Berkeley, 199
UCLA, 200
Union Square Investors, 290
Union Square Ventures, 284, 289
Unsubscribe.com, 292
Unum Therapeutics, 266
Urban Escapes, 152
USAA, 205
Validated learning, 273
Vast.com, 290
Venrock, 264
Venture Fund, 267
vice, 119
Viking Global Investors, 264
Virgin America, 210
Vittana, 292
Votizen, 278
Voyager Therapeutics, 267
Vungle, 294
Warren Buffett, 256, 257, 259, 287, 295
Wealthfront, 151, 278, 292
WebVan, 252, 260, 275
Weiting Liu, 175
Wellington management, 264
WePay, 154
Wesabe, 232, 233, 234
Wharton School, 289

Whoopie Goldberg, 252
Wilfire, 294
WordPress, 192, 232
XFire., 290
Y Combinator, 289, 308, 310
Yahoo, 47, 97, 196, 242, 294, 308, 310, 311, 350, 351, 352
Youbet.me, 168
YouTube, 61, 343
Yummly, 330
Yves Behar, 335

Zapier, 124
ZenBenefits, 345
Zendesk, 204
Zendrive, 292
Zenefits, 125, 179, 215
ZenPayroll, 127, 128
ZeroFox, 136, 137
Zite, 343
ZocDoc, 163, 164, 289
Zuckerberg, 42, 43, 188, 189, 197, 289
Zynga, 289

Made in the USA
Las Vegas, NV
16 November 2021